Elliot Donahey is an *out* young queer boy—artistic, empathic, and full of secret passions. He is a boy seeking protective shadows where he can hide from those who don't understand him…and to provide him with the means of surviving one more hellish day of high school.

When Elliot finds himself in the arms of Marco Sforza, a boy who is made to bask in the light of fame and success, shadows and light take on a whole new meaning. Marco's rising star as the quarterback of the Mercy High Avenging Angels may come crashing down around him if his relationship with Elliot is discovered. And Marco's past of playing a ladies man convincing his teammates he's *one of them* will pose problems that Marco's teammates have to deal with.

Can Marco and Elliot find their romance in the sun, or will those who profess to be close to them tear them apart?

Before the Fall

Angels of Mercy, Book Two

SA Collins

A NineStar Press Publication

Published by NineStar Press
P.O. Box 91792,
Albuquerque, New Mexico, 87199 USA.
www.ninestarpress.com

Before the Fall

Copyright © 2019 by SA Collins
Cover Art by SA Collins Copyright © 2019

This is a work of fiction. Names, characters, places, and incidents are either the product of the author's imagination or are used fictitiously. Any resemblance to actual persons living or dead, business establishments, events, or locales is entirely coincidental.

All rights reserved. No part of this publication may be reproduced in any material form, whether by printing, photocopying, scanning or otherwise without the written permission of the publisher. To request permission and all other inquiries, contact NineStar Press at the physical or web addresses above or at Contact@ninestarpress.com.

Printed in the USA
First Edition
November, 2019

Print ISBN: 978-1-951057-56-5

Also available in eBook, ISBN: 978-1-951057-52-7

Warning: This book contains sexually explicit content, which may only be suitable for mature readers, homophobic slurs, and homophobic violence.

For Paul Berry

Chapter One

Fallout

Seven a.m. came far earlier than either of us wanted. I was still buried beneath my boyfriend who was softly snoring against my neck, a small pool of drool escaping from his lips and down the back of my shoulder, sort of gross and at the same time utterly sexy of him. I realized what a freak that made me about Marco. I mean it wasn't lost on me that I thought him literally drooling on me was sexy.

How fucking weird and kinky is that? Is drool even considered kink?

"Babe..." The phone was incessantly beeping to beat the band and I just couldn't reach it as he'd pinned my arm closest to the phone beneath him. He was so relaxed which made him infinitely heavier. His mouth began to move along my neck, followed by his tongue rasping against it. He was awake.

"Honey, I can't get to the phone. Mom will hear."

He lazily reached up and fumbled with it—not even bothering to look. He knew my passcode—no secrets between us. Well, at least by the end of the morning there wouldn't be. I vowed in the middle of the night I'd tell him about Angelo and deal with the fallout. The phone stopped as he moved my body into place so he could relieve the morning wood. He licked his middle finger and then reached down and prodded my hole.

"Mmmm, still wet. Good. Need lube?"

I shrugged, marveling how automated the whole process was—not that it lessened the passion one jot.

"Wanna slick me up first?" Which meant he wanted me to blow him for a bit.

I nodded. He smiled darkly and climbed up the length of me. Within a few seconds he was burrowing deep within my mouth. I rested my hands on his ass as he fucked my mouth. The taste of him never ceased to amaze me. He was very pungent, but in a sexy spicy sort of way; it never failed to press every one of my buttons. The scent of him, and this particular part of him, got me horned up right quick. After a few leisurely thrusts of his cock into my mouth, his right hand left the wall above my headboard, and gripped the back of my head. Deep throat time. I made sure to produce enough saliva for him; he liked it wet and sloppy when he skull fucked me. I had no intention to disappoint. I know some may think it sounds harsh, but you'd have to know Marco and me. This was simply how we were. Like a well-oiled machine—and not in a weird animatronic sort of way either.

"Okay?" was all he asked. Not that he'd wait for a reply. It was more of a signal he was going in full throttle. I opened my mouth to swallow him down. The foreskin slipped back as the head of his cock made contact with the back of my throat. It had taken us some time for me to learn to suppress my gag reflex and to breathe around him when he was in that deep. But he was an excellent teacher and I was the star pupil in our arrangement. He leaned forward just at the right time when he felt me open up fully to him, and deep throat fucked me for a while—his precum oozing in a steady flow into my mouth when he retracted. It was a sloppy wet mess. We wouldn't have it any other way.

"That's my boy. So fucking hot when you do that, baby."

It was all the encouragement I needed. If I could've smiled I would. I'd let him fuck my mouth and throat for as long as he'd like when he said those things. Fucking hog heaven when we got like this. Each time he extracted himself from me his cock was raining back down into my mouth. It was a very, very sexy sight; one I knew all too well. I opened my jaw wide and slipped my tongue out like a hungry bird wanting the worm. He chuckled, knowing how his cock drove me crazy with desire. I did desire him. He slipped back down again, saliva oozing from the sides of my mouth as I welcomed him back home.

"So close, baby. I wanna fuck now. 'Kay?"

I nodded again and let him slip away from me momentarily while he moved back down. I savored the flavor of him as he did. I ran a quick hand over my mouth to clear away the spittle.

As if by instinct, I hoisted my legs so he could judge for himself how ready I was for it. He fingered me again to determine if it was to his liking; I was good either way. I actually liked it when it burned a little at the beginning. He seemed satisfied that I was ready, and he began to fuck.

He did it slowly and leisurely at first, whispering those sweet soft nothings in my ear while he claimed what was his. I held him for all his worth, which was quite a lot. He chuckled as he continued to slowly, achingly push his way in and out.

"I'm not doing it right, am I?"

"Huh?" I murmured. It felt just fine to me.

"Wait for it..." Then he began the slow swirl of his hips that never failed to push me into the pain versus pleasure part of me, massaging my prostate like a muthafucker. Fucking euphoric heaven. My toes curled and flexed—that was definitely the spot. He glanced at them and smiled. "That's my boy. Just enjoy it, sweetheart. This is as much for you as it is for me."

"Okay, but we can't take too long. Mom will be getting up in about an hour or so." How I managed to get that out between panting over his arduous fucking I'll never know.

He laughed softly.

An hour was barely enough time for Marco these days. When we screwed and had the luxury of time on our hands, he could easily eat up an hour, bending me into positions that would take us to new highs of ecstasy. He looked into my eyes, never missing a stroke into me as he did so. This boy loved to fuck.

"She came in like what, 3:00 a.m.?" he whispered to me without altering his rhythm in pounding me into oblivion. That's my man—the Superman of fucking.

"Uh-huh. But she can never sleep past 8:30 or 9:00. Don't know why that is, but it is. That's the latest we have."

"You gotta be at the shop...ooh, fuck baby, that spot is so sweet. I need to fuck there for a bit."

My breath hitched as he did. I licked along my lips as he really went to town inside me.

"I love you so much, Els. You know that, baby, don't you?"

"Of course. I love you too."

I watched him, not sure if he could read the betrayal I felt in the back of my mind regarding my fuck with Angelo. Nothing had come of it—not really. Not that Angelo or I wouldn't have wanted it to if Marco weren't in the picture, but I still was feeling a tad guilty about it.

My guy who could fuck me to oblivion suddenly stopped fucking.

"What happened?"

"What?"

"Don't lie to me, Els. I can see you're hiding something."

"Can we like focus on one thing at a time? Like letting you finish and then we can talk about it?"

He pushed himself up onto his arms so he could really look at me. He raised an eyebrow but not in a sexy kind of way. His eyes—piercing, with a small degree of fear coloring them—were asking unspoken questions of me. He turned his head slightly again to the end of the bed behind him. Silently, he reached some sort of conclusion about whatever he saw, and he slowly resumed the fuck, only now leaning into it with more vigor. He wanted to get it over with so we could talk. I thanked the bed gods that between the memory foam mattress and the bed being literally bolted to the floor and wall, to compensate for the slight unevenness of the floor, I didn't have to worry too much about noise other than what would be coming out of our mouths. He hiked his leg up so his foot was near my right shoulder, forcing my right leg higher so he could truly have unfettered access and fuck me relentlessly. It was a brutally angry kind of fuck, but I think we both needed this. The anger was definitely palpable between us—weighted, though for different reasons.

"Burns..." I whispered.

He nodded with a grunt, as he jackhammered the fuck out of me. It was a painful and grueling pummeling, but we were in it together. With each prod of his prick, he was burnishing the pain out of us, using my body like a boxer would a punching bag. I was okay with it. At this point I probably deserved it. Marco liked rough sex on occasion and so did I. This was definitely one of those times. His foot was next to me, his toes curling into the bedding to secure his footing, my right knee next to my face. He wanted me to feel this. The stern turn to his brow, the focus of his gaze, he wanted me to know I was his and his alone. I swore when we got like this he couldn't actually feel his cock being teased to release. It was like he checked out and just fucked me mercilessly. Within my heart of hearts, I secretly enjoyed it when Marco became obsessed with fucking me like this, using my body to drive his passions and scratching the itch only he could reach within me. Sometimes it was what men needed. We understood this kind of pain. So I was there for him. It was a good kind of hurt, an ache I never wanted to recover from. It's part of what bound me to him.

A long trail of precum oozed from my cock, pooling into my navel; I was responding to his assault. He kept it up, watching me as a single tear slipped from my eye. He leaned down and licked it ever so gently with a whisper touch of the tip of his tongue, but never wavering on how hard he was pounding me. I marveled at how our bodies could do that. One part feather soft and gentle, the other fiercely brutal. His right hand pressed down upon the underside of my left knee, opening me further. Being limber for Marco had become a high priority for me. For us, really. He was snapping his hips the way that had never failed to drive me insane with desire, struggling like hell not to scream loud enough to bring the roof down—say nothing of waking my dead-to-the-world mother.

Sweat mingled with a few tears that had escaped his eyes. He was very angry, a tempest-like well of anger. His eyes darted to my curled toes; the arch to my foot would rival a ballet dancer's. He knew what he was doing to me. He nodded with his satisfaction over how I was responding to him. Despite the brutal voracity of the fuck, he could tell he was still pleasuring me in a profound way. He was claiming me for himself—pressing against whatever he thought I'd done. Fighting for me while we fucked.

I bit down on my lower lip, reaching out to hold on to his ass, ensuring I could limit how far he'd withdraw before plowing back in. I had a few relentless tricks of my own to play, so I bore down on his cock. His eyes widened, mirroring my own as I increased the pressure on that leviathan piece he was using against me—his bull-sized balls slapping against my ass. I was milking the pain away, I was leeching it like a painful venom from him as I increased the pressure on his prodding cock. A few more strokes and he lunged forward, pressing for his release within me, though I knew the fear of what I might spout at him later was roiling in the back of his mind. For now, at least, he'd set it aside, but it was there nonetheless, stalking us both like a hungry wolf tracking its prey.

As he came his mouth aggressively latched onto my neck and sucked hard along the tendon he favored. He spent himself deep within. The bite from him was painful. I hissed as he continued to shudder with release. My right arm flailed against the pillow, my fingers straining to gain purchase. He was bending me to the point of breaking, and still I reached for him, to please him even though I was in such a state of complete orgiastic annihilation. I milked him with each successive thrust—being sure to increase my hold on him as he withdrew; the sigh he gifted me was punctuated with the anguish he'd been feeling. I soothed his back as he released his hold over my body. Like an overspent rubber band, my body gave in, collapsing as he left little kisses along my neck and face. He let me relax as he straightened out, resuming his dominance over me. His body engulfed mine, surrounding me.

For the moment, I was still his and he was mine.

His mouth moved along my neck in a series of small puckering kisses advancing slowly to my jawline and eventually finding my mouth. The whole time we kissed I couldn't help my mind wandering back to last night with Angelo and how very similar it all felt. The familiarity troubled me. There was no apparent reason I could fathom why it felt so. I eventually broke the kiss. It was time to come clean. He slowly withdrew from my mouth, though a small stream of saliva still ran from his lips to mine, bridging the distance between us. We're very sloppy kissers.

"Was that more for your pleasure than mine? It's been a while since you've done that. Was it all about you?"

"I'd never leave you like that." He wiggled his eyebrows, only there was little in the way of true feeling behind it, to let me know we weren't finished just yet. It was a half-hearted attempt at the familiar salacious gesture. It was true enough. Marco could go again within a matter of seconds from blowing his wad. Marco loved to fuck. He loved to fuck me, though I could see he was tabling that for the moment.

"But you can't throw something like that at me and then expect me not to react. So, spill it."

"I was trying, but you came too fast."

"Elliot..." He sighed with the superior tone a parent uses with an insolent child.

"Okay, okay. I get it. Serious talk time. But first, let's get cleaned up."

"You mean you don't want to finish our fun after?"

"Yeah, well, after we talk it'll probably the last thing on your mind."

I began to move off the bed, but he grabbed my arm, stalling my progress.

"What happened? Please tell me...should I be worried?"

I shrugged. Not good. Fear quickly burned across his eyes like an unchecked wildfire. His hands became more forceful, turning me roughly on the spot, his eyes burrowing into my own. He knew I couldn't look away very easily when he did that. It was the one thing he'd conditioned me to do with him. In a way, I needed to know we were good, even if his gaze held very little warmth at this moment.

"Elliot, you're freaking me out. *What happened?*" That last was a bit louder than we should've been. I put my hand over his mouth, and he shook it off. The anger in him was very real. I was threatening his world. I shushed him. And he looked slightly over his shoulder at my bedroom door. We both waited a beat to hear if his outburst had woken my mother. Several quiet seconds passed, the only sound being our breaths and a few birds twittering outside. He slowly turned his eyes back to me. I shrugged out of his vise grip and relented. I rubbed where his hands had been. The only time he had ever manhandled me was during sex. This was altogether different.

"Well, it has to do with the game. Well, sort of."

"The game? What do you mean?"

"Well, just let me finish, will you?"

He sat back on the bed Indian-style with an elbow to one knee propping his head up. My eyes immediately darted to his crotch, damned near my favorite view of him. I always had a thing for Marco's cock after a good fucking. It would remain slightly engorged, not fully hard but very clearly spent. It never failed to make my mouth water, let alone my ass twitch—eager to get him fully aroused again. Old habits are hard to break.

He snapped his fingers in front of my face. "Eyes up here; you can play later."

"Yeah, still not so sure that will happen after I tell you what I am gonna tell you."

"Did you cheat on me?"

There, it was out. I knew he'd get to it before I had the courage to say it because it was his worst fear, or so he said. Yeah, like my leaving him would totally wreck his life. There were any number of people, of both sexes I was sure, who would love to bump me to the curb and take over.

"No!" I paused, never a good thing when you're trying to be on solid ground while presenting your argument. "Well, not really. Not technically."

His head came off his hand. His eyes grew darker, if that were possible, the green intensifying from brilliant grass to saturated moss—dense, dark, and foreboding. I definitely struck a nerve. I held up a hand, stalling him before *his* imagination ran away from us.

"Just hear me out, okay? This isn't easy. It shows how incredibly naive and gullible I am. You're right. Okay? I know you've told me before, but until last night I really didn't have any idea to what degree you were right. So let me be the first to say—yes, you told me so."

"Okay, glad to hear it, but it doesn't tell me what you did that has got you so worked up. And if you're worked up about it, then, baby, I'm fucking freaking out. So just spill it."

I sighed, giving in to how hopeless it was to stall any further. The cat was out and running rampant all over the place. No use denying it any longer.

"You know how I really don't fit into your world, right?"

"What? Are you kidding me? You are my world. Always will be."

"Yeah, thanks for that, but you know what I mean." I pointed a finger at him—"Jock"—and then at me—"Queerbait... Simple logic on how it all plays out, right?"

He sorta nodded, but I could see he was really anxious for me to get on with it.

"So that first game you played I was really sort of pent up, you know, stranger in a strange land, and all of that shit." His eyes were pleading with me to cut to the chase, but for me the chase was part of it all. I needed to explain how Angelo came into my world and how much of it he consumed when we were together, how haunting it was to be with him, the familiarity of it. That's what I needed to put into words, only now, with Marco facing me with a fearful look in his eye, I didn't have the wherewithal to sort it out correctly. My tongue kept getting in the wrong place. I fumbled like I'd just gotten a new tongue piercing or had a stroke and couldn't make my face work right.

"Anyway, so I was really nervous that first night. No one to sit with and I was really trying to be there for you because it was so important to you that I was there."

"I was soaring, babe. You made me feel, argh, there aren't words to describe what a high you put me in that night on the field. That stadium was packed, but there was only one pair of eyes I was playing for: you."

"I know, sweetheart, but from my side, it was pretty fucking scary, Christians at the Colosseum kind of scary."

He nodded. Again, urging me to press forward.

"That's when he showed up, out of nowhere."

"Who? Some guy making the moves on you? Who the fuck is he?"

I sighed and rolled my eyes.

"Will ya just wait a goddamned minute for me to finish, 'kay? *You're killing me, Smalls...*"

His mouth became a grim line with my calling a "time out" on him.

"So, then there was this guy, a foreign exchange student—from Italy, no less."

"From Italy?"

"Yeah, complete with the accent and the whole nine yards. Kinda hot in that he reminded me of you a bit. Same build, and parts of his face even."

"So his face looked like mine?"

I could already see Marco tracing out guys on campus who might look like him. It was a lost cause. I'd been looking for Angelo off and on for weeks and never found him.

"Well, sort of. You see, that's the strange part... I never saw all of his face. Not at one time, anyway."

"What? Baby, that makes no kind of sense."

"Well, you remember that first night? How cold it was?"

He vaguely nodded that he recalled it somewhat. I guess under a crap-ton of football gear maybe it wasn't so cold to them. Hell, like I didn't know any of that shit. Maybe it didn't bother him at all. Perhaps he was acclimated to it.

"Well, the guy walked up as I was trying to figure out where you told me to sit. I was all confused and lost."

Marco smiled; he could totally see me dazed like a lost fawn seeking out his mama. His cock stirred between his legs on the mattress. He loved dominating me, and when I felt afraid it stirred quite a bit in him. I had to be careful. Now was not a time to get that ball rolling again.

"So the guy sort of took pity on me, I guess. Or maybe 'cause he was new to the school he just wanted to make friends at the game, ya know?"

He nodded. I pressed forward. Only now, it got tricky.

"I talked with him and our conversation flowed fairly easily. I figured he was so new no one had bothered to tell him what a social faux pas he was making by even speaking to me. Anyway, so then he introduced himself. His name was Angelo."

"Huh" was the only thing to burst from Marco's lips. Not a *who the fuck is Angelo*, but a simple acknowledgment that he now had a name.

"He said he was here from Italy but had an affinity for 'the American Football' as he put it. And he seemed to know a lot about it."

Marco pushed me back onto the bed and pulled the covers over us as he settled himself on top of me. Not to fuck, just 'cause I think he could sense I was closing in on the whole "not technically" moment he was dreading. He propped his head on a crooked arm, lying half on and half off me onto his side, not quite smothering me, but close. He slowly trailed the index finger of his left hand on my chest as I continued with my story, tracing a lazy figure eight around and in between my two nipples.

"We sat and watched the game together. But I never saw his face. Not totally. Just from the bridge of his nose up. He said it was because of the cold night air. No, wait. That wasn't right. No, it was because he had a cold and he didn't want me to get it. That was it. I remember now because at the time I knew it made him European."

Marco's brows knitted together. My logic failed him a lot. Hell, it often failed me a lot, so he wasn't alone on that score. I'd just learned to go with it.

"I mean, any red-blooded American boy would've just thought, *hey, don't sit so close to me if you're afraid to get sick, suck it up, that's what I am doin'*—that sort of attitude, ya know? Not Angelo, he was very considerate. Spoke through the damned woolen scarf the entire game. Never saw more than his eyes. They were green like yours. Same sort of brow line too. Not nearly as handsome as yours though."

We both knew I was lying here, but I would always give the one-up to my guy. At least, I was still hoping he'd be my guy by the time I finished.

"Yeah, I get that. Now *you're* killin' me, Smalls. Get on with it, already."

"I'm trying, I'm trying...but you need to understand the context."

He harrumphed but allowed me to press on. I could tell I was frustrating the hell out of him though because he ran a slightly shaky hand through his wildly curled hair.

"So, here's the deal. I don't know why. I can't really even put my finger on it. But for some reason the guy seemed really familiar, like I'd known him like, forever. Really comfortable to talk to and be with. It was safe. I was safe. Feeling so fish out of water and all that, he was my rock in raging waters, you know? I mean, it wasn't like I could just run down on the field and get huddled next to you on the bench while you were playing, ya know? I was by myself. I guess I coulda hung out with Greg and his family, but on that first night it was just me."

"You said you'd get a ride with Greg. What happened with that? You mean to tell me you walked from your house all the way to school?" He didn't even wait for my reply—probably because he knew me and how I worked. "Elliot, you coulda been hurt or something. What were you thinking? Those roads from your house down to the school are not well lit. Baby, don't do that. If you need a ride, then let me know. I'll figure something out."

Part of me relished how much he still cared. I guess he sorta saw where this was all heading. It couldn't have been easy for him to connect the dots ahead of where I was in the tale and still have enough love to spare. I knew I was eating that boyfriend cred like crazy. I needed to wrap this up.

"Okay so, like, that game we shared his blanket and he explained how football worked. So I got into it. I finally saw you in a whole new light. So yeah, yay, Marco. I was all jazzed up for the game to get rolling. And then you all made your entrance. I got all flushed just watching you take command. Totally reset my whole outlook on you. I fell in love all over again."

He blushed and smiled. At least I could capture these moments in my head in case I tanked in the next few minutes.

"So anyway. That game things went okay. You won."

"The team won."

"*You* won." I wasn't letting my guy think I saw it differently, even if he did. He was my hero, always would be. "Anyway, we went our separate ways, and I got in the Impala and waited for you and—well, you know the rest."

"So how's that technically not cheating? 'Cause you what? Shared a blanket and some quality friend time with another guy?"

"No, not exactly."

His gaze got dark again. He realized we weren't out of the woods yet.

"So I kept going to your games and I never saw the guy again. Just me, learning how to cope being by myself in the stands, which is fine. I'm cool with it, in fact. But it was the game last night when he showed up again, dressed as the Red Death from *Phantom of the Opera*."

He sorta shook his head like he had no fucking idea what I was talking about.

"Aw, honey, you are such a straight boy in a gay world."

He looked like I stung him with that comment. I couldn't figure out why though. I had to trust it would come out in the wash at some point.

"Anyway, he was all dressed up, even had prosthetics on the upper part of his face. See what I mean? I never got to see it as a whole. What's up with that? So I said that to him. Well, that and where the fuck had he been—he said he'd go to the games with me so we could watch them together, but I didn't see him at any of the other games. He said something about how schoolwork was bogging him down since English wasn't his forte. I got that, but Jesus, he couldn't come to a single game since the first one? That was just a bit weird, especially because he was so knowledgeable about the game and in particular about the Angels."

"He knew about us?"

"Yeah, he said he had looked up what he could on the net when he found out he was heading this way."

"Did he say where in Italy he was from?"

"If it came up, I don't remember it. He short-circuited my thinking from time to time. To tell you the truth, he was kind of electric."

"What's that supposed to mean?"

I reached out and grabbed Marco's hand. It never failed to send a shiver up his arm. He loved me touching him. I needed to have him understand and I knew the words would fail me—but the touch, he'd get.

"Do you get it now?"

He nodded. "So you had the hots for this guy?" His voice sort of cracked, fear tinged with a little anger visibly washing over him.

"No, not exactly. It was that he was familiar. I don't know how else to explain it. Electric is all I can come up with."

I released his hand, though his eyes kept watching mine. I knew he was troubled by what I said. And if that was trouble, I was a bit worried about the next part.

"So, fast-forward to last night. He was all dressed up in a massive costume. I couldn't really see him totally, but after a few words I knew it was him. We took seats high up in the stands, primarily because his costume was so damned big. By the way, whoever thought a Homecoming and Halloween theme should go together oughta be taken out and beaten severely. Really lame idea."

He nodded, though his gaze had gone blank. I wondered if he'd checked out or something.

"So he watched the game with me only this time it was far more pointed. We held hands, discreetly. Nothing more, and no, unfortunately that's not the not technically cheating part. I'm getting to that."

"There's more?" Suddenly his attention was back to what I was saying.

I nodded, not bothering to hide the shame I was feeling, and I was deeply ashamed. I loved Marco. I knew I did, and facing the very real possibility that this could be our undoing caused knots to form in the pit of my belly. Maybe he'd understand. I mean apparently it was a hard night all the way around.

"When things didn't, uh, go right, at the Homecoming announcement, I had to leave. I just couldn't watch it all go down. Please understand, Marco, how much I was hurting inside that I couldn't be there for you. But I knew Cindy was going to paw all over you—and I so didn't need to see it."

"Yeah, about that. I may have something to confess there as well."

He looked extremely distressed about his mini-confession. It was as if I'd just gotten sucker-punched. No air, nothing. I mean, I knew what transgressions or mistakes I'd made. But just the thought of Marco doing something he was ashamed of or afraid of how it would affect me had me really worried.

"Never mind. I don't think I want to know. I don't think I can handle it right now."

It was the truth. Suddenly I was afraid of where my mind went racing—even if I hadn't put a real name to it, I had a real strong gut reaction to what he wasn't telling me. Only one thing could have happened last night to put that look on his face. I couldn't hear him say it. Better not to know. But what if it were true? What then? I didn't know. Would I give up on Marco? I didn't think so, but with that skank, Cindy, anything was possible.

He fucked her.

I don't know why my mind went there, but it did; all on its own. I tried to push the images from my mind: his mouth on hers, her claws into his flesh, the look in her eye knowing she was taking him from me. And no doubt she knew I was involved with him on some level—I just couldn't wipe the vision of her with that malicious pointed glare, draining him, leeching my man like some sort of parasite. *Just the thought of him losing himself with someone...* My eyes widened with that.

"You know what? I think you need to leave."

"What? Baby, no! Please, dear God, no. Els, I swear I'm not sure. I really don't know what happened. I wasn't telling you a lie. I don't really know. I think someone drugged me, put something in my drink. Things got really foggy, and there are parts I can't remember very well. I'm really scared. I think I messed up, but I don't remember any of it! It wasn't me. I swear! I'd never hurt you, never!"

His voice was rising. I knew I had to get him calmed the fuck down or I'd have Mother-dear banging on the door. I gave him the iciest stare I could muster.

"Marco Raphael Sforza, you better check yourself and keep your voice down and get a fucking grip!" I rasped to him in the tersest whisper manageable.

He immediately froze. But the look of longing, of pleading with me—those eyes, those beautiful, beautiful eyes moist with the possibility that I was sending him away. So much love there and he was desperately afraid it wasn't enough, that he'd damaged us beyond all repair. In truth, I didn't know how I really felt about it. I was raw. And I was jumping to conclusions. Hell, he said he couldn't remember what happened. So maybe he was drugged; that might be true. While Marco was crafty when he needed to be, he was not a habitual liar. I believed him when he said he couldn't remember. But what did that mean for us—in the here and now?

I knew how this looked. It wasn't lost on me. I was being a little bitch to him about it. I mean I knew I couldn't keep him to myself forever. You only had to look at Marco and know he was the kind of guy who attracted temptation. I wasn't that delusional despite what he'd said about it, but he just didn't realize out of all the people in the world he could've stepped out on me with—why'd it have to be *her*? It may not have been fair; it may not have been totally right. I sort of believed him when he said he was coerced, whether by drink or drugs, maybe both. But it didn't mean it went down any easier, 'cause it didn't. Like the anti-Mary Poppins, it was like swallowing a spoonful of acid to make the shards of glass go down. It cut *as* it burned.

I took a deep breath. "Look, I think we need some distance to sort out what went on—on *both* our sides. I'm not proud of what happened with me either. But you have a mystery to solve, and I so can't be there when you do. After you've sorted it, then we can find a time and place to talk. Okay?"

"Els, *please* say you won't leave me. I couldn't bear it, baby. I just couldn't. This was robbed from me; you have to understand that. You just have to."

"I don't *have* to do anything," I spat at him with far more conviction than I had a right to, given my own tryst with Angelo.

That stunned the hell out of him. A new round of silent tears spilled from his face. I sighed and brought him to me and kissed each eyelid, shushing him.

He slowly backed away, pushing me from him. I couldn't help but feel his eyes roam over me. Gauging what, I wasn't so sure. Something new had threaded its way into the room and loomed large between us. This was a side of him he'd never shared with me. I guess he still had a few surprises up his sleeve. Fucking girls seemed to be just one of the many things I didn't know about him. This unknown worried me. I tried to regroup and get control again. Under this new gaze that wasn't so easy.

"What I mean is, I don't *have* to do anything—*if* I do anything, it's because I *want* to. I think I believe you when you say you don't know what happened. You've never willingly lied to me before. I don't think you are now. I think you are genuine in that you feel like you were raped or coerced or whatever. I get that. But I can't deal with it, at least, not right now. Not with Cindy involved. You don't understand how much that bitch and her best friend have tormented me through the years. And now it appears she's gotten her claws into you, taken that away from me... Can't you see? I can't deal with that. Not her, and certainly not right now. I think we need a little time to think about what we've both done. Like I said, I'm not proud of what happened on my end. Though let's be clear, it was in no way anywhere near what *you* might have done. But it doesn't make it any more right that I let it happen."

And that is the biggest lie. The worst mistake I made. But it's out there now. No pulling it back. Yet, I know my transgression was equal to his own, if not greater in that I wanted it—even if it never ran its full course. It had been Angelo who'd retreated, not me.

He watched me, eyes slowly catching fire, brilliantly flashing—it seemed familiar and a little bit *not*. I thought it was sort of out of place given how fucked up we were right now. Brother, did I ever have it wrong.

"Yeah, you convince yourself of that all you want. But I can see it there, Els. Right fucking there." He pointed one of his large index fingers right at my eyes. "I'm not the only one who fucked up last night, right?"

I stammered, unprepared for this new assault; I was caught completely off guard. "Is that so-o? I am not sure wha-at the fuck are you talking about..."

He got right up into my space. Only this time it was unlike any he'd ever shown me. This was pointed, dark, menacing. I took a couple of steps back which only had the effect of bringing him in closer until I was backed up against the wall next to my bathroom door, his hot breaths scalding me instead of inflaming.

"I'm not the only one who fucked around last night, it seems."

"But I told you—"

"You told me *dick* about it, *babe*. So, I had to fill in the blanks and I'm not liking what I am seeing. Should I spell it out for you?"

"Wha–at?" I rasped, trying like hell to figure out how he could've sorted it so quickly.

He turned abruptly from me, and I slumped against the wall, so thankful for his retreat. That is until he got to the bed. He whipped the top sheet back, exposing the fitted sheet beneath.

"This..." was all he said.

"What?"

"Get the fuck over here and I'll show you *what*..." he tersely whispered to me.

It was so hard to do all of this and not wake up my mother down the hall.

I peeled away from the safety of the wall and I saw it, evidence of the fuck between Angelo and me, a smudge of lube, unmistakable against the tan-colored sheets, incontrovertible and utterly impossible to refute or dismiss.

"*We* didn't fuck there. I spotted it the moment I came in when you had the bedding pulled back. But I knew what had happened to me—so I had other things on my mind. But it was there, stalking me, stalking us. For a few I wondered if we had fucked at the end of the bed before. And then I realized you didn't have these sheets on the bed the last time I spent the night. So, you can try to convince me all you want that it wasn't what I think it was. And the fear in your face makes it clear I'm not far off the mark. Mine may have been coerced. I was definitely drugged."

"So you say..."

"You said you believed me before..." He pressed his point, weakening mine.

"Yeah, well, so, maybe I was wrong about that."

"What I think you were wrong about was giving up on us so quickly. One fucking night of one awful decision after another and we both seriously stumbled. But I never thought you'd go there willingly."

"He was aggressive…" Another lie.

"So, he what? Raped you? Looks to me like lube was involved… couldn't be quite what you're making it out to be. If it's rape, then he wouldn't stop to lube up. Just spit and fuck *if* you were lucky. Simple mechanics in the heat of the moment. So, you both knew what was happening. So, what the fuck?" He took a deep controlled breath. "Babe…" The tears began to fall, breaking my heart.

"Sweetheart…" I tried.

He held up a hand while the other he pinched across the bridge of his nose, clamping his eyes shut from the horrific evidence of my affair on the bed.

"Yeah. We need the fucking space you want all right. I can't…I just can't right now." He moved past me and picked up his shit and started to quickly dress.

"Baby, I…"

"No, Els…*not* now," he mumbled as he got his pants and shirt pulled on.

"So, we both fucked up…so yeah, I get that."

He stopped abruptly and glared at me. "I got fucked up and something bad happened. I own that. But you…you fucking tried to pull one over on me." He pointed to the bed and that fucking stain.

He was right, and I started to tremble all over—watching him quickly pull himself back together. Within seconds he was dressed and started to make his way over to the window.

"Marco?"

He stopped, panting with frustration or anger. I really couldn't say which at this point. He was a monolith of a man, towering and expansive in ways that never failed to strike awe and adoration from me. Even now, as he pulled away in retreat, a darkness swirled around me. I was becoming light-headed with the possibility that I wouldn't have his love any longer.

He turned around and came at me like a wave. He pulled me tightly into an embrace, though it was an empty victory in that he wouldn't look at me nor did he kiss me. *Is he putting an end to our relationship? Is this it?*

He relaxed his grip a tiny bit, watching me for a moment before releasing me fully so he could bend down and grab my black boxer briefs from the floor—something from my room. It was absurd, but it was the tiniest light at the end of the tunnel. We just might make it after all. He rounded on me, making me jump again.

"I'm hurt. I'm mad. And I am *so* fucking sorry for failing you. But I also am in so much pain from what happened that you won't even admit." He indicated the bed. "But I think you're right. Time to give us perspective, to sort out what we really feel about all of this."

I nodded, my eyes misting up from how everything was falling apart, how I'd let it all happen so easily.

He held up the boxer briefs in front of me. "I'll fucking fight for you, Elliot Donahey. You're *mine,* goddammit. I don't know how all of this got so fucking out of hand, but this isn't how it ends. I swear it isn't. I don't know how long it will take for us to put it all back together. I don't even know if you want to."

"I do! I swear to you I do..."

The grim line of his mouth stalled me from speaking further.

"We'll see." He shoved the boxers into his back pocket, gripped the back of my neck, and pulled me forward, but rather than kissing me on the mouth, he left a soft kiss on my forehead. As horrible a consolation it was, I knew I deserved nothing better. But I figured I had to find a way back to him, didn't I?

A moment later and he was gone, leaving me standing there naked, raw and completely in shock.

My phone vibrated. I picked it up—four words gave me hope on that small screen.

I'll fight for you.

Chapter Two

Spanning the Distance

Ever a man of his word, Marco did as he promised. He dutifully kept his distance. It was a strange feeling. At first, every hour I spent away from him while going through the motions of my workday became a bit easier to accept. I was lapsing into my former life, the life I had pre-Marco.

While it was easier than I realized, I hated myself for the ease with which I could lapse into my old world, a world without him. Inwardly I despised myself for how weak I was. I was a coward, choosing to give up, toss in the towel and not fight for him, fight for us. *He's the greatest love of your life, and this is how you repay that?* His last words haunted me.

I'll fight for you.

I stared at his text message from this morning. Clearly, he was the better man in our relationship. Equally clear to me, I was *not* his equal. Part of me lamented this in ways that drove me to tossing all care to the wind to wail and moan and devolve into a maelstrom of despair and remorse. I didn't deserve Marco.

The trouble with all of that was it was such utter bullshit. I mean, not that he'd fight for me. I hoped he would. I prayed he would. I just didn't know if he ultimately would. I had to trust in how he was a man who did what he said he'd do.

As for me, yeah, not so much. Once the realization of how I was lying to myself, rationalizing it all away took any resolve I had to think I was in an okay place. For a while it soothed; it calmed ruffled feathers. That was the lie, just me trying like hell to put it all on him, on what he did, and how it justified what I'd let happen with Angelo.

That was the tipping point. What I'd *let* Angelo do? I hadn't *let* Angelo do anything. It wasn't on him. Not really. That was all me. I'd instigated it. I'd pushed him down that horrible set of events. I'd wanted everyone to hurt as much as I was.

Mom had gone to the grocery store shortly after I came home from work, so I took that moment to collapse, to give in to the torment I'd held at bay all day at the Q. My inner Yoda/Gollum crept out from the dark recesses where he lived within me.

Fucked Cindy, did he? So what? Not the only man on the planet he is, right? Somebody will want damaged goods. Get your shit together and move on, you must...

I somehow had convinced myself it had nothing to do with me. Not really. I mean, it was his body, right? He could fuck whoever he wanted with it. Yeah, that was how I felt about it. Or so I tried to convince myself to make it hurt less with the result being I didn't buy a single goddamned word of it.

And this revealed the ultimate lie about myself, the one I never had the courage to admit, only now with the enormity of his absence, I could no longer deny it: I was a fraud. I talked a good game. I knew what to say and often when to say it, like I had some wellspring of life experience to back my shit up.

Who the fuck am I really kidding? I'm eighteen for fuck sake. I can barely get from one day to the next without epically failing in some way.

I wasn't a master of my domain, a man who could say with any real authority I knew my place in the world and had a right to demand it all. I knew I spoke well and truly beyond my years, but it was all a way to cope with how absolutely fucking scared I was of *everything* in my world. Marco, my parents, school, and the fucktards who wandered its halls. It didn't matter from what part of my world it came, I was drowning in a sea of trying to just cope—flinging complex thoughts and ideas at people like emotive stones. Hoping against all hope that if those stones didn't hurt, well, at least they'd distract them while I made my getaway.

It was *all* a great lie.

I saw what worked for people much older than myself and thought I had the fucking wherewithal to apply it to myself, like TV could give a boy like me life lessons I could apply and make things work. For the most part, it had been nothing but my big mouth and pure luck—plain and simple.

The sad part about it all? I simply didn't have a plan B in the grand scheme of all things me—and now it was showing. Epically showing.

And really when you come right down to it, what about me? I wasn't the total Saint Elliot last night, either. How could I possibly blame Marco if I went off the rails as badly as he had? That was the question I didn't have an answer for that satisfied, that would fill the void in my heart for what I'd done to him. No...

To us.

Oh, I had a quick and dirty answer for how I felt. But it was a lie. A fucking flat-out lie. I was just as culpable, just as maligned, and just as wrong to have gone as far as he did. So, we didn't climax. Angelo had entered me; we'd clearly begun to fuck. It was brutal, it was intense, and I had relished every fucking thrust of it. But it was also wrong. He nearly came, for fuck sake.

Angelo.

Angelo's gaze when he pulled away tormented me. Such rampant hunger there to take me away, to sweep me from Marco's grasp and have me all to himself. So erotically familiar and foreign all at the same time. Powerfully alluring. But in the end, nothing but a fool's paradise, as they say. Romantic, heady, and deeply captivating to have a foreigner sweep into your life and want to take you away. But how long could that one play out? It would never work. None of it would. I was a fool to buy into the whole damned thing. He'd get over me. He'd find a new life back home in Italy. I was certain of it. My eyes focused on each curve of those letters on my phone.

I'll fight for you...

The phone buzzed, and the screen was replaced by Marco's glorious face. I nearly dropped the damned thing because it surprised me when it went off, as if he could sense I was reaching out across the ether to him. I was reaching and as usual he was there.

His smile glowed from my phone, and tears fell, blurring and obscuring his glorious and transcendent beauty. It kept buzzing, waiting for me to answer it—each throbbing, rattling motion pleading for me to answer his call.

One more ring and it'll slip to voice mail. I declined the call—hating myself to hell and gone for doing so, knowing he wouldn't let it go. A beat.

No voice mail.

Another call.

I let it ring through, sagging against my pillow and weeping like the fucking social retard I was. And I am not the type of person to use the word *retard* with ease. If I used it, I fucking meant it. And in reference to me, I meant it. Deeply. I was an inept and undeserving boyfriend. He was mythic; he was a god. A god who stumbled, but didn't they all in those mythic legends? Why should my guy be any different? I was the little fag boy who belonged in the shadows. I deserved to be cast back there—where I belonged.

No voice mail.

I should've answered. A reminder that there were a great many things I should've...but didn't. I rolled over in my bed, clutching the pillow closer to me.

Silence, oppressive and weighted, pressed in around me.

The phone buzzed.

I picked it up and looked at the text from Marco.

> *I get it. I'll leave you alone. Good night, my dearest love...miss you—M*

I broke.

Sunday was a fucking slog fest. I was pissed. I was sad. I was a fucking over-the-top dick to anyone who had the misfortune to cross my path. Foul didn't begin to describe it. It was a good thing I was exiled to the store. And thank the creator of all that was holy no one actually decided to show up at all. I couldn't've handled it. So instead I cleaned; I scrubbed. I kicked; I pounded; I walloped. I was a fucking mess, and I took it out on *everything*. Nothing was spared my wrath, wrath that was saturated in guilt.

Yet, through it all, every time I spared a look out the front of the store—which was far more often than I wanted to admit—I noted that Marco had remained true to his word: he stayed away. No car in the parking lot. No drive-bys. Zero. Nothing. I was crushed.

I never felt so utterly alone, so completely small and unworthy.

It was further proof I didn't deserve him.

I wanted my bigger-than-life boyfriend. I wanted him to pull me to him and let me disappear into him. I wanted him to take me back into oblivion. He could make me disappear from everything and everyone if he'd only take me back.

I just wished I were worthy of that.

I didn't know when I would be, or if even I could. But I did know one thing: I loved him so deeply I knew I'd go off-the-rails crazy if I didn't get my fucking shit together and tell him what's what. Admit to my own infidelity. Admit how royally I'd fucked things up all on my own. It had nothing to do with Homecoming, his parents, or what he *might've done*.

And that was key here—what he *might've done*. I was a fucking fool on a truly epic scale to think I could put that on him with no proof except for my wild imagination. And I knew I couldn't trust that.

If what he'd said were true, and Marco never lied openly to me about anything, then I had to believe him. Fuck, as I thought about it, he'd admitted to it even when he wasn't sure he'd done anything bad at all. He had copped to it, took it like a man, and owned up to the *possibility* that it was true. Marco had always been honest with me. And how had I repaid him?

By being a bitch-assed panty-waist, that's how.

So instead I beat up a sack of frozen fries until I knew it was a mashed-up mess inside. How did I know that? Simple. Because my fucking high-tops punctured a hole in the side of the paper sack which only drove me to make a far greater mess. If someone did wander into the store by mistake, my fucked up emotive state would take care of it right fucking quick. They'd run out of the store screaming there was a fucking cray-cray gay boy raging a personal war against the potato.

I didn't care.

I wailed as I pounded and hurled the mashed potato all over the fucking place. It didn't matter. I realized cleaning it up afterward would give me something to do. And I did it all in a frenetic and maniacal pace.

At the end of the day, tired and worn with my emotive mental ramblings—not to mention the sheer physicality of it—I stood there, bitter and tormented, with the store even more spotless than when I came in.

I gazed out of the entrance of the store, into the waning light, staring at the space in the lot where he'd said he always parked when he was watching me over the summer before he confessed he loved me. I glared at that space through tears streaming down my face.

As empty as the hole in my heart.

I hated myself for that too.

His words still haunting me...and how much I wanted to believe them.

I'll fight for you.

Monday.

I stood there in front of school, debating if I was going to actually do this. I noticed Marco's car was nowhere to be seen. Then again, I arrived on the lot a good thirty minutes before school was supposed to start, mostly because I was up really early seeing how I couldn't get a fucking wink in all night long. I didn't even care what I was wearing. I hadn't shaved since Saturday, so I knew I looked disheveled with my four whiskers showing along my chin. Fuck it, I didn't really care.

I looked down at my clothes, noticing for the first time what I'd put on. *Fuck me.*

Along with some torn-up slightly stained jeans, I was wearing a pajama top, not that anyone but Marco, my mother, or I would know. But it was one more tick in the column of the fucking things I'd lost control of. I was not particularly a fashionista by any stretch of the imagination, but Jesus, at least I knew how to put clothes together, so I didn't look like some sort of escaped mental patient.

"Though apparently, not today," I murmured.

I hitched my hoodie a bit tighter, trying like hell to hide my fashion faux pas, and pulled my backpack up higher on my shoulder. I needed to get to my locker and get shit swapped out for the new day and head to class.

As I slammed shit between my locker and my bag, Cindy's voice—in that irritating supersonic pitch that could strip the paint off the walls if she'd just put a little effort into it—stopped me cold. I closed my eyes, wishing it all would go away. No such luck.

"Beautiful, what a cunt-tacular way to start a morning," I groused to myself.

I didn't want to look. I tried like hell *not* to care what the bitch was up to. Most of all, I didn't want to see Marco with them all. I knew minus me, it's probably where he'd be—it would be familiar to him. And they were forever hanging out together, jocks and cheerleaders—just like clockwork. I heard Sony echoing whatever Cindy said as if she were some speaker set to an auto delay or on a serious amount of reverb. This was invariably answered by a couple of the jocks who were totally pussy-whipped into following the cheerleaders around. Guess if it was the only way you could get some snatch, then maybe I oughta have pity on them.

Yeah, that's it. I'll pity them all. I slammed my English Lit book into my backpack and started to zip it closed when I heard Beau's voice rumble. My eyes closed again involuntarily—as if I thought for one moment that if I didn't really see him, he'd go away. Just the sound of him was enough to bring fear on the rise. Without Marco at my side, I'd never felt more vulnerable.

"C'mon, Sforza—you are *seriously laggin'* this morning. Whass the matter witchoo? Too much of a hot night out with Cindy again?"

To which she cackled like the hyena she is. I couldn't help myself; my eyes snapped to where they were down the hall to find Marco bringing up the rear. I could practically hear Cindy's smile crack her makeup-spackled face.

Catching that I was watching them all, she lunged for Marco's arm. I noticed he had his hands firmly planted in his jacket pockets. His hair was a bit unkempt, and his clothes weren't quite en pointe. These were subtle changes in his appearance, but I noted them just the same. For some stupid reason I couldn't fathom, I took solace in the fact that if I was miserable, then he should be as well. It was petty and it was absolutely illogical, but it also felt so fucking gratifying to see it in action.

Well, I guess I solved that little mystery for today: I'm still a dick. Can tick that off. I have it covered. My general douche bagginess is plodding along, unabated, full steam ahead.

I stopped zipping my pack to see him glance my way, and I noticed he hadn't shirked himself away from Cindy's grasp. It was all I needed to see as they meandered their way out to the quad and Mount Olympus. Well, that's what the geeks at Mercy called the multitiered garden in the main quad, mostly because the top level was the Jock Domain. All the sports jocks really, but primarily it was the football team who called it home turf, though if you lettered, you were in—a bona fide member of the club: the Titans and Gods of Mercy. It had been that way long before we came to this school, and I was fairly certain it'd be the same long after our elderly bodies had grown cold in our graves.

Cindy pulled Marco along by his elbow with her arm firmly tucked in with his. I couldn't quite tell what the look was he gave me. Even across that great distance, as they were literally on the other end of the building from where my locker was, I should've been able to read what was going on. When we were together, really together, I could've read that look and known exactly what he was thinking. Two days later, and he was becoming a nonentity to me. He was slipping away. It was a very sickening feeling, like fingers slipping through my intestines—raw, horrifically moist, and harrowing. Maybe that was the whole point.

I didn't know anymore.

I finished zipping up and slammed the locker shut only to hear Cindy and Sony's laughter chase me down the hall and up the stairs to Mr. Crowe's classroom. Once ensconced inside, I stared out that same bloody floor-to-ceiling window I had for the past several weeks, only this time it felt far different.

Cold. Distant. Painful. I chose to focus on cold. Cold would inure me to the rest.

Yeah, that will be my guide now. Indifferently cold. Damn near fucking austere with it. That's how I can get through this.

I practically heard the queer villain sneer in my thoughts, like one of those James Bond movies where the villain seems so gay—bald, bitter, and petting a puss...cat. That was the dark mood I was in right now. Seeing Marco with his own, when he'd often railed against their narrow-minded ways, only solidified my position. He'd defected, plain and simple. I was the aberration.

I watched them from that lofty, eagle-eyed view of their small, narrowly defined heterosexist views on how the world worked. Marco sat on the side of the cement planter with everyone else around him, still Jupiter-like in that the court was his to command. Cindy, as Juno, by his side. Or rather like a scene out of a made-for-TV movie about a jock football player and his cheerleader girlfriend, so commonplace a story I thought it pathetic. Maybe that's how it should be. Maybe that's what he truly needed. Maybe Beau and Cindy had the right of it all along, and I really *was* the villain in this story. I ran my finger along my neck, pulling at the ball chain dog tags usually hang from, only mine had one helluva expensive ring on it. Marco's promise ring.

I watched as his eyes drifted up to the window. Even now, magnet to steel, he couldn't help checking on me. On any other day, he'd spy me and would make his getaway to come to me. Not this time. I was okay with that. It made things *easier*.

Real fucking easier, goddammit.

I slowly pulled up the chain from around my neck, making sure he could see what I was doing, making sure the ring was visible. It was large enough I was sure he knew exactly what it was. I grabbed my backpack and slipped the ring, chain and all, into it and zipped it up. It was quite the little production, but I wanted him to understand I wasn't going to be wearing it. I was clear about what he seemed to want, so I was going to give it to him.

He could never say I stood in the way.

Cindy said something and they all started to laugh at it, and he spanned the distance with a look—dark, pointed, dangerous—and then he laughed right along with them, just as loudly as they did. But his gaze was in my direction, as pointed as it had been before he joined with whatever insipid thing that Cindy said. The humor never reached those dark green penetrating eyes.

Disgusted, I grabbed my shit and moved away from the window over to the front of the class, sat down, and set myself up. A few moments later Cheryl Petersen came and stood at the end of the table. I glanced up from my phone as I was checking email to find her staring at me from under her bangs that hung nearly as low across her face as mine.

Cheryl could be a quite pretty girl if she weren't so consumed with hiding it with drab clothing in muted colors sure to obscure any femininity. This non-look was capped off with Doc Martens that looked like they were vintage—from like the '90s or something—virtually assuring her single status. Cheryl was on the thin side with the exception of her full hips and rather round ass, the kind of girl's butt guys seemed to like. She had full lips and a rather longish face with carefully sculpted brows over intense brown eyes.

"You're sitting here today? Not in the presence of his regal mightiness?" Her head jerked to the row Marco and I usually sat in halfway up the classroom.

"Is there a problem?" I asked as I arched a gayboy brow her way.

She just shrugged and frowned in a way that said she really didn't have an opinion on it one way or the other.

"Suit yourself. But if *I* had *that* beside me every morning, I'd be first girl on campus to ensure I never lost that seat."

"Yeah, well, between you and me, it ain't all it's cracked up to be, sweetheart. Believe me," I deadpanned as I went back to an email from my father since we'd missed our Skype chat this weekend.

She slapped her backpack onto the table beside me. "Yeah, well, I guess you'd know, wouldn'tcha?"

I stopped reading, letting my phone slip quietly to my lap, and looked at her. She plopped down with all the grace of a linebacker, far heavier than a girl of her size should be able to do. Cheryl was resilient, for sure—her manner of rolling with new information demonstrated that to me far more than any fleeting conversation I'd ever had with her before.

"What would make you say something like that?"

"Ah, c'mon now, it's not such the big secret you both think it is. And if you are sitting here, away from his über-wowness of a fuck-stud, Marco Sforza, then it can only lead to one conclusion: there's trouble in paradise. So, what'd he do at Homecoming?"

"Why do you think it had anything to do with Homecoming?"

She sighed like she was disappointed we had to play my little game. Only for me it wasn't a game; I was serious. I needed to know what she meant by whatever Marco and I were doing was known to others around us.

"Why are you acting like that?" I pressed her to answer.

Unfazed by my aggressive tone, she simply shrugged. "Oh, because you both were as lovey-dovey as can be after you left the stadium with him that afternoon before the Homecoming game, and now, one weekend and a school dance later, you both are about as far apart as you can get."

She eyed me as I slumped back into my seat, her eyes blossoming with gleeful delight.

"That's it, isn't it? Am I right?"

I nodded briefly. "But how would you..."

Two other girls meandered into the room but paused as they heard my voice escalating in pitch and intensity. I was quick enough to bring it back down to Earth. I leaned in toward her with an intensity to my whisper. "How could you possibly put all of that together? Who *else* knows?"

She rolled her eyes as she started to dig out her English Lit book and Surface tablet.

"I saw it for myself as you both left school that afternoon—some of us play hooky every now and then. A girl *can* see things, ya know?"

She watched me as my brows stitched themselves together over our *not* being a school secret. I guess she decided I needed some pity.

"Don't worry, sunshine. The people who'd've figured it out aren't really the ones you should be worried about. They'll keep your shit safe. They'd have no interest in ruining one of our own. In a very odd way, you're probably a bit of a hero. I mean the geek boys won't get the whole boy-on-boy action—well, there might be a few who do, come to think of it. But the rest of us girls"—she wiggled her eyebrows to ensure I got her meaning—"well, we wouldn't necessarily mind seeing a bit of that. Boys like their girl-on-girl action, and well, we geek girls...we have our own little peculiarities."

"Yeah, well"—I swallowed roughly and wiggled a finger in the general direction of her forehead—"you'll just have to keep that all in your head because whatever you've imagined, it never happened."

She smiled, tsking her tongue in a way that always sounded a lot like pigeons in tap shoes to me. So irritating.

"Tsk, tsk, tsk. You think I didn't spy you slipping that necklace with that helluva ring into your backpack?"

My eyes widened a bit.

"You were staring so intently, I just had to find out what or rather, *who,* you were looking at." She watched me for a second longer before she connected the dots for me. "I can follow imaginary dots too, silly boy."

"Okay, so you've figured me out. It doesn't matter. It's over."

"Is it? Wow." She frowned again. "You disappoint me. I'd've thought with the way you two were so into each other it was a forever kind of love. A Romeo and, well, Julian sort of love, ya know?"

"I think you mean Romeo and Juliet, don't you, Cheryl?" Mr. Crowe remarked as he walked in and laid his things onto his desk before turning around and beginning to write up the day's lesson plan. This effectively ended my curious conversation with the quiet, unassuming Cheryl. For a moment, despite my irritation at how easily she'd stripped me down, I sat there silently admiring her, seeing her for the very first time with open eyes. She was, in a very real sense, the female version of me, in just about every way possible. Well, except of course for the lady parts, 'cause, uh, I *so* didn't want to contemplate that.

My awe-inspired admiration for all things Cheryl ended as I heard Cindy's cackle of a laugh echo down the hall. No doubt she was walking

Marco up to class. *Doesn't the bitch realize how phony she sounds when she laughs like that?* And wasn't it supposed to work the other way around? Marco should be walking *her* to class. Well, what the fuck did I know? Maybe girls walked their guys to class now, sexual equality and all that shit. Straights fucking baffled the fuck out of me. Geeky girls loving boy-on-boy action was included on that list despite my newfound admiration of Cheryl. It was all simply too weird.

I didn't bother to glance toward the door. I was beside myself with wanting to see him up close—I really was. This was my chance. Part of me was screaming inside to just turn and face him as he came in. I started to. I saw the toes of his trainers as I heard him beg off Cindy's clutches with a promise to sit by her during next period in American Civics. That did it. I was over it all. I slapped my arm up onto the table and put my head into my hand, effectively screening him out with my wall of bangs he was so enamored with when we were together.

I spied those trainers stopping at the end of my table. I could see them under the crook of my arm.

"Good morning, Elliot," he rasped out quietly.

I sighed, pulled slowly away from the table to look up at him, careful to do so from under my brow. A part of me relished how much it would hurt him to do the one thing that drove him bat-shit crazy with lust for me only now in a completely different context, if only to get him back for letting that leech Cindy hang on to him.

I smirked slightly, allowing it to come into the smallest of smiles, but then said nothing. My eyes traveled to meet his and I saw it. So much pain there I nearly broke. His eyes were misting, glistening. This was incredibly hard for him. I was a fucking dick from hell to pull this crap on him. I took in a slow deep breath.

"Morning," I murmured, the smile slipping from my face. I was in pain too.

"C'mon, Sforza, got our chairs in the back, all set up for us." Beau slapped him on the shoulder and pulled him away. I didn't bother to look back. Gods of my fathers, he looked like shit, unshaven, eyes slightly pink, worry dressing his brow. I was sick to my stomach. I looked down at the floor between my feet.

"Mmmm-hmmm" was all I heard from Cheryl as she opened her English Lit book to the page Mr. Crowe had indicated where we'd be starting.

My god became mortal.
I wanted to curl up and die.

I am not sure how or why things went the way they did. Actually, to be honest it was a bit of a blur for the first two periods. I didn't take a single note from the lectures Mr. Crowe and Mr. Grant had doled out. Mostly I doodled my initials combined with Marco's, constantly going over and over it, my chin resting on the side of my fist against the table with my eyes firmly to the paper and all of the wasted ink in front of me, tracing those damned initials of his.

The buzzer for our next class went off, and we had to stroll our way over to Calculus. Normally I looked forward to this class. Greg had been my one constant through most of my days at Mercy. I so needed him now.

"Dude, whassup?" was all he said as I plopped down onto the chair next to him at the front of the class. "No offense, but, you look like hammered shit."

"Well, my looks mirror my mood, then. Mission accomplished," I murmured with absolutely no conviction in my voice. I was sort of surprised at that, given inwardly I was a fucking mixed-up wad of confusion and hurt.

"Wow, you really do have it bad."

He leaned forward so his head was level with mine which was fairly buried in my backpack because I couldn't find my damned calculator.

"You and Marco okay?"

I stopped my treasure hunt for the elusive calculator as he popped his head up and looked back into the classroom to where Marco usually sat among the cheerleaders this period. He returned his wide-eyed gaze to me and gripped my wrist rather hard, stopping me from digging around into my pack any longer.

"Fuck me. What happened?" he asked in earnest.

What the fuck is it to him all of a sudden? For the life of me I couldn't figure out how Marco and I had kept everything on the total DL around school, and yet everyone I knew seemed to know our shit.

"I knew something went down at Homecoming, but Laurie Taylor was giving me the eye at the dance so I got a bit tied up myself." He wiggled his brow for a second, and I knew he had given up the virgin card. I smirked. *Good for him.* And I meant it too. Inwardly, I found some fucked-up way to be happy for him about that. He was my best friend at school and all. Someone else ought to be happy if Marco and I couldn't.

"Shit. This *is* bad," he offered as he let go of my wrist when I glared pointedly at it.

"Yeah, well, last I checked, it was still my shit to deal with," I blurted out, immediately regretting it. I closed my eyes and ran a hand over my face. "Dude, I'm sorry I said that. I know you're just letting me know you give a fuck."

He slowly shook his head. "You have *no idea* how invested I am in it."

I sat up at that.

"What the fuck is that supposed to mean?"

He was about to tell me, but Mr. Barrett began to bring the class to order so we had to put our social crap aside for the next fifty minutes. I didn't think I could last that long. I grabbed my shit and began to cram it into my backpack any way I could get it in there. I zipped it up as far as I could in a hurry and bolted to Mr. Barrett's lecture podium.

"Yes, Mister Donahey?" He looked at me with his half-lensed specs.

"I'm, uh, not feeling well. Can you give me a hall pass so I can go see the nurse?"

He pointedly gave me the once-over, and I was so thankful I looked like hell because I knew he'd comply.

He reached under the podium, pulled out a slip, and hastily filled it out and passed it to me. I noted that he glanced up into the class in the general direction where Marco sat.

Does everyone know about us? Jesus H. Christ...

I didn't look at any of them as I dashed out of the classroom and into the hallway.

I got about halfway down the hall when I found a custodial closet. Discovering it unlocked, I opened the door, slipped inside, and threw my pack onto the floor. I sagged myself down right next to it with my back against the shelves, and I silently let the tears flow. Thankfully, I had one of those Kleenex packs in my backpack because within minutes I needed to blow my nose something fierce. After about five minutes of that, I got my shit together and trudged my way over to the nurse's office.

"So I got your text. What do you want?" I said as I slumped onto the seat in the stadium next to Greg.

"Dude, what the fuck is going on between you two?"

"Okay, one, how the fuck did you know about it? Which leads me to two, how does *everyone* seem to know about it?" I pulled out my phone from my pocket and turned on the front-facing camera. "Nope, it ain't written on my forehead—well, that's a relief. So, what the fuck gives?"

He shrugged as he dug out his lunch from his backpack. He handed me an extra apple juice box. Greg always seemed to have an abundance of them in his backpack. He was addicted to apple juice, it seemed.

I took it, popped the straw in, and pulled a long draw on the apple goodness inside—allowing myself one brief moment of unfettered *ahhh*.

"Dude, I can't speak for everyone else you lumped into question two, but as for question one, I've been there since day one."

It was his turn to drink as he laid out his sandwich in his lap.

"What do you mean since day one? We got together in July. Seeing how it was summer vacation, I am fairly certain you *weren't* there."

He shook his head as he bit into his sandwich. I had to maddeningly wait for him to get the food masticated enough so he could actually talk. Normally I had an aversion to people talking with their mouth full, but I was willing to set that aside just so he could answer the mofo question.

"No, Elliot. First day of our sophomore year. I was in it from back then, only to be fair, I really didn't know I was until Marco had me well and truly on the road to playing Cyrano to his Christian."

"What? What kind of crazy are you saying?"

"It ain't all that crazy, Elliot. Think about it. Marco was second-string quarterback to my older brother, Kevin. The two were bound to hang out together, so he spent quite a bit of time at my house. He made the connection that you and I were passing acquaintances, which admittedly at the time we were. Nowhere near the bromance thing we've got going on now. It didn't take me long to sort out that Marco had a thing for you, which was over-the-top huge back then, because he hid it rather well. But after—" He wiped his mouth with a napkin he extracted from a pad of them he had in that Mary Poppins backpack of his. "After it was out, he fucking had me as his personal butt monkey between you two."

I sat there stymied at the whole thing. I knew Marco said it went back that far, but I had no idea Greg had been recruited to the cause, with me being that cause.

"It totally makes sense now. All those conversations, and that lunch at your place! Oh my god, I never knew..."

"That's sort of the point, isn't it?" he chuckled.

A beat between us as he attacked his sandwich like a homeless man and I distractedly nibbled at my own, trying like hell to recall the events of my sophomore and junior years, seeing where he happened along there. I just didn't have a whole lot to grab onto. Not knowing about Marco's interest in me, I had to admit most of what I did recall about him was that first period in my sophomore year and that stupid chair game he and Greg used to play to sit next to...

"Oh. My. God. The chair game..." I stammered.

He nodded. "And the light finally goes on, ladies and gentlemen. Jesus, for a quick-witted gayboy, you sure are slow on the draw sometimes."

"Fuck you."

"You wish, Donahey."

A tear escaped my eye before I even knew it was upon me. He stopped.

"What the fuck, Elliot? Jesus, man, *what the fuck* happened?"

"You just don't want to know."

"Uh, yeah, I kinda do. I mean, either way you cut it, Marco's gonna come for me soon. I need to know the lay of the land before he gets to me, and what you want me to do about it."

"*Me?* Why me?"

"Look, I may be Marco's friend, but I was yours long before he came along. I know where my loyalties lie."

I smiled warmly at him. He really was a very good friend. Why hadn't I treated him more like that? I mean, I wasn't a dick to him. At least, I couldn't recall ever being like that. I hope I hadn't. The way he was being with me right now led me to believe I hadn't.

"Well, I wouldn't want to put you in an awkward position between the both of us. It wouldn't be right."

He chortled.

"Yeah, like I have a way out. Be serious for once, Elliot." He shook his head as he took the last bite of his sandwich. Then with his mouth half-full, he continued, "Elliot, whether or not you want to recognize it, I am knee-deep in your and Marco's romance. So, you need to come clean. What the fuck happened at the dance that I am not aware of, and more to the point, why are you acting so fucking guilty?"

"Me…uh, *guilty*?" I stammered even harder with his accusation.

"As a jailbird. What gives? I've never seen you so miserable and pent up all at the same time." He leaned way into my comfort zone, far more than he ever had. "What the fuck *did you do*?"

I leaned way back, trying to avoid his probing gaze. "Personal space, dude. Jesus!"

He didn't relent one jot. "Yeah, so not my concern right now…" A spark seemed to ignite in his eyes. "Oh, my god! You fucked another guy! *Fuuuuuck*!"

Greg got up and began to pace around.

"What the fuck, Elliot? What were you *thinking*?" he barked at me. "Do you know how hard I had to work to get you to even give the guy a chance? *Do you*?"

He was back in my grill again—his hot breath buffeting my face. I could've just leaned forward a bit and kissed him square on the lips. For the briefest moment, I wondered what it would be like.

What the fuck, douche! Haven't you done enough damage? That's how I got into this mess.

"Yeah, all right, I get ya. Bring it down like forty-seven billion decibels already!"

"No, I don't think you do. Fuck, Elliot, how *could* you, man? How the fuck could you *do that* to him? You've no idea how long and how hard he fell for you."

"Well, don't be so quick to put it in past tense, jackass. And by the way, since we're doling out the guilt trips here, what about his boning that cunt Cindy?" That put a stop in his step. "Yeah, didn't get that little memo, now didja?"

"*What?*"

"Yeah, you didn't see that one coming, huh? He seemed to have missed cluing you in on that little nugget of Sforza boning grandiosity, didn't he?"

He smirked.

"Boning grandiosity? Elliot, really?"

"Well, I'm still flustered, dammit."

He leaned his back against the railing with his arms crossed, the smirk slowly mellowing to a grim line of concern along his mouth. "Marco and *Cindy*? He fucking *hates* her. What the fuck is *that* about? And more to the point, how the fuck do *you* know about it?"

"Because I could tell he was unfaithful. Just like he could about me. That's how we are with each other. No secrets, goddammit. Not one damned bloody secret." I was wailing a bit. I couldn't stop myself. It was like one long bullet train of remorse and regret.

"Okay, okay. Calm down." He sat down next to me and gently rubbed my back as I put my head into my hands. "You just have to take a deep breath and tell me what happened."

"I fucked a foreign exchange student who goes here."

"A foreign exchange student? That's not possible."

"What are you talking about? I know what I did, and with who," I said as I grabbed one of his damned napkins sticking out of his pack.

"Dude, I am not gay, right?"

"By looking at how you dress, that's a given," I snorted as I completed wiping my nose.

He chuckled in response, probably shocked that I could still kid around with him even when he knew I was in such a completely fucked-up state.

"Yeah, well, when new meat hits the campus each year—I notice. We only had five students in the foreign exchange program this year. Four girls and one guy. So, unless you've switched teams..."

"Oh, yeah—like that's gonna happen." I snorted.

Greg mirrored the sentiment.

"What's the guy's name?"

"Angelo—and before you ask, I don't know his last name." I held up a warning hand to stall his next comment. "I know, I know. That makes me sort of a slut. Except I only had the one time with him."

"And you put out that first time?" He whistled. "You really are a slut."

He smiled at me and nudged me even though his last comment cut a bit deeper than I think either he or I realized. To show I still loved him as my best bud, I nudged him back, though I really wanted to bitch-slap him instead.

"Yeah, okay. Maybe that last was a bit harsh. But you gotta admit, it was a little bit funny."

I suffered a small smile for him. "Yeah, okay."

"Anyway, it's not him."

"What isn't?"

"Your foreign fuck buddy."

I gifted him with a slanted smile in that *fuck you* sort of way. "He's not—"

"Yeah, yeah, tell it to someone who actually cares."

"You care…"

"About you, sweetness, yeah. We'll be BFFs forever. You'll color my hair and I'll do your mani/pedi's for-eh-ver. Dude, really?"

"Well, you said you did," I groused, pouting more than I probably should've.

"I do." I shrugged, so he nudged me again, a bit harder. "C'mon, you know I do."

He kept on nudging me, so I kept doing it back, until we ended up slapping at each other like two preteen girls.

"Enough already! Jesus, be careful or you'll turn *me* gay."

"Well, at least I know I'll end up with a good boyfriend then." I wiggled my eyebrows at him. He smiled.

"You know, if I were gay, I'd so be your boyfriend."

"Aw, that's the sweetest thing you've ever said to me." I rolled my eyes though I couldn't disguise my blush.

"No. Really, Elliot. A small part of me really does love you like that. It's infinitesimal in size and scope when compared to the females of the species, but it's there, nonetheless. I wish I could be there for you that way. We really click. I've never known anyone who could mentally keep up with me. None of the girls do, that's for sure. You've ruined me that way."

"Dude, it's you who have to keep up with me. Need I bring up Maria again?"

"Yeah, yeah. Okay. But you gotta admit, I am fairly good for a straight guy."

"Solid. You get the honorary gay gold star."

"Wow, gold star status. That's gotta count for somethin', right?"

"It does. You get full access to my complete fucked-upness. Aren't *you* lucky?"

He chuckled but let that one slip by.

"So, Angelo?"

"Angelo."

"We don't have a foreign exchange student named Angelo. His name is Emilio from Madrid, Spain. Supposedly he's quite the looker, but I wouldn't know about such things."

"Well, that's because I'm the only guy for you, it seems." I put my head on his shoulder and smiled broadly, batting my eyelashes at him.

"Uh, ewww, so not playing with your parts, dude." He jerked his shoulder up, forcing me to sit back up again.

"Yeah, yeah. Don't spooge your burgeoning gayboy love all over me," I chided him.

In an instant the humor left his eyes; they became harder.

"No. You're *Marco's*."

He got up quickly and with purpose. He grabbed his pack and stuffed the remnants of his lunch back into it.

"Now, I don't know what your shit is, what you have to work through, but Jesus, Elliot, start acting like he's yours and you're his. You got me?"

He leaned forward and put his hands on either arm of the seat I was in and looked me squarely in the eye—pointedly pushing me into the most uncomfortable place I could be without Marco doing the pushing.

"But..."

"Uh-uh. Not a fucking word," he growled at me. "This is your BFF who cares more for you than I really want to admit right now because I know what he's gone through to get to you. I know how hard it was for him. I may not be gay. I may not understand what it is between you two, but goddammit I will *not* stand by and watch you two implode. Now get your faggoty ass together. Do what you gotta do, but so help me I will kick you within an inch of your life if you hurt him. I love you both, goddammit! I will not watch this happen. So, *fix it*!"

And with that he was gone.

I sat there for a good three minutes just trying to catch my breath, the look in his eyes etched forever on the back of my eyelids. I couldn't *un-see* it, no matter how hard I tried. Unmissable, undeniable, ever present. I knew he was right. I had to set it right. I had to find a way to claw my way back to Marco. Instead of heading to Art, I grabbed my shit and headed off campus.

I needed to think.

The day was slowly devolving from just another overcast day to darker clouds creeping closer to Mercy, mirroring my mood completely as I made the slow trek back home.

I huffed as I rolled over on my bed. Too tired to sleep, too exhausted with all the emotions raging within me that found no hope of peace shook me to my core. I didn't know how to deal with it. Cindy's clutching at Marco, seeing her with him plagued upon my mind.

Could he be seeing Cindy?

I tried like hell to push it away from my mind. Part of me knew he wouldn't—not ever—consider such a thing. But still...the look on his face when that leech of a girl gripped his arm and how he didn't pull away. I had to admit a girl like Cindy would use Marco's moment of despondency to make her move and overwhelm him, deceive him, hell, even coerce him if needs be. There was nothing the bitch wouldn't do to get to my guy.

But he isn't yours anymore.

I grabbed my phone and made my way to his texts. Those four words the only lifeline I had to him now:

> I'll fight for you.

I needed answers.

Greg told me to get my shit together and fix this. I just had no way of figuring out how. Furious for lapsing into feeling sorry for myself and not tending to Marco, I hastily wiped away tears that had started to form.

Get your shit together!

I leaned over the side of the bed and wrestled my laptop from the backpack, spilling half its contents across the bedroom floor in the process, and quickly made my way to the web. I pulled a tissue from the box I had along the headboard cubbies and blew a large collection of snot, wiped my eyes, and gathered myself together to see if I could find something out there that could help.

I searched Marco's social media accounts. Nothing. Not on YouTube, not on Facebook, Snap, Insta, or Twitter. He hadn't posted a thing since our fateful morning where we decided to take a break from one another. He'd just ceased to put anything out. That was bad.

My brow furrowed as I contemplated my options. Desperate, I decided to start searching the Sforzas in general. While it wouldn't give me anything to work with to find my way back to Marco, it might expose an article or two that would shed some light as to what was going on in his life. It was as good a place as any to start.

There were several articles about his parents. I focused on one about the season opening for the San Francisco Opera ritzy gala that recently happened in San Francisco. Marco's parents were prominently featured with all the other socialites and benefactors. The article had a picture of the Sforzas dead center. His cousin, Francesca, just to his mother's right and Marco just beyond his father's left were also in the picture. But there was another boy between Marco's head and his father's, tucked there in the shadows and turned slightly away from the camera, as if looking back into the crowd. My eyes narrowed as I tried to zoom in on the picture. It only maddeningly turned into random pixels, pushing the boy's face further into obscurity rather than clarifying it. Yet, I couldn't help but think that, in some way, he was a Sforza as well. The slightly turned profile so close to Marco's.

The caption was equally interesting and supported my theory: *Opera benefactors Vincenzo and Sofia Sforza (center), attending with their son, Marco (left) and niece, Francesca Sforza (right). Other members of the family were also in attendance.*

I kept searching, now fascinated with the Sforza clan as much as what he was up to since we split. With Marco's words about his family ringing in my ears, I began to try different combinations of social events or contributions the Sforzas made. I couldn't explain it if someone asked me why I was doing this, but somehow it gave me a little connection to him—even if it was a connection he tried desperately to keep from me.

I clicked through several links to articles that seemed to be saying generally the same thing about how great the family was with their philanthropic generosity for social and artistic causes. As I got to the bottom of the second page, however, a related link in my Google search caught my attention:

Sforza Family Conspiracy Theories.

"What the fuck?"

Conflicted, that's what was coursing through my body and making my finger quake the tiniest bit as it hovered over the trackpad on the MacBook. Sweat formed quickly along my upper lip and I hastily wiped it with the sleeve of my shirt. I couldn't shake the feeling of Alice peering into the looking glass at this moment. If I clicked the link, I knew I might fall into the proverbial rabbit hole—and a dark one at that.

"Don't be silly...they're rich, of course they're gonna have trolls and haters saying shit about them."

I bit my bottom lip, my finger shaking even more. I pulled my hand away like I'd put it too close to the fire and shook out the nervousness trying to take root there.

"C'mon, you know how this works. They're famous. People are always gonna try and take them down. You know them."

But did I? I mean, really? All I knew was Marco. And maybe to a smaller extent, his cousin, Francesca. Hardly the deep dive into their personal lives and how they operate as a family. If Marco was to be fully believed, and I had no real reason to doubt him, they were dysfunctional like any other family. Maybe with all their wealth that only amplified it for them. I didn't know how the rich moved about in their world despite what I told Marco about watching *Downton Abbey*. Marco was very careful to temper his wealth around me. I had to remember there was a whole side to his life that he kept from me—to protect me, or so he said. Given what I was reading now, I could kind of see his perspective on it. Their life, glamorous as it was, probably came with a high emotional price tag.

Before I could talk myself out of it, I pounced on the link and watched in rapt horror as page after page of shadowy theory sites started to fill the search before me. Each one a little more ominous than the one before—a definite rabbit hole. Just how far did I want to trek into Wonderland? That became the burning question. I didn't fool myself into thinking I was on some fanciful journey like Alice's. From the short blurbs in the search results, it appeared the family had their dark side— far more real than anything Lewis Carroll could dream up within the pages of his drug-induced classic work of literature.

Yet, the Sforzas were monolithic in Italian history. You bet I searched them out to figure what I'd gotten myself into once Marco and I became a thing. I learned they had risen to prominence during the Renaissance only to have their fortune and favor dashed in the 1600s when they were forced to relinquish a fair amount of their holdings and slip back into the ether of the royals of the time. The family laid low for centuries, moving stealthily in the background of the surviving duchies of Italy—and the world—until their phoenix-like rise from the ashes of oblivion into the Olympic stature they enjoyed from the beginnings of the Industrial Age to the present. A hold on several markets and governmental influence and power they had no intention of relinquishing now they were back in the game.

One thing I discovered rather quickly; it was never good to poke a Sforza. The men of the family ruled like the ancient gods of old. Their words were absolute. And, if history and literature were any sort of guide, gods don't take kindly to being threatened or provoked. I'd witnessed the reaction in Marco whenever my mouth said something stupid or offensive to his ears and he wouldn't have it. His anger intrigued and frightened me in equal measures. I knew he'd never harm me, but the fire in his eyes at those moments made me tremble inside whenever he drew near. I did not deceive myself that every time Marco brought me to him, I was playing with fire. Sforza men were passionate, decisive, and voracious in how they lived life. And somehow, by some odd stroke of luck or divine provenance, my urchin life mingling with stratospheric Marco's seemed nothing short of destiny. Marco always spoke of *us* in those terms.

I'll fight for you.

Hesitantly, I scrolled the search results when one entry caught my attention more than the average fare of dark corporate maneuvers and the like. Those didn't interest me much. Well, not at this juncture at any rate.

One post, from a blog that seemed to trace the darker side of the family operations—beyond the scope of their corporate or social media personas—tracked the individuals within the family. That link, and the brief excerpt accompanying it, threaded me with dread.

My finger quaked over the link: *Whatever happened to Antonio Balducci?*

The small blurb after the titled link made my blood run cold:

Probably the most troubling story for the family is that of Marco Sforza and his one-time close friend, Antonio Balducci. The Balduccis—close family friends of the Sforzas—had a grandson, Antonio, staying for the summer of 2008 in the familial home in Torino with his grandmother, Silvia Balducci. His association with the Sforzas began with a DJ gig they contracted him to perform for a family birthday party. It was then Marco Sforza became intimately associated with Tonio, as he liked to be called by his friends, and could often be seen with the young Sforza heir zooming in and around Torino together.

Marco's name was mentioned in the extract blurb of the article. His name. Not just the family's—his. Suddenly the room felt hot, even though I broke out in a cold sweat just staring at the mention of his name in relation to this missing boy. The shaking had progressed from the index finger of my right hand throughout my body. Like a leaf desperately clinging to life on the tree, its delicate texture caught in the thrust of an impending tornado, I trembled in fear.

Somewhere in the distance thunder sounded, making me jump in the process.

As if the MacBook would suddenly swallow me whole, I quickly pushed the laptop from me and scooted far up the bed, my back pressed to the headboard cubbies. Wrapping my arms around my bent legs, I huddled there, unable to move further. I would've climbed the damned wall if I could. I needed to put as much distance between me and the article as I could in that moment. I stared at the screen from across the bed.

Despite my growing efforts to minimize the terror, the link beckoned me. As if haunted by my childhood past, it felt as if a ghostly hand emanated from the screen, mocking my favorite Bugs Bunny cartoons as a boy. I could practically feel it caress the side of my face, gently pulling on my chin to bring me back to the laptop.

Okay, I gave in. So sue me. A boy was missing from the look of it, and there was my boyfriend's name in the blurb. How could I not *not* read it?

I lay flat on the bed and clicked the link, steeling myself against whatever would come from it. What could Marco possibly have to do with any of this? That's what I wanted to know and wished I never saw the damned thing at the same time. Was this the guy he said he was with? I gently closed my eyes, took a protracted centering breath, forcing myself to calm the fuck down before I opened my eyes to read the damned post.

> *Though there are many sites and blog entries discussing various nefarious efforts by the Sforzas to shape the course of the modern world, no story carries more intrigue and mystique than that of the disappearance of Antonio Balducci, grandson of Silvia Balducci, a close family friend of the Sforzas. Indeed, the Sforza and Balducci families have had quite the history together for generations, going back to their secretive involvement in Mussolini's death. So, to hold Antonio's disappearance against the mired conspiratorial accounts of Mussolini's demise and coming out on top provides clarity of just how troubling Tonio's brief association with the Sforza clan and subsequent speculated*

demise truly is. He had a much-rumored bromance with a teenaged Marco Sforza (see inset picture below). They were often seen whisking throughout the streets of Torino on Tonio's Vespa with Marco clutching to the boy so tightly that many within society circles in the city questioned the truer nature of their relationship. We are not here to debate whether Marco's association with Tonio took on this level of intimacy—though it is highly likely given the accounts of those known close business associates and friends of Tonio, some of whom are at the pinnacle of their fashion careers, often speaking out on the nature of Tonio and Marco's bromance. They don't mince words when recalling the last night anyone saw Tonio.

"You had to see the blowout that happened the night of Tonio's birthday. We all were waiting for the arrival of Marco Sforza. Everyone gossiping on how it would all play out. Many of us know Tonio wasn't specific when it came to who he took to his bed. That was never the issue; it was the association with the Sforzas that raised everyone's brows. He was definitely playing with danger when associating so close with the heir to the Sforza family. He thought he knew how to handle Marco. Maybe he did, but certainly he underestimated what the family would do once they found out," Marissa Tomasini commented days after Tonio's disappearance became the news of the town.

Many only speculated on the events that transpired that night. What we do know is at some point during the evening Marco ascended the stairs with his gift for Tonio—who had secluded himself in his bedroom for a more intimate gathering away from the main party. Whatever occurred upstairs is unclear. Marissa, who was in the room when it all went down, for some reason that continues to mystify to this day, refuses to speak further on the matter. Could the Sforzas have gotten to her as well? What everyone can agree is that Marco was in the room for no more than five minutes before he descended the grand staircase of the house in a hurry, meeting up with family member Pietro Sforza, and Ekaterina Petrova, an up-and-coming runway model, halfway down the stairs where both Sforza boys assaulted Tonio before making their hasty exit.

None of this is troubling as you can't toss a stone far in Torino circles without hitting a party where some sort of fisticuffs occurred during the course of the night. Italian passions run high, even here in Torino. Yet it is in the ensuing hours after the party ended around midnight that things begin to get murky. The family van Tonio used to move his DJing equipment from gig to gig across Europe was found outside of Torino near the town of Villanova Canavese along the Stura di Lanzo. The van was empty and expertly cleaned of anything that would provide a lead for the authorities to pursue. Within a couple of years, and thanks to a lack of evidence, the case grew cold. Oddly enough, it was the Sforzas who stepped forward to handle the funeral arrangements when Signora Balducci finally declared Tonio legally dead. In her best friend's grief, the matriarch, Signora Sforza, took on the arrangements and subsequent celebration of life ceremony before an empty casket was interred in the family mausoleum on the Balducci property. Tonio's body was never recovered.

This is not the only such entry regarding the darker aspects of the Sforzas' movements behind the scenes. While the family fell out of power and prestige in the late 1600s, their rise as a powerhouse of influence from the dark recesses of the global shakers and players cannot be denied. With their growing ascent during the industrial revolution, the family has worked tirelessly to blossom into a global operation with vast holdings across many industries, both in textiles and manufacturing as well as high tech and medical research markets. Would it be so beyond the scope of the Sforzas' reach to rid themselves of Tonio Balducci were he moving too close to the heir apparent to the Sforza empire? Other names within the Sforza family have been associated with Tonio's disappearance over the years for many people were not pleased with his presence–accusations and speculation the Sforzas flatly deny.

There was more, but I couldn't go further. Marco had hinted about the existence of a boy in his past; I didn't know if Tonio could be him. Why did he go missing and was now presumed dead? I'd joked with Marco about their family being so powerful that I often worried I might do something so epically embarrassing the family might "take me out"—something Marco was adamant would never happen. He resented even the speculation I'd put on it. I made sure never to do it again.

Still...

I clicked a link to pursue related article posts along this line only to get a *404 page not found* error. When I tried to go back to the previous page, it too came up as a 404.

"What the hell?"

I remembered I'd turned off caching on my browser, so everything was feeding in real-time which meant whatever I was looking at had instantly been removed or taken offline. I went back to my hit list from Google and tried one of the other links only to run into more 404s. A couple of entries down I tried another one and was successful in getting to the site's referenced link, only to have it break when I went to a subsequent linked page and the back arrow taking me to a 404. It was as if I was being watched and someone didn't like what I was looking at. I immediately glanced around my room, suspicious that a hidden camera was placed here. A flash of lightning and roar of thunder—no doubt I'd angered the gods—made gooseflesh prickle across my skin.

"That's ridiculous. Marco wouldn't do that."

But his family? Yeah, suddenly I wasn't so sure anymore. There were times when Mom and I weren't home. We didn't have a dog or something to secure the house from entry beyond standard locks on the doors and windows. And sometimes even those weren't secured when we weren't home. I had to have a talk with Mom about that.

Biting my bottom lip, I tried to search for this Pietro Sforza under Google Images. There was nothing. Not a damned photo to be had. How can you exist in this world today without any presence on the web? There were plenty of entries about Marco: YouTube vids, pics, general postings across social media, but nothing on this Pietro. This was troubling. I didn't know what to think.

"Best to leave it..."

I closed the laptop and hastily dropped it back into the backpack next to the bed. I pulled the pillow close, my head spinning with the conspiracy theories I had stumbled into out there. Before long, whether due to fatigue from the drama of my day, or because I grew weary thinking about that blog entry, eventually I fell asleep.

Tuesday was more of the same. I'd see him around; he'd look my way, his eyes almost pleading for me to give in and tell him I was ready. But I didn't and so he descended further into a disheveled hell. The weekend was approaching, and with each passing day he seemed to look worse. Each passing day, I hated myself even more. But I just couldn't find a way to come clean, to cop to the fact I was so wrong about all of it, how embarrassed I was by it all.

By Wednesday afternoon there was a rumor that Marco was sick. People were really sort of worried—like *the second-string quarterback might get his shot at stardom* kind of worried. I even spied Cindy trying to get Marco to eat some lunch up on Olympus and he was having nothing of it. I couldn't watch, and not just because Cindy was there. He was hurting because of me. He was unshaven, and with Marco that mattered; his clothes were rumpled. His eyes were bloodshot, and he looked careworn. It had only been a few days since he'd left my bedroom and we'd parted.

But true to his word, he kept away. Except for that Monday morning, which I soon came to realize was his testing the waters between us, when he'd said good morning, he hadn't said one word to me.

On the way home I heard the rumble of the Impala behind me. I didn't look back. I didn't want to scare him off. Truth be known, I was happier than I'd ever been that he was following me, even when he'd sworn he wouldn't. I was okay with his breaking the agreement between us. If I were truly honest, I wanted him to pull up in front of me to stop me from going any further, and haul me into the car and take me away from all of this. I'd let him do it. I would.

Without any further hesitation I turned around, fully ready to tell him that, when I saw the car veer off and take a side street, disappearing from sight.

I ran home, tears streaking along the side of my face and down onto my neck.

I burst into the house and tore into my room—diving onto the bed and crying, beating and berating myself for being so utterly foolish, for not manning up and doing what I needed to do. This was my shit, not his. I needed to own up to what I'd done and beg his forgiveness.

I rolled over in bed and pulled my phone from my pocket with shaky hands. I had to do this. I had to call him and let him know I was ready.

I brought up his contact and waited a few seconds—my finger hovering over the send button to initiate the call. I took a deep breath and pressed it. I was ready. I could do this. I only hoped it wasn't too late.

"Hello?"

Cindy *Fucking* Markham. What. The. Fuck?

"Elliot? Is that you?"

I didn't say anything. I couldn't. My own worst fucking enemy and she was right there, with Marco.

"Look, you little faggot, leave Marco alone. Can't you see how badly you've hurt him? He's only tried to be nice to you, and you go along and fuck up his life. What kind of sick twisted little fag boy game are you playing with him?"

I couldn't listen anymore. I hung up the call. I dropped the phone beside me and rolled onto my stomach and let the tears pour out.

Fine, he can have her. He can have the whole damned thing. I want out.

At some point I fell asleep—the sheer amount of crying I'd done had worn me out.

"It's over..." was the only thing that came to mind when I woke in the middle of the night. I didn't know why she was over there. It mattered little now.

The week progressed in a slow slog. I worked and I cried. I beat up another bag of fries until I was wearing half of it. Cindy Fucking Markham's face was on each fucking fry as I pummeled it across the fucking storeroom.

Mom saw I was struggling. How could she not see it? I wasn't very good at trying to hide it. She tried to talk to me about it. At first I nearly bit her head off. But then I came to her room late that night and begged her forgiveness. I told her I was a shit and I was sorry for making things harder for her and not better. Before she could ask anything further, I begged off that I was extremely tired, which hadn't been a lie—I was fucking exhausted over it all, and I left her to ponder my dour mood.

Throughout the week I kept trying to see if he was posting to Facebook, Instagram, or Twitter. But he was remarkably silent. He wasn't a social media guru by any stretch, but he did have nearly everyone following his Twitter account at school. Being the quarterback sort of guaranteed that status. I was one of the many followers, a nameless face in the crowd. Only it had been my face he said he prized above all others. Now, I wasn't so sure.

Wednesday would've been a bit more removed from it all were it not for my running smack into the cheer squad as I made my way off campus heading home.

As soon as I turned a corner, I came to an immediate stop seeing Sony and Cindy standing with a couple of other cheerleaders heatedly gossiping. I made to turn and go in a different direction when the rest of the squad came up behind me, cutting off that option.

"Well, what do we have here ladies? Queerbait Ladybird Donahey."

The gaggle of girls tittered and darkly smiled at my sudden predicament. I quickly tried to gauge how I'd get out of it. Short of me scaling a large cement planter holding a potted Japanese maple, my options were few to be had. From the looks in their eyes, they knew it too. I wasn't ruling out the planter escape, but before I could make my move, Cindy and her ilk closed ranks around me.

"Ya know, what I can't get is why someone as hot as Marco would even find something remotely interesting in you?"

"We, uh, had to do that project. It's not like I could avoid it or something..." I hated the tremble in my voice. I was showing weakness to them. That never ended well. I had to remember I was able to hold my own against Cindy and Sony when they cornered me before Homecoming. Where was that guy when I needed him now?

Simple, you don't have Marco to back you up. That's why.

"Cut the crap, faggot. We know you've been eyeing him, stalking him, trying to weasel your way into his life. The boys on the team have seen it. It has very little to do with schoolwork. And...I get it."

Okay, this was new. She seemed to pull back, her venom less prominent now.

What. The. Bloody. Fuck?

She crossed her arms, her eyes grew cold, and I knew she wasn't letting up. This was merely the coil before the strike. I swear for a moment her eyes almost looked serpentine to me. I began to sweat all over.

"He's quite the hunk of man meat. I'll give you that." She paced back and forth as if I needed to be schooled in what a catch Marco is. "And that wad of cash his family has doesn't hurt, either. But! Let me make this very clear so you don't go pushing on those fucked-up gay boy fantasies you got rolling around that head of yours. Marco would *never* want you in that way."

For reasons I couldn't explain, I snorted.

So not good, gayboy!

"How would you know? How do you know we haven't already?"

No, no no nonononononononononononono! Gayboy red alert!

I was epically blowing it. Now was not a time for superhero gayboy to bitch his way out of this.

My response seemed to stall them all. They wore exasperated looks on their faces. As if they'd heard my voice in a light they never considered I'd ever have the cojones to pull off. Hey, way I figured it, these girls have been at the center of my world of hurt at school. I've watched them leech the boys—parasites, the whole lot of them.

"It's not like Marco would be attracted to the power your pussy wields."

There. I went too far.

Fuck. Me.

"What did you say?" Cindy uttered in complete shock at the ballsiness of my last statement.

"I just don't think Marco would associate with someone, or any of you, who gives it up for nearly every guy on campus." I glanced around at the whole lot of them, seeing the rising vehemence in their eyes. This was bad. Very, very bad.

One of the cheerleaders pushed me from behind, and I tried to recover but the toe of my trainer caught on an upended part of the sidewalk and I stumbled. My hands went out and landed on Cindy's breasts.

"What the fuck, faggot?"

And she backhanded me with a closed fist. I staggered back only to have a couple of cheerleaders grip me from behind, pulling me up to face Cindy. The side of my face started to swell, no doubt a bruise beginning to form where her fist had collided with my face.

"What's going on here?"

We all turned around, me with my hand covering Cindy's assault, to find Marco's teammate, Enrique, standing there.

The cheer squad parted as he made his way to me.

"Little fucker grabbed my tits!" Cindy spat at me.

"Well, we all know that wouldn't be a solo experience, would we?" Enrique snorted.

The girls gasped at his comment.

"Fuck you!"

"Not a chance in hell, sweetheart. You okay, Elliot?" he asked. Real concern started to take root there.

Why is he being so nice to me?

"Yeah, I, uh, tripped on the broken path and fell into Cindy. Sorry, uh, Cindy. My bad."

Enrique turned to them all. "He apologized, though I have some doubt as to his *simply falling* from where I stood." He glanced around the group, defiantly pressing his position to them all to challenge what he saw. Thankfully, they didn't. Instead they all turned, ponytails bouncing around as if they hadn't a care in the world.

After they'd cleared out, among giggles from several of them, Enrique turned back to me.

"You sure you're all right?"

I nodded, more embarrassed than anything.

"Thanks, uh, I think I can take it from here."

"I can give you a ride home if that would help."

I glanced around, unsure if I should chance being alone again. It wasn't beyond those bitches to get their pussy-controlled zombified boyfriends to seek me out and have another go at me. Maybe I should take Enrique up on his offer.

"Yeah, sure. That'd be great, uh, if you don't mind."

"I don't mind. Not at all. C'mon, let's hit it."

I followed him out to the parking lot and climbed into his Beamer. Not one of the low-end models either. Enrique rode in style. He was cruising in a maroon 640i.

Does everyone live in the lap of luxury but me?

"Don't sweat it, Elliot. Marco asked me to keep an eye out for you. He knows you're feeling vulnerable," he commented as we made our way out of the parking lot.

"I'm on—"

"Yeah, I know where you live."

Okay, that was shocking.

"Oh, uh, okay."

We drove for a bit, neither of us continuing the conversation further. His last words about Marco ringing in my ears.

"What do you mean about Marco?"

Enrique smiled; he was a really good-looking boy. Seems he was an all-around good guy too. As we made the turn onto the street that would lead to mine, he leaned a tiny bit in my direction, his right arm bent onto the center storage compartment between us.

"I know about you and Marco. He explained it all to me. So, I get it. My younger sister is bi. She just came out to the family about a month ago. I love her like the bright sun, so I'm all about the ally status." He winked at me as if that were some queer ally secret signal. The *I'm so cool with the supreme Qweeness* in a gayboy like me sorta wink.

"Oh." I mean, what do you say to something like that? I didn't have the words. Which, if you knew me, is extremely rare. But it gave me hope. My one-time boyfriend was looking out for me even now. Greg was right. I had to put this back together.

We rode the rest of the way in relative silence until he pulled up in front of my house. I was only too glad Mom had the store for the rest of the day since she had errands to run this morning and she needed to relieve Aunt Marsha this afternoon. I didn't have to contend with her worrying over my slightly red face. I pulled down the visor to check the mirror before I got out. It didn't look too bad. It might not even bruise.

Enrique turned slightly in his seat. "Here, let me take a look."

His hands slowly retreated from examining my face, his touch so gentle. Who knew a jock boy other than Marco could be this nice?

"Just put something cold on it. Got some frozen veggies in the freezer?"

I nodded, wide-eyed at this little exchange.

He smirked. "I don't think it'll bruise if you get to it as soon as you get inside."

He removed his hands and smiled warmly.

Still mesmerized, I decided now was the time to make my escape before it got any weirder.

"Uh, thanks. For the ride, I mean. Well...for all of it, really."

"Sure thing. And, Elliot?"

"Yeah?"

"I know you and Marco are going through a rough patch, but he's still there for you. He will always watch over you. You let me know if any of the guys are messin' with ya, okay?"

I slowly nodded, still bewildered by this whole damned day.

"Great." He slapped my knee, bringing me out of my dazed stupor.

I opened the door and mumbled my gratitude again as he powered up the car. I waved him off and then dashed in the house as he made the U-turn in the cul-de-sac just beyond our house before heading off into his afternoon.

Once inside I dumped my shit at the kitchen table and opened the fridge to discover some frozen peas. I grabbed them and applied them to my face as Enrique had instructed. I turned my back against the kitchen counter and just stared straight ahead, not bothering to focus on anything. How could I? This was some seriously convoluted shit my gayboy warning system had no way of preparing me for.

Thursday was surreal. I walked and moved about in a haze, a fog that never cleared no matter how brightly the sun shone upon me. It was Rod Serling/*Twilight Zone* surreal. Black-and-white TV surreal. A nightmare from which neither Marco nor I could awaken. Colorless and bleak.

Each day was slow and only provided more of the same. Every time I saw Marco on campus, he was surrounded by his jock buddies with the cheerleaders swimming around them like those pesky fish that hang on to sharks. Leeches, the whole lot of them. And I'd left Marco to be leeched away. I had no one to blame but myself. Marco's eyes would find mine. It was automatic between us. We could always sense when the other was near despite how hard we pushed against it. We found each other. Binary stars—only who was leeching whom?

Friday's prospects appeared to be no better, only by now I had given up completely as well. My homework slid into oblivion. I had never been this way with homework. It was but one way my collapse was being broadcast to everyone around me. Whatever little ability I had to make myself presentable had dissolved into a miasma of clothing so disparate it bordered on being comical. Comical if it weren't so bloody sad.

Enrique seemed to keep an eye out for me and engaged the guys on the team whenever he spotted them looking in my direction. I made a mental note to tell Marco I appreciated Enrique's offer of friendship and protection when I figured out how to get things back on track with him. By Friday morning it had long passed into being unbearable. This was the ether beyond bearable. Unchartered territory.

Starting with breakfast, Mom had begun to realize something was very wrong with me over this past weekend. We didn't talk about it, but I could tell she was putting it all together. Thankfully she gave me my space. No doubt, she realized I'd only rail at her about not knowing what it felt like to be gay and to be rejected.

Only, hadn't I been the one who had done the rejecting?

"You sure haven't been eating much lately," she said softly as I toyed with my egg-in-a-basket breakfast that morning. In truth I'd had maybe, at best, half a forkful of the sloppy goo.

"Not much for food these days."

She watched me over the rim of her coffee mug. It was a large mug she held aloft with her delicate slender fingers. I had her hands, her build. But I had my father's eyes, and according to her, I had his heart. All in all, not a bad combination, I'll grant you. My dad was a very good-looking guy. Way I'd figured it, if I had one-tenth the handsomeness he possessed, then I was doing fairly well for myself. Maybe I'd snag another guy at some point in my life. He wouldn't be Marco, but...

She slowly set her coffee down. There was a softness to her I hadn't witnessed before, a concern I hadn't seen since we'd both cried that day when I fell down the ravine.

"Can I help?"

"I wish you could, Mom. I really do."

"You and your boyfriend having problems?"

I nodded, trying like hell to stop the tears from forming.

"Bad, huh?"

"Very..." I croaked and stopped because I didn't trust my voice to go any further.

She folded her arms on the table and leaned forward a tiny bit.

"Things weren't always perfect between your daddy and me, you know. Relationships are work, Elliot. But if you really feel for him like I can see you do, then you have to be willing to work through it, to fight for what matters most."

I nodded, the tears starting to really flow. She got up, came around to me, knelt down next to me, and pulled me to her.

"I love him, Ma. I really, really do. I just don't know how to fix it," I bellowed, not caring for one damned second what she thought or that I was spilling my emotive guts all over the fucking kitchen.

"Shhh, I know, baby. I can see that. I do."

She gently rocked me, placing my head on her small shoulder. She was a bird of a woman, but my daddy often said she was the strongest bird he'd ever known. I sorta got that right now.

After a few minutes of her comforting me, I pulled back and reached for a napkin to blow my far too wet nose and wipe away the tears from my face.

"Now, what you're gonna do, is you have to face whatever it is you're running from." I started to say something, but she held up a hand. She wasn't having any of my bullshit right now, whether it was true or not. It simply wasn't on the table.

"I know you, Cassiel Elliot Donahey. You are your father's son. Your heart is bigger than you realize. You feel things deeply. It's always been a worry of ours, your daddy and me, but I just knew I'd have to be the one to pull you up by the bootstraps and throw you back in the game. It's just how you and I are, baby."

I nodded. She was right. It was how we were.

"So, you're gonna go to school, and sometime today, you find a way to pull him aside and talk. I don't care if you gotta ditch today to have it out. This is far too important for either of you to go on like this."

"I'm fairly certain he's doing better than I am with this."

"Maybe, or maybe that's what you've been wanting to see, because it makes it easier for you to push him away. You ever think about it like that?"

"No."

"Well, ya see, now you've got a new perspective to consider. But, either way, you gotta have it out. So, I am giving you full permission to take a day off if you need to." She lovingly slipped my long bangs from my face to behind my ear. "I just want my baby to stop hurting. Okay?"

I nodded again and wiped my nose. Maybe having a caring mom who was knee-deep in my romantic shit wasn't such a bad thing after all.

There was just one little problem with my mom's big plan to get Marco back: he hadn't shown up for school today.

The rumors were running rampant. Now I was worried. I attempted to call him again this morning. No answer. It wasn't looking good. First up, that Wednesday night Cindy had answered his phone. Maybe he'd given up on us. It was the only thing I could think of because surely he could've seen my phone number in his call history, couldn't he? Unless of course Cindy somehow had deleted it. But she'd have to know a helluva lot more about Marco for that to happen.

It just wasn't adding up. And that's what worried me.

I asked to go to the bathroom during Mr. Grant's lecture in American Civics. Instead I padded off to the same custodial closet that had been open before. Lady Luck seemed to be on my side yet again; it was still unlocked.

I gently turned the handle and, small miracles—I was all about the small miracles these days—found no one inside again. What the fuck did the janitor do all day? *Shut it, Els, just go with your good fortune and concentrate on finding Marco.*

I pulled my phone out, pulled up his contact, and called.

Ring

"C'mon, Marco, pick up."

Ring

"Where are you, baby?"

Ring

"Jesus, Marco. It's me... Pick up the damned phone!" I was getting desperate now. His cheery voice bubbled from his voice mail. I remembered his recording it after we'd had a serious make-out session. You can sort of hear me in the background giggling, and there was an audible smile to his voice.

"Hi. You've reached Marco Sforza, I'm, uh, so not available right now, if you'll leave..."

I pulled the phone from my ear, tears falling from my face. I hung up without leaving a message. He'd never refused my call before. Not ever. This was bad. There was simply no other way to see it. I sagged a bit. I slid to the floor of the closet, pulled my knees up, and rested my head on them for a moment, allowing myself to wallow in self-pity. I was definitely that—pitiful.

Who knew how long I'd been there? The period bell hadn't gone off, so it couldn't have been too long, though time was beginning to be a nonentity with me. I wiped my face roughly with the back of my hand and clambered my way back up to head to class—dejected, forlorn with grief. Inwardly, I felt a piece of me begin to die. And I didn't mean that metaphorically; it was literal pains of death. My love for him was dying. I hurt and it was acute and piercing.

But one thing was clear: Marco had moved on. He had Cindy, I guessed. I'd fucked up. Royally. No other way to see it.

I don't remember the rest of the morning. One foot in front of the other, not that it was a conscious move on my part. I was just going through the motions, following the masses and hoping like hell I didn't wander into the wrong class. By the time I reached PE, I realized I had gotten very lucky with my daily wanderings. I really wasn't paying attention, hadn't been since I'd gotten onto campus this morning and discovered he wasn't there.

I begged the coach to just let me forgo tennis for the day and I would spend the period running around the track. I needed to shake things out. I needed to regroup.

I fucking hated regrouping.

I trudged out to the track, watching the other guys who were actually on the track team get a workout. If I tried to keep pace I'd probably end up on the ground dying a slow, breath-catching death—slow suffocation not only from a lack of air, either. I was already feeling emotionally suffocated.

So I ran, choosing to keep my own pace, one foot in front of the other—just like I had been doing all day.

Yeah, I can do this.

The day was already becoming unseasonably warm. A high pressure system had settled in the past couple of days though it was starting to show signs of waning, in effect cutting off the usual Pacific Ocean air-conditioning that always kept things temperate. Today, the air was nearly stagnant, little gnats and other insects flittering around. I swear I swallowed a few as I cleared the far end of the track where a small flurry of them were swarming. Another lap and I was beginning to let my mind go, slipping further into a vegetative state. With each step, and a rising pant to my breath, I felt everything melt away. Maybe that's what I'd do— run until I fell down in a heap of exhaustion, barely have enough energy to breathe, let alone form a thought, least of all a thought concerning Marco.

About ten minutes in, I took a break. I don't know who I was kidding. While I was a decent enough sprinter, long distance was more my style, but I was woefully not prepared to hit the ground running like I had. It'd be like my trying to bench-press two hundred and fifty pounds right from the start. I was gunning for a disaster.

Luckily enough for me, my survival instinct kicked in and forced me to get a drink of water from one of the fountains. I wasn't stupid though. There were only two you could reasonably chance to drink from near the stadium. One was halfway down the field. Seeing how I was at the end farthest away from the main part of the school, there was one a helluva lot closer—tucked just to my right alongside the visiting team's equipment/locker room. So I ambled over, running the end of my gym shirt up to my forehead to wipe away the great amount of sweat I'd worked up.

As I approached the building, I thought I heard something nearby. I stopped and looked around. Might just be a deer in the forested area that ran right up to the school property line here. It wouldn't be uncommon in these parts.

I looked around briefly before deciding it was nothing to concern myself with. I drank deeply for a few seconds and then slowly stood up to face the track again. I picked up the hem of my shirt and pulled it up to my mouth before realizing I still hadn't cooled off as much I should. I whipped the shirt off instead and ran it all over my face and neck to get the sweat off, just taking a bit of a breather.

"Marco, where the hell are you?" I mumbled.

As if the gods were listening to my small plea, strong hands gripped me about the waist and pulled me quite forcibly around the corner of the equipment building—out of view of everyone else on the field. I began to struggle, not realizing who had me until I was forced into the equipment closet with my backside shoved hard up against one of the utility cabinets. A beat later and my head collided with it as well. Before I could shake the black dots from my vision to see who it was, hands slammed on either side of my head. Tremendous heat emanated from whoever had grabbed me. I could tell before my vision completely cleared who it was: *Marco*.

I knew his scent anywhere. When I did come around fully, I found him huffing; like a bull raging for a kill, his breaths buffeted against my face. Instinctively I breathed him in.

Jesus, how I've missed this...

"Are you through with your little time-out?" he gruffed at me.

I opened my mouth to say something, anything, even just to tell him what a fucking asshole I was and beg him repeatedly to take me back. I messed things up so badly I couldn't find the words to begin.

"Never mind. I don't care. So you can save whatever you have rolling around up in that sweet, beautiful head of yours. Goddammit, Els, I can't take it anymore. It's killing me, babe. You're mine!" He pounded his finger on the metal cabinet right next to my ear, driving his point home for me, as if his anger hadn't already gotten my attention enough.

"*That's* how this works. I am *yours* and you are *mine*. *Nothing* will ever change that. Now I'm not happy about you fucking around with some other guy…"

"We didn't—"

"I don't care right now! Well, I do, but not now."

"I swear I wouldn't…I, he stopped…"

He shook his head once, stalling me from making more of a complete ass of myself than I already was.

"Not now. 'Cause right now, this very second, Cassiel Elliot Donahey, you will swear by all you hold near and dear to your heart that *nothing* will ever shake us again. That I am breath and life to you as you are to me. I am through with this shit. Do you understand me? Do you?"

I opened my mouth to tell him so, but a sharp lift of his chin stalled my saying anything, so I kept my gaze firmly locked with his, and nodded just once. He huffed for a few seconds longer, to where it was becoming a bit awkward. I didn't know what to say or do.

He did.

He grabbed me from the cabinet and pulled me forcibly to him, one hand firmly on my ass pulling my hips roughly into his, with his other hand cradling the back of my head and his mouth—sweet Jesus, his mouth collided with mine. His scruffy beard was rough against my skin. It burned, it scraped, and I happily endured it all.

He was ravenous.

He devoured me.

As the kiss deepened, he guided me to the floor and within seconds had my shorts off.

"Fucking shoes…" He ripped those off along with my socks. "Toes. I fucking love watching your feet, babe. I missed you so damned much."

I nodded. I knew I wasn't supposed to talk. This was about his taking me back. I'd endure whatever he was going to put me through, as long as

I was his once more and I knew, I just knew I'd never put us through this again.

My own stupidity, my arrogance, got in the way. He was incredibly angry with me. I saw it. I felt it in the way he was manhandling me. I didn't care. I deserved this. I'd cut him in ways I never should've.

But even in this, in his fury to reclaim what he said was his, he grabbed my T-shirt and shorts and bundled them up to put underneath my head. Comfort, he still found it within him to comfort me.

"Are you good?"

I nodded. Keeping that maddeningly stupid tongue of mine stilled against any other dumb-assed thing I wanted to say. He nodded once in curt acknowledgment before he popped open the button fly of his jeans and out popped that hellaciously beautiful cock of his.

I watched in rapt wonder, choosing to let any angst I had slip away from me over his little caveman fucking he had going on to pull me back to him. He was a fucking disheveled mess. Aside from the unshaven aspect, his hair was droopy in a way that said he hadn't kept up with any of his normal godly grooming regimen. He may not have even showered this morning—either that, or I had missed the hell out of his musk. I heard him pop the top of the travel-sized lube he had on him—it may have been a spur-of-the-moment thing with him, but I knew he always kept a small bottle of it in the Impala.

Worry lined his face. I'd truly frightened him. He was still glorious, that much was evident, though my little stunt had worn him down. I'd done this to him. I'd made him mortal—and one should never make a god mortal. It never ended well. I had leeched all his light, and now it appeared he had come to take some of it back.

Chapter Three

Eyes to the Horizon

Thank the gods the visitors' equipment room was on the outer reaches of the school. Our makeup sex had been wildly erratic, fevered, and deeply gratifying. When he came in me, I swear I learned the value of praying and of having my prayers answered. Only *he* was my god; he was life itself to me. I'd never make that mistake again. I'd never send him away. And I know what they say about never saying never. Well, I didn't see any way I would let that come to pass again. After what I'd put us through, I felt I would endure anything from him if he kept me close.

He spent the next several minutes kissing me hard. He was incredibly rough with me, whether to punish me for ever considering sending him away, or just because he was so happy to have me back, I wasn't sure. To be honest, I didn't care.

I won.

I got my man back.

He was mine and I was his.

I gathered my shit together, reclothing myself as best I could from that little equipment room to make my escape to the gym since the shower bell had sounded. He told me to get my ass out to the car as soon as I was showered. I told him Mom had given me her blessing to miss school if it meant spending the day with him.

He smiled softly at that. It was a first for us; a parent had given us their blessing. For Marco, that was huge. It was a bit for me too.

Maybe one day we could really have it all.

Twenty minutes later he and I were parked along the cliffs. The wind had shifted, shoving the edge of the high pressure south. A wall of rapidly darkening clouds swirled in the distance. The air, once stagnant, had shifted along with the pressure. Cooling breezes now buffeted against us as we lay on the hood of the Impala, wrapped up in each other with our backs against the windshield, legs entwined, with my body nestled along the right side of him, my hand resting flat against his left pec, my head directly over his heart.

We were alone.

We were together.

We were one.

"Babe?" I asked him softly as my head lay against his chest, relishing that I got to hear the most gratifying sound again—his beating heart against my ear.

"Hmmm?" he hummed to me, kissing my forehead softly, his whiskers still tickling me.

"I am sorry for putting us through all of that." The tears came without being called. "I am so, so sorry. I am such an asshole for doing all of that. When I thought I lost you..."

He nudged me from lying against him so he could watch my face fully. Eye to eye. Riveted once again, electric. A gentle thumb sweeping my tears away.

"When did I ever let you think *you'd* ever lost *me*?"

I sniffled. "When you came in on Monday morning with that skank hanging all over you. I saw how she was acting and how you weren't shrugging her off."

He smirked. "Only you could see me at my lowest and think I was being amorous." He shook his head and kissed my forehead again, leaving his lips against them as he spoke.

I looked up at him. A line from one of Jay Brannan's songs lilted through my head, capturing this moment, revealing with poignant clarity what had once been a haze of confusion and hurt. "Ever After Happily" was Jay's take on how the fairy-tale ending as it was understood by the masses didn't apply to boys like us. We had to learn to write our own rules for happiness. It was now, resting on the man I knew I'd love for the rest of my life, that the last few lines of the song rang true. I softly sang them to Marco now.

"*Starting today, I'll tell the story my way. The King of Imperfection, takes back the Prince of Mistakes...*"

"What?" he asked me softly.

"Nothing, just something that finally makes complete sense to me, words from a song that perfectly distills this moment. I don't think I'll ever hear them the same way again."

"Oh. Well, what I can tell you is, my heart was breaking that whole time, babe. I thought I had lost everything. Nothing or no one around me was going to change that. Only you could change that. Only you could release me from the hell I was in. To be honest, I don't remember much from the time I left your house on Saturday morning. It was a slow descent into hell."

I pulled back to look at him fully. Even now, I saw the radiant light from within him shine again. It was still subdued. I'd hurt him quite a bit. I'd give anything to take that from him. I'd let it visit me tenfold if I could make it all better for him.

His eyes narrowed as he looked back out on the horizon as I nestled back in against him again. His arm around me squeezed me just a bit tighter.

"It isn't over yet; you know that," he said quietly. His foreboding tone mirrored the graying sky.

I looked up at him. He nodded once to the clouds in the distance over the Pacific. I cast my gaze that way and saw them. Not soft white and billowy like you'd expect the fog when it rolled in to cool things down as was common in this part of the state. No, these were ominous, foreboding. You could smell the storm coming. Rain, quite a bit of it, it seemed, circled us like wolves.

"Cindy?" I asked him.

"Um-hmmm," he agreed.

Dammit.

"Though not just her. I don't think she acted alone. That night had a lot going wrong for it."

"You can say that again..." I deadpanned.

"That night ha-a-d...hey! Ouch!" I tickled him and bit his right pec hard enough to get his attention for his cheek.

"Well, that'll teach ya." I smirked, though it faded all too quickly as I watched the storm taking shape as it moved toward us. I turned and followed his gaze before he turned to face me. We kissed, softly, passionately. He plundered my mouth and I willingly submitted to it all. When we finally parted, I sighed and so did he.

"There are parts I still can't remember," he said softly while carding his fingers through my hair. I closed my eyes, relishing his touch once again.

"There are parts I wish I could forget" was all I offered.

He let it go.

So did I.

"I know it's not good to not talk things out, babe. But for now we'll just let it go. We both know infidelity happened on both our sides. Mine was perhaps more coerced than yours but…"

"Nothing fully happened, just so you know. I mean, it got out of hand, but we never did…you know."

He was quiet. It was an uneasy quiet. A troubling quiet.

"Thank you for coming clean on it. But if it's all the same to you, I don't want to know any more."

I nodded. "Can I tell you one small thing I learned from it?"

I took his silence as an approval.

"I learned that no one, no matter who he was, was ever going to equate to you. I know I kidded you once that I had nothing to compare you to. Well, now I have. There was no comparison. I am sure he'll make some guy happy down the road. But it won't be me. You're the only man for me, Marco. I swear it to you."

He still hadn't responded. He could be like that. Marco wasn't the talker I was. It didn't mean his silence was a bad thing, just maddening when I wanted some sort of confirmation from him.

I waited, listening to his heart, to the rhythm of life coursing through him. When I finally couldn't take it any longer, I begged him to say something.

"I thought you already had your confirmation that I still love you" was all he said.

I lifted my head from his chest and looked at him—not bothering to hide the confusion on my face.

"You were just listening to my heart. I thought it would tell you everything you needed to know." He smiled softly. "Babe, whatever is coming our way, promise me we'll always face it together."

"On one condition."

"What's that?" he asked softly.

"Will you—"

His phone buzzed. Marco extracted it from the inner pocket of his letterman's jacket. A text message from Cindy. A quirk to his brow as he looked at me.

His finger hovered over the screen to unlock it and read the message.

"You might as well. You know we'll have to deal with it one way or another. The storm on our horizon?"

He took in an audible breath and let it out. I found I mirrored the action right along with him, unsure of what we were about to encounter.

I watched over his chest as he tapped his way to the text message from her.

It contained only four words, words that shook us to our core.

The words?

We need to talk...

Chapter Four

Coiled Like a Cobra

We stewed over that little text from Cindy. We were still battered from our last epic fallout, and now here was Cindy tossing us a new one.

He didn't answer her.

I didn't know what he'd say if he had. Part of me didn't want to know. It was all too real and biting and had the potential, with whatever she'd have to say, to put a stop to our plans.

Saturday, we spent apart. He said he had some things to catch up on that he'd allowed to lag while we were separated. I understood, as I'd practically let my life fall apart during that time too. I was still digging myself out of the homework hole I'd created for myself. Luckily, my teachers were only too happy to help me out as I was a good student who had only shown this one small dip in my academic achievements.

I did make time to head over to Greg's to tell him we were back together again.

"Jesus, thank the gayboy gods you both got your shit sorted. I didn't fancy having to kick either of your asses over that romantic debacle," Greg confirmed as he tossed the basketball soundlessly into the hoop before passing it to me for my layup.

"Hmm, especially because Marco takes such good care of mine." I knew it was cheeky as all fuck, an unspoken agreement between us that I would goad the boundaries of his oft-denied gayboy tendencies to know what *really* went on between Marco and me on an intimate level despite his protestations to the contrary. In many ways, I believed Greg to be a latent bisexual who hadn't quite yet come to terms with it. But that was his journey to make on his own time, not mine. I had to remember that and not goad him too much. For now his squinched face was all he'd give me as a reward for my cheek.

"Aanyway..." he drawled with no small point to his expression that we were collectively moving on. "I seriously am glad it's over." Another effortless shot through the hoop as he passed me the ball so I could repeat the same moves he just did to show him I could, to which he grinned in appreciation of my efforts.

He leveled a sharp finger in my direction. "Though we'll have no repeats of that in the future. Do I make myself clear?"

I held up my hands at chest level in complete surrender. He nodded; the message was received and acknowledged.

I walked up to him as he leisurely bounced the ball, signaling a time-out of sorts.

"There is something I do want to talk about that came out of the whole shit show. If you don't mind."

He nudged his chin in the direction of the house, silently indicating the way we boys do, communicating a complete sentence nonverbally with a single move.

Once we settled with our backs to the side of the house, Greg planted the ball between us and rested his left arm on it, sort of leaning in my direction.

"Okay, spill it. What gives?"

The longer I hemmed and false-started to say what was on my mind began to weigh upon Greg's face more and more.

"Elliot—" He broke my fish-out-of-water moment, finally gave me some relief from my not knowing how to bring up my research into Marco's background with him. "Just take a breath and tell me. And please, for the love of all that is holy, please do *not* tell me it involves your mysterious fuckbuddy!"

"What? No!" I shook my head and then smiled more than I should've given how I'd fucked up and needed to own it and not take my transgression so lightly.

"Okay, then what is it? It can't be that big, can it?"

I sighed, finally resigning myself that I had to say something. I'd started it after all.

"I don't know how big it is. It's just...well, it's about Marco. No, that's not wholly correct. It's about Marco and his family." I clenched my eyes against the memory of reading that damnable blog post, wishing I'd never clicked on the stupid thing. I decided on a different tack.

"Okay, like, we know Marco has a past, right?"

"Els, we all do."

"You *know* what I mean. There's urchins like ourselves..." I began. Greg tried to speak up to counter my assessment of our status in life, but I held up a hand to stall him from giving me any of his lip. I needed to get this out. "And then, there's the godlike family of the Sforzas, right?"

Greg sort of nodded that he accepted my little summation, allowing me to continue.

"So, like, when we were apart, I wanted to see how our separation was affecting him. So, I did a little searching around on the net. I quickly noticed he hadn't posted anything to any of his social media accounts, so I decided to try searching his family, and...well..."

Greg's hand gripped my right forearm to stall me. "Elliot, I'm gonna stop you right there. You know how famous and rich they are. You had to know what you were getting yourself involved with, right? I mean, on some level. When you date someone as rich and famous as Marco and his family are, you *know* in this day and age there are going to be conspiracy theorists, detractors, trolls. You know how this works. You can't buy into that. You *know* and *love* Marco. You have to believe in that."

I turned to face him. "Oh! I do. I swear, I do. But it's just...I found something I don't quite know how to deal with–or even if I should."

By this point my gaze left his face and I stared at the ground between us, ashamed for even wandering down this thicket of gossip and innuendos. Greg was right, I should know better...but, still, Tonio. Marco's Tonio at that. No, I needed to have my say and see what Greg thought about it all. I pulled out my phone and pulled up the bookmarked reference I found on another site that commented on the original being removed under suspicious means but had captured the posting in screen caps. Nothing on the internet truly disappears. I needed to remember that. My desire to put voice to what I saw began to wane a bit.

"Never mind. This whole thing is pointless."

Greg snatched the phone from my hands and began to read what was there before I could do or say anything further. I decided to wait and get his unfiltered reaction to the whole thing. His brow furrowed a couple of times, but he handed me the phone back and shrugged.

"So, some dude disappeared mysteriously. Look at the circles he moved in. It may have nothing to do with Marco's family. Coincidental, I say. But hey, if it bugs you so much, then ask him. He won't hide anything from you. If I am sure of anything, I am sure of that."

"I know. But if I do ask, won't he take it that I think there *is* something to hide?"

Greg contemplated my point for a second or two. "Not if you ask him honestly. Show him what you found if you don't want to hide anything. I am sure it's fine. Guilt by association and nothing more. I mean, c'mon, have you ever had any moment in your time with him that would suggest they'd do anything like that? I mean, really?" He snorted at my even suggesting as much.

"Well, his cousin is a badass and that does give me pause."

"Good point. She is a badass. But still…it's Marco. You know him. Far better than most of us I'd say."

He was right. This was all so foolish. What did it matter if Marco had some sort of fling with this Tonio guy? I wasn't around. He didn't even know I existed. I can't put that on him. It wouldn't be fair and I knew it. I resolved to let the whole thing go until at some point when we've had quite a bit of time away from our breakup where I could pursue it if it still bothered me even as my resolve to never bring it up again began to grow.

"You're right. It's silly."

"It's not silly. I never said that. You love the guy. You want to make sure you understand everything about him. I get it. No secrets and all that stuff. But really, are you gonna get your tips and pointers about his past from a website that has something to grind against the family to begin with? If it was such a cloud of suspicion, why didn't you find any real news sources making that sort of association with this Tonio's disappearance?"

He was right about that one too. I hadn't considered that part.

I nodded. The moment passed. Greg reached out and ran a hand over my head, ruffling my hair.

"Dude! Not the hair."

We both laughed as he goaded me into getting back up and finishing our hoop practice.

Marco called me at home that night while I was readying myself for bed. I pushed all thoughts of the website from my mind and concentrated on what he wanted to talk about for once.

"I haven't answered her text at all. Not formally, anyway."

"It might not be the wisest thing to do, babe. We're gonna have to face it sometime."

"Yeah, I know. I just am not so sure about what happened that night. I get pieces of it, and they're sort of in conflict with one another. It's all too confusing. I try to sort it all out, but all I get for it is a headache and a churning stomach."

"Okay, I hear ya. But, sweetheart, I did have quite a bit of time at work to think about it today."

"Uh-oh, that can't be good for me."

"I'm talking to you now, aren't I?"

I heard the smile in his breathing. "Oh, yeah, huh?"

"Dork."

"I'm your dork, though."

"Are you?"

"Never stopped, babe. But yeah, I've been thinking about a lot of it too. You're right in one way. This is not going to end well. I mean with Cindy being involved and all. If there's one thing she is, she is opportunistic. And I am sure whatever plan she cooked up that night was not all her own doing."

That was a little revelation. Perhaps I did need him to rewind and replay what *had* happened—at least what he could remember happening.

"Baby?"

His breath quickened when I called him that. I knew he was truly worried about us, where we stood. The fact that little term of endearment came so easily to my lips must have been like water to a parched man, soothing his dry, cracked heart and bringing it back to life again.

"Hmmm?"

"I know I said I didn't want to know what happened after I left Homecoming. But I was thinking about it. I think you better tell me what you remember. Anything you think was important."

"Important, huh?"

"Yeah, it might be easier for me to help you fill in the blanks and all."

"I see what you mean, but I'm really nervous about it."

"You nervous? I don't think I've ever—"

"Oh, I've been plenty nervous. And every time I have been, it's always because of what I'm afraid you'll think of me. You have no idea how hard I work to make you happy."

"It shouldn't be work."

"Not like that. I mean, I am very mindful of everything I do—so I will never be an embarrassment to you. That's why this whole Cindy thing has me so fucking pissed off."

"That's good. Anger, yeah, we can go with that. I'm fairly pissed off too. Probably for the same reasons. I mean, I buy the whole rape thing. And while you had to be hard to do it, it depends on what was slipped to you that may have taken even that choice away from you."

"You mean like some vitamin K and Cialis all in one little pill? Make you all sexy and sensual but hard at the same time?"

"Okay, not what I was thinking exactly but, yeah, okay. Could be."

"I don't know. It was definitely something. A combination of something. 'Cause I wasn't just feeling sensual—like touching was the most incredible high. Didn't matter who I touched. My skin was on fire. But that came later. Earlier on, after you left the field, I was just pissed. I hated the whole damned thing."

A beat where all I could do was hear him breathing. I gave him that; he seemed to need it.

"The second half of the game I was so pissed off I was trying to throw the game away. Unfortunately, our team bridged the gap from the wild balls I was throwing. The coach was chomping at the bit, howling at me after each offensive series when the defense was taking the field and I was on the bench, giving me hell and what for about why I was intentionally throwing the game. Finally, at the end of the third quarter with the coach's threats of pulling me from the game, I gave up and began to play our planned strategies and pulled well enough away from the other team to a resounding victory. It made me even more pissed at the whole thing. Naturally, my parents were ecstatic. They had achieved a Homecoming King in me and a championship game that put us in the play-offs. What's more, my mother's well-spent money had nearly unseated you as my consort. With the school board pressing that decision to set your victory aside, my mother's best-laid plans were put into play. And they were both at the dance to gloat about what a victory it was for the Sforzas and what a moment it was in our little town's history that now bore our family name. I'd done right by them."

He was huffing. I wanted nothing more than to soothe him back down.

"I was beside myself with how angry I was with all of them. I became a fucking tiger I was so mad. My father and I got into a terrible fight. I had never talked back at either of them the way I did that night. We still aren't truly talking at this point."

"Babe, I'm sorry."

"I'm not. They can fucking stuff it for all I care at this point."

"Marco, they're family. I know what family means to you."

"But a bloody family doesn't hang your ass out to dry or pimp it out for their own glory."

"Yeah, you've got a point there."

"More than a fucking damned point, babe. I was whored out. Nothing short of it."

"Whored?"

That seemed a little strong to use in this situation, but they were his feelings, so I had to go with it.

"Yeah, 'bout that—I, uh, I'm sick with the possibilities. I would never hurt you, Els. Never. You don't know how completely this whole set of events has turned my world upside down. I hate it. I fucking hate every goddamned bit of it, that it has touched you. It makes it all so dirty to me." He was fighting tears, the sniffling percolating and punctuating each word. "I took three showers today. Fuck, babe, I didn't even work out. It's all so fucking dirty to me."

"Shhh, it'll be okay."

"Will it?"

"You'll still have me, if you still want me, that is."

Now it was my turn to panic. He could so easily walk away now. It wouldn't take much of an effort on his part. My heart kept skipping the longer he paused in answering. An audible shudder came out of his mouth. My hand shook as his breathing buffeted against my ear. Oh, god, here it comes.

"Baby, I'll always want you. Always. It was you I was worried about not wanting me anymore. How dirty it's all become. It's tainted us. It's…"

"You don't know that for sure. *We* don't know for…"

"I know. I fucking feel it in my bones; I know, and I hate that I do. Christ, I hate myself."

"No, don't say that."

"But I do."

"Marco! Stop it!"

He sniffled loudly. I practically heard the tears spilling over.

"I wish I could. I really do, Els. I just have failed you miserably."

"You did nothing of the sort, sweetheart. Well, not intentionally, at least."

"How can you…" He struggled to put it into words; my heart was breaking for him. This couldn't have been easy to come to grips with. All day at the shop I had prepared myself for this very revelation. I thought I had. It seemed like I'd run it down in every possible permutation of what could happen and how it would affect us, if there still was an us after all had come out in the wash.

"It's quite simple. I love you. That's how."

He cried audibly. My heart was being shredded with each sob from his lips.

"I've changed my mind. Come to me, Marco. I can't bear for you to be alone through all of this."

"No, it's not right."

"Why? I don't understand. So, you might have fucked her. You wouldn't have had the first affair in life. Given the circumstances, I think I can handle it."

"Ah god, Els. Don't you see?"

"No. I don't. And if you're going where I think you are, you can just stop right there. You are still the same man who said he loved me."

"I do. God help me, I do. More than my own life. More than anything I could ever hope to be."

"God help you? Why?"

"That's not what I meant. I mean God help me because I'm not good enough for you. Not the other way around. Never that. You're sweet; you're my Elliot."

"Yeah, well, we both still need to heal from this. And like you said, we should do it together, right?"

"I guess, yeah. You never did finish what happened between you and this Angelo character."

"It got hot and heavy, you know that. Are you sure you want me to say?"

That was greeted with silence. Usually never a good thing, but with Marco, you never really knew. Not really.

"When it happened, I knew it was so wrong I put an end to it—right quick. I was nice about it. I didn't think it necessary to be rude. But I was firm. I told him we couldn't ever again, that I was yours and you were mine. I meant it. He tried to tell me if it were true, then why was he there with me and you weren't."

Okay, so I knew I was editing the hell out of what had really happened. He knew we'd fucked or at the very least had started to—even if I'd never fully laid it all out for him.

"I had quite a bit of shit happening on my end..."

"Baby, I know that. Fuck, I threw it right back at him and said so. But then he came up with if I meant so much to you, why didn't you just throw the towel in on the whole Homecoming thing and join me off the field. Fucking walk away from it and all. I didn't have an answer for that. To be honest, it just hadn't occurred to me. I don't believe it occurred to either of us."

He snorted. Not in a way that held any derision in it, more of an acquiescence of our mutual failing to see the obvious out. We'd both failed each other that night. So I said so.

"Neither of us is to blame, sweetheart. That's why you have to come back to me. You were right. I see that now. That's why we can't let them win. Come to me. Let me make you better."

Silence.

Then breathing. Soft, quiet breathing. Mulling it over, more like.

"Come on, baby. Come back to me. They can't win. They just can't."

"'Kay...but, baby, I'm not..."

"Not another word about that. If I say you are, you are. Now, Marco Raphael Sforza, get your glorious hard-muscled ass over here, strip down—"

I heard him crying through a smile, but I had to press on. He needed this. I needed this. We'd get through it. We would. But I'd learned my lesson. It would only get better if we did it together.

"—and climb back into my arms, for fuck's sake."

"Baby, I so don't deserve you..."

"Yes. Marco, you most definitely do. I say you do. If you love me, then that's enough. So, get here, strip down, climb into my bed and into my arms. Tonight, we sleep together. Parents and friends be damned."

He came to me, tired, worn out, humbled. It was my job to rebuild him, to let him fall completely apart so I could put him back together, greater than he was before. He snuck into my room close to 12:30 a.m. He didn't even tap on the window. In truth it had been well over an hour since we'd talked, and I was growing concerned that something had happened, that he'd changed his mind.

I paced around my room, not sure if I should call him. I mean I didn't know if he was intercepted by his parents and they were having another argument or, I don't know, could be really anything from the sound of how their family worked. I had precious little to go on there. Sure, I'd been to the house. I'd witnessed for myself the pristine austere home. Cold and museum-like didn't even begin to cut it. The only room I liked in their house had been Marco's. It was the only one that held any warmth, though I did wonder why my boyfriend had so many pictures of himself in his room. Seemed a little too "selfie" for my tastes. I mean I knew I had some good pictures of me I liked, but I sure as hell wouldn't put them up in my own room.

I sighed, murmuring to myself, "Why are you thinking about that? You've got bigger fish to fry!" By chance my eyes darted to my bedroom window and I saw Marco standing there looking at me. He didn't even have a coat on. Just standing there, shivering in the cold. I ran to the window and opened it to pull him inside.

"Where the fuck have you been? Baby, you're so cold. Get undressed and get into bed."

"Elliot, I don't know 'bout this... I shouldn't..."

With all the sass I could manage without totally flaming out, I pointed an index finger at the bed, and through clenched teeth I said, "Marco, get undressed and get into bed. We are going to sleep. *Sleep*, that's all. I know what I said earlier today about not knowing how we'd get through this, and I was stupid enough to send you away that morning. Yeah, well, I was a fucking idiot for thinking that. I lied earlier when I said it was good for us. You were right; being apart is never a good thing for us. You need to try to remind me of that whenever I go off the rails on our relationship, deal?"

He nodded, though still hadn't bothered to unbutton his shirt or his pants. So I tugged at both, and within a few seconds, only because he went commando, his cock sprung from his pants the moment I jerked on the button fly of his jeans, and he was bare to the room. I briefly basked in the glow of his glorious body, luxuriating in that he was fully naked. I pushed him into the bed. He sort of lumbered to it while I went back to my bedroom door and locked it. Then I grabbed my chair from my little writing desk and ran it up under the doorknob as an extra security measure. I knew this would only buy me a little time to hide Marco should my mother get curious in the middle of the night.

Finishing with that, I sprang for the bed, shucking myself out of my boxer briefs, and within seconds I had my man, cold and slightly clammy from the night air, bringing his massive body on top of my own, the way he loved to sleep, his head softly tucked into the crook of my neck.

"Love you, Els. I love you so much, baby. You've no idea how scared I've been. I thought... I thought..."

"Shhhh, not now. Sleep. I've got you. I won't ever let go. 'Kay?"

He nodded and left me little kisses—over and over as he started to lull us both into a deep and dreamless sleep.

Thank the stars above that neither of us snored—much.

Around five thirty I awoke to Marco's stirring, my shoulder once again wet with the pool of drool from him. I smiled at the absolute domesticity of sleeping with my man. He brought a hand up to wipe his mouth, lazily smirking in the dawning light, our whispers to each other the only sound in this silent early morning.

"Hey, baby. Feel better?"

He nodded without saying anything. "Sorry 'bout the drool, honey."

I shrugged. *Par for the course.* "Yeah, well, that's you all over..."

He snorted and maneuvered to grab the lube from the headboard as he shifted slightly in between my legs to relieve the morning wood. I slowly dragged my fingers along his muscular back while he prepared us for a good morning fuck.

"You know I like waking up to you doing this...you know that, don't you?"

The dark lust coloring his smile went straight to my cock, not that it needed much convincing.

"Good, because it'll be part of our morning ritual when we're married."

"Oh? Just after we're married?"

"You know what I mean, baby."

I nodded. "I am yours and you are mine. I know."

"Always."

He suckled upon my neck as he pressed for entry. I brought my legs up alongside him to give him full access to the depths he so liked to plunder within me. These were the long languishing thrusts I'd come to relish as he moved within me, making my body ache for more, my toes alternately curling and flexing as he pounded my prostate, bruising me as he did so.

"You are so beautiful when we fuck, babe."

"Only then?"

He smirked. "Stop fishing..."

I smiled and then bit down on my lower lip as he found the one spot that drove me wild. I hissed to him softly, "Ooh, right there, lover."

"I know. I got you. Just let me do my thang. I love making your toes curl—so fucking sexy. I so want to shoot a video of that someday. I could watch and stroke to it for hours, completely edging as I watch you writhe under me in pleasure. So fucking hot."

I nodded, only because I could barely contain a thought while he mercilessly pinged that small point within. My breath came out in short pants as he swirled his hips against it, nudging it, making my cock twitch with his efforts. I came—slowly but with such a sweet intensity I was growing to love.

"You good?" He wanted to know if he should hurry up and finish himself.

I nodded. "Keep going. I'm in it for the long haul if you are."

"That's my boy. I'll get you to shoot a couple more times before I blow. You good with that?"

"Shhh, show, don't tell, baby. I'll take whatever you have to give me. It's never over until you say so. I know that."

"God, I love you so much, Els."

And he went to town plying his cock and that sublime muscular body of his for the better part of an hour. The light in the room slowly illuminated the lustful way he watched my eyes—studying me, watching for signs of pleasure that I'd reveal to him in the quietude of our coupling. He'd see them, chase them, capture them, and then bend them to his will. I came twice during that fuck. My chest and belly a puddle of goo that he mashed between us, with gentle words of encouragement that he loved to see me paint myself with cum and could I do it again for him upon command. After my second one though I told him I was really spent, and he smiled and gave in to his own pleasures. When he came, I could feel him pulsing for a good half minute, spending that large wad within me. We lay there in a pool of cum, sweat, and absolute bliss. I was undone.

"I gotta say, those quiet fucks fucking nail it for me."

He smirked. "Els, you don't have to tell me. I know. That's why I do them. I know you like it rough too. But I get to watch you more when I can drive them out of you slowly, methodically. Plus when I shoot, it's so fucking awesome because I've edged it for so long."

I smiled as I slowly extracted us from the tangle of the bedding and dragged him to the bathroom. I yawned softly.

"Oh, a couple of Thursdays from now I'm gonna be gone for a day," he added. "I thought I should tell you about it now. Just during the day though. I'll be home in the evening."

"Oh? How come?"

"Stanford meet and greet."

"Ah." A beat. He was watching me in the mirror on my closet door. "Want me to tag along?"

"I'd love it if you did; you know I truly would."

"I feel a *but* coming on…"

He smirked guiltily, and with a little shrug he continued, confirming my thoughts.

"But it might be kind of awkward, what with football coaches and all. Not that I'd care about them knowing about us. Hell, I intend to tell them. Be upfront about it. But this is the dog and pony show, and you'll just be bored. And besides"—he pulled me into his arms—"I don't want you around other hot and studly men. I couldn't take the competition."

I tried my level best to look completely unconcerned. "I wouldn't see anyone but you, lover boy. Why shop around when I know I've already got the best? Everything else is a cheap knock-off."

He went to kiss me, but I put a finger to his lips. Instead, I produced a toothbrush I kept in a drawer for when he stayed over, and we both took care of business before sharing a minty-fresh morning kiss that lasted for several minutes.

I turned on the shower, and we slowly bathed each other. He fucked me again for a bit, but we didn't give in to it. I sucked him off, tasting what he'd put up inside me earlier that coated his cock, fucking heady mix of flavors. He came again down my throat, whispering how beautiful I was to him, my eyes never leaving his as he emptied himself within my mouth.

I got him dressed and told him to meet me at the shop later. I needed a bit more shut-eye, and he needed to get back home before anyone was the wiser. We kissed softly for a few before he took his leave of me. I nodded off for about an hour when my mother knocked on my door to make sure I was up and getting ready for work. That going back to sleep thing was so not a good idea. I was groggier than if I'd just chosen to stay awake. *Won't be doing that again.*

The day passed rather uneventfully, with the sole exception that Marco was extremely attentive to anything I mentioned, even in passing. I let him practically wait on me hand and foot, which was quite comical given there wasn't much for me to want when all I had to do was the usual stocking, cleaning, and occasional cooking for the wayward customer. Oddly enough we had far more this particular Sunday than any other I could recall. For some silly reason several old people from the Baptist church decided to reminisce about their youth and descended around one o'clock for an afternoon lunch with Blizzards all around. Beau's father, Reverend Hopkins, commented that he wasn't aware Marco worked at the Q. I hastily informed the reverend that he had stopped by so we could discuss our English project which we had to present on Wednesday. It was a testament to the solidity of Marco's and my relationship that he was there for the hand-off and played his part to perfection. The reverend and his crew seemed to buy it, and for a while I actually had shit to do in the store. Mom wouldn't believe the daily tabulations from today's receipts.

For the most part, Marco stayed in the back, making sandwiches or working that beast of a fry machine. He was such a dream because I never had to ask. He just knew where he was needed and chipped in without much prompting on my part. I realized I could have said things couldn't be better, but with everything still swirling around us, a veritable school of piranhas in the water rending emotive flesh from soulful bone, I knew we were not out of the bloody water yet.

As if he could read my mind, as soon as our last customer from the lunch rush was out the door, he tossed the towel he had in his hand over his shoulder like a seasoned chef and said, "I threatened Cindy with a criminal investigation."

I practically tripped over myself when he said that. He lurched forward to help me not drop the load of frozen French fries I was carrying to the mini-fridge near the fryer. He helped me hoist them up.

"Close your mouth, Elliot, unless you're trying to catch the wayward fly that's been buzzing around here for most of the afternoon. Wait!" He flicked the towel in the air, slinging it in one slick-assed move. With a loud crack I twisted around to find said fly convulsing in its death throes some eight inches behind my left foot. He smiled like the Cheshire Cat. "Got 'im." Then he slipped a finger under my chin to gently close my mouth for me.

"Eh, uh, what do you mean you threatened Cindy? When the fuck did this all happen?"

"Yesterday. I actually did talk to her. I know it's sort of a lie, but I didn't want to concern you with it until I'd processed it all. But I did it when we were taking a break from seeing one another yesterday. By the way, babe, I am so down with never doing that again. I know what you said about making the heart grow fonder and all that Hallmark card shit, but that's not us. Never will be. So we're so not ever doing that again."

He chucked the towel onto the prep counter. I hastily snagged it and flung it into the linen hamper and went to retrieve a fresh towel from the rack which I gently placed onto the counter beside him.

"So you saw Cindy, yesterday?"

He nodded slowly, trying to get a read on how that made me feel. Yeah, good luck with that. I wasn't sure how I was feeling. If he could read something from me on it, then I wanted him to tell me 'cause frankly I was a mass of conflicting waddle about it.

"Yeah, she came to the house, if you can fucking believe it. Beatriz answered the door."

"Beatriz?"

"The maid—she happened to be cleaning in the library. You know, the one with all the books you kept peeking into?"

"I did not keep peeking." He smirked and arched a brow at that. "Well, I happen to like books, that's all. I can't help myself..."

He smiled warmly, if only for an instant, my old Marco shining through the haze of confusion we were treading.

"I wouldn't tell you to be any different. Remember? You're perfect for me just as you are."

"I still don't get that, but"—raising my hands up in mock surrender because I knew how he was going to respond, and I had every intention of heading him off at the pass—"I know it's not mine to get. I remember."

He nodded that all was right, as it should be.

"I take it this is what she texted about?"

He shrugged and sort of nodded. I wasn't so sure how to take that, but I decided to let him finish his story anyway.

"Anyway, so Cindy came over and, not knowing my position in the matter, Beatriz let her in, then paged me over the intercom that I had a visitor. Well, when I got to the top of the stairs, there she was, chatting away with my mother no less. I fucking nearly hit the roof I was so livid. Luckily for me, Mommie Dearest spoke only superficially at either one of us, knowing full well that her best-laid plans were still going along swimmingly, but I wasn't a happy participant and she didn't want to press her luck with me—at least not without my father being around."

As he detailed yesterday's events, I realized he couldn't look at me anymore. This was extremely distressing as we had a routine of always being comfortable looking into each other's eyes. I sort of leaned down to catch his attention that had drifted off course a bit.

"Hey there. I'm up here."

"I know."

His eyes finally found mine again and I walked toward him as he turned from the fryer to lean against the prep counter to wrap me in his arms. I rewarded him with a gentle kiss.

"Anyway, so I walked her to the library where Beatriz was still cleaning. I am sure she thought I'd walk her up to my room, you know, that somehow that fucked-up moment gave her license to eke further into my private life. I wasn't having anything of it."

"Mmmm, 'kay."

"What?"

"Nothing, not really. Just absorbing. Go on."

He paused, trying to gauge where the hell my head was and probably cursing the gods above that he didn't have telepathy, which would come in handy right about now, only to realize what a mixed blessing it was in the long run. My randomness would probably drive him bat-shit crazy.

"Yeah, it would."

"What would what?"

"Drive me bat-shit crazy, what else?"

"How the fuck?"

He laughed and it was rich and deep, from his belly kind of laugh. So musical, well at least to these careworn ears that had heard nothing but fear and fretting over what could be for the past several days. It was a welcome sound.

He pulled me tightly into him, his lips upon my neck. "Because, my sweet, I know you far better than you think."

"Well, I don't care what it is. I'm just glad we're that connected."

We kissed softly for a few seconds. I just luxuriated in it, allowing myself to take it in for the brief respite this moment afforded us. I knew it wasn't going to last and I'd need this small humorous moment to cling to when all that craziness would come to pass. And I *knew* there would be no escaping that.

"So, uh, what were you saying about Cindy and something criminal?"

He smiled darkly at my wanting to take a dig at her if only to let him know I wanted to hurt her as much as she tried hurting us.

"That I was going to open a criminal investigation. Yeah. I know it's a bit weird because I was coerced into sex. The whole teenage boy crying wolf over having to fuck a girl—I realize how weak that defense would sound. I know it would be near impossible to use it as a defense, but I can put the scare into her and whomever she was colluding with. The rape thing would never hold; maybe the whole drug thing won't either. But it at least put the fear in her that we weren't going to get together, not that it was ever a consideration on my part. But she didn't know that, actually. Sadly, I don't think she knows it even now."

"What? You can't possibly—"

"She's a cheerleader, Els. They trade on their looks and danceability. All they've got are looks and poise, not much else for her to fall back on. I mean, you remember her biology presentation on sexual reproduction cycles that first year we met? God, *that* was painful."

"Yeah, and you'd think for a slut like her, that'd be a shoo-in, wouldn'tcha?"

"Hey, now...looks like I fucked that..."

My eyes narrowed.

"Yeah, let's not bring that up *ever* again between us, shall we? I mean I realize she'll probably try to rub my nose in it at some point. And uh, ewww, smegma-coated fish much?"

He rolled his eyes as I pressed on.

"Well, after she finds out about us... Speaking of which, what are *we* going to do about that?"

"What? Before the season is over? I told you I was all for it. I'll do it tomorrow at school. Fucking announce it on the school audio system. Hell, I've got enough followers from school on Twitter I could tweet it now, if you'd like. I told you I was all in. You were the one staying my hand."

He pulled his phone out, but I quickly removed it from his hand, kissed his palm, and slipped it gently onto the counter behind him.

"Yes, I think you should hold off. I just wanted to hear it from you. I wanted to be sure we're on the same page, that's all."

"We're always on the same page. At least, I try to be—but you can be so *elusive* at times," he said with a hint of exasperation to his voice.

"Yeah, well, we're going to have to work on that a bit more then, won't we?"

"Lots of personal one-on-one sessions, I'd imagine." His eyes flashed.

"Definitely. Maybe even undercover sort of work."

He mock gasped. "Ah, undercover work? Oooh, sounds like that could be very *interesting*."

He kissed me again. My heart was breaking a little bit for him. It couldn't be easy. He'd been coerced into sex, felt dirty from it, and thought it would be the ruin of us. I had to admit I was swallowing quite a bit of crow in putting it behind us, even if I knew we hadn't heard the last of it. But he was worth it. He loved me unconditionally. I'd given him plenty of opportunity to bail on me, and he never once contemplated it, at least so far as I'd been able to sort out. *That's certainly saying something, isn't it?* I looked into his eyes. Like Greek fire, they burned brilliantly. They only did that when he watched me intently, as he was doing now. Yeah, he was worth just about anything I'd have to endure.

"I better be..." he murmured into my mouth before I pulled back, my eyes narrowing at how he was doing this whole mind-reading thing he had going.

"Okay, you need to stop anticipating my thoughts."

"You're just easy for me to read, baby. I know you thought it was strange that I wanted you to watch me while we fucked. But it was then you were at your most vulnerable, and it was then your eyes let me see into your soul. That's what I fell in love with. You opened up to me and I fell—I fell so hard for you, babe. You've no idea how spellbound you have me. I'm trapped and I have no complaints. Your love is like water to a thirsty man. I only feel alive when I'm with you."

"That's rather a dangerous prospect, isn't it?"

"Oh yeah? In what way?"

"Well, if something should ever happen to me..."

He gripped the back of my head with his big hand and pulled me tight against him.

"Shhh. Don't ever speak of it. God, Els, I couldn't bear it. I just couldn't. I can't even waste a moment thinking about such a thing happening."

"Well, we don't know what the future brings, what will come our way. I could walk across the street…or some thug could jump me… Any number of things could happen. You can't be everywhere at once, hon."

"After we graduate, you just wait and see. I'll figure out how, once we're free from all of this…"

"The Q? Really?"

"Not just the Q, but—" He looked around at the shop, then smiled.

"Well, yeah, I can't wait to get you out of here too. But not just here, I mean out of Mercy. I want us to leave the very next day after we graduate. Start out on our own. Find an apartment near Stanford."

"I haven't been accepted yet."

"Letters have gone out. I got mine and I know you'll get yours. You're so fucking smart, Elliot. I know you'll get in. Then we'll have our little place where I can make love to you all day if I want to."

"While that seems like fucking heaven on wheels…" I flushed from what he'd said.

"Literally…" He giggled, not bothering to hide his lust.

I smirked, mirroring his mood. "Well, we *would* have to show up for class sometime."

"You know what I mean."

"Yeah…" My smirk blossomed into a full-on smile as he tightened his grip on me slightly. He nuzzled into my neck, leaving little nips. I started to giggle and he went for gold. It was as messy as it was glorious.

Chapter Five

The Wrath of Jupiter, the YouTube Edition

Monday came with all the calamity of a tsunami. The incessant buzzing from my phone stirred me slowly to life. It was 5:45 a.m., and Marco was ringing in after he got back from his morning run. We chatted quietly for a few minutes before I had to really get going with my day. That part was good; it was my normal morning routine, albeit a bit earlier than usual. It was my man, so I didn't mind. Everything else went to shit shortly thereafter.

This shit storm I speak of got off to a wondrous start as I was pulling my morning toast from the toaster oven. I hadn't even gotten to decide on butter or jam or both when I was sucker-punched by my mother. She said it with such ease I knew she had it brewing in the back of her head along with the coffee percolating in the coffeemaker.

"The next time he spends the night, I want to meet him. I should know who's under my roof."

I didn't answer, not really. Just sort of nodded. There was no reason to deny what she'd said. I knew that much. I pulled my toast onto the plate and quickly applied some butter. She slapped a slather of egg whites with a little cheddar on my plate. This was the least healthy thing she'd ever made for me. I was grateful for this *decadent* offering. I moved to the table where a glass of OJ and a couple of large dahlias in a vase were waiting for me. I plopped down, a little uncertain where my mother was going with this.

She sat down to her breakfast of yogurt with granola and her requisite cup of joe. We ate in silence, that ominous cloud of her knowledge of my boyfriend's activities gathering above my head. When she couldn't stand it, she broached the subject again.

"I don't understand why you think you have to keep him a secret from me."

She sipped her coffee. I was scarfing my food down just to get the breakfast interrogation time over with.

"You might as well slow down. We have fifteen minutes even before we have to leave, and you'll still be early." Then wonder of all wonders, she dug deeper to really rattle my cage.

"You're both being safe, aren't you?"

"Christ, Mom. I so don't want to talk about this with you. Give me a little cred, will ya? We're exclusive."

"That didn't answer my question which makes me think, *no, you're not*."

"We did in the beginning, but we're exclusive. You have to know him. It isn't like him to stray from who he's with. Very honorable and all that and can we *puh-leeze* stop talking about this? He's gone through so much since Friday. I'm keeping him together, but it's been rough."

"I don't care about rough when your life is in the mix."

"Mom!"

"Don't you Mom me, mister! I didn't carry you for nine months to have you throw it all away on some football jock and his raging teenage hormones!"

"Look..." I almost said his name, caught myself just in time to pull back; I huffed slightly with frustration before I grabbed a Zen-like moment and regrouped. It was best not to piss her off; I had to tread lightly. "If you knew him..."

Wrong fucking tack to take, moron. I just wasn't awake enough to deal with this.

"Pre-cise-ly my point. That's *exactly* what I want. I need to meet this young man who is boning my son. If you both are playing it loose and wild, then I need to look this kid in the eye and make sure for myself he's on the level, that he truly loves you as much as you say he does. That he *is* exclusive to you."

"All right, fuck! I'll figure out a time to introduce you. For fuck sake, give it a rest, will ya? Homecoming was a bitch for both of us, and we're a bit raw from it."

"Language, Elliot." She sipped her coffee, her eagle-like gaze doing its level best to unnerve me. It was working. Then it appeared it was time for a new salvo across my bow. "So why would Homecoming be so awful? That was like what, two weeks ago?"

"Never mind. It just was, okay? Can we please let it go for the moment so I can finish breakfast and you can get me to school?"

She watched me intently for a few seconds before she went back to her yogurt. I shoveled the last bit of egg whites into my mouth along with nearly an entire slice of toast.

"Elliot, don't be rude. You weren't raised in a barn. It wouldn't hurt to have a little decorum."

I was up and to the sink to rinse off my plate and stack it in the dishwasher before I padded off to my room, not bothering to rise to my mother's bait.

I texted Marco to go straight to school, that my mom was driving me in. No way out of it. He called me within seconds of it being sent.

"Why's she driving you in?"

"Because she cornered me this morning saying if you spend the night again, she wants to meet you. She must have fucking heard us."

"I don't see how. We're fairly quiet when we've fucked there."

"Yeah, well obviously not. She asked if we were playing safe. You know...as in condoms."

"What'd you say?"

"I told her the truth. Yes we were, and no we're not. We're exclusive so..."

"Fuck! Elliot. Do you have to be so fucking literal with her?"

"She's my mom, for Chrissake! It's not like lying to her comes naturally. It's not how we are. I'm sorry. I did my best to contain it. I really did."

"No. She's right. I should've introduced myself earlier. Hell, I dunno. Probably should've asked her permission and all."

"It's not like we're getting married, lover."

"Not yet. But we will. I swear to you we will."

"Make an honest man out of me, huh?"

"Always. You're the most honorable thing that has ever happened to me. I want to do right by that. Only way I know to let the other guys in this world know you are mine. Best not to fuck with that if they know what's good for 'em. That's all I'm sayin'..."

"Yeah, well. Not like we're going to be talking about that any time soon. We've still got to get through high school for Chrissake."

"Okay. But it doesn't mean she isn't right. We should do the meet-the-parents dinner thing, I guess."

"Oh, I so hope there isn't a reciprocal element in that statement. I don't think I can handle the posh Sforza surroundings and family culture."

"I wouldn't subject you to that until after we're married, or at the very least engaged. Believe me, I'm doing you a *huge* favor."

"Mmmm-kay. I guess I'll catch up with you in English, then?"

"'Kay, babe. I can't wait to see you again. I miss you so much when we're not together. Now we actually sleep together I just can't sleep well without you."

"Yeah, I sorta know what you mean. Restless kind of sleep. Me too. Can't wait until we can do it all the time."

"Uh-huh. Exactly my thinking on it. If meeting your mom is what I have to do to get a little closer to that, then so be it. I gotta do it sometime. Better on her terms, so she sees I'm not afraid of her, that I'll stand up for my guy."

"You're so smart about these things."

"I'll do anything for you, babe."

"But you shouldn't have to. It should be effortless. It is for most couples, isn't it? Why not us?"

"You'd think, but I bet I could easily find any number of guys who are struggling with the whole 'meeting the parents' fear factor. I don't think this is something that is unique to us."

"I guess. But still, the whole meet-the-mom thing, so weird for you, right? I can try and put it off. Say you're wrapped up with the whole extended season and shit, *only*..."

"Only, what?"

"Well, she somehow knew you were here the night before last. And if that is true, which, given her recent line of questioning I have to believe it is, then before you can spend the night again, we gotta do the meet 'n' greet. Given that neither of us can sleep very well without each other being there, then either we get this over with or, dammit, we're gonna be real tired by the end of the week."

He snickered. "Yeah, and I'm dead tired from just one night without you." A beat. "Sooo?"

"Okay. I'll figure out something."

"Well, I guess it can't be this week—the final game and all. And Mom and Dad are still on my ass about the whole Homecoming fiasco and my cold shoulder to Cindy. The fucking tramp ran into Mom in town yesterday while I was at the Q with you. Spilled it on what a jerk I was to her. I got home to another fucking slugfest."

"He hit you? That son of a bitch..."

"What? No! Oh my god, Els. I can't believe you went there."

"Well, you are Italian...what the fuck would I know?"

"Seriously? Now you've gone all wop-ass on me? Where the fuck did that come from, you corn-holing mick?"

"Mick? Are you fucking kidding me?"

A beat. Goddamn him and his twisted sense of humor. *So not the right time to do this...*

"Fucker..."

"I so had you though, for like a *few* seconds."

"Yeah, okay. God—how the fuck do you know me so well?"

"Two words: two years. Told me everything I needed to know."

"I totally missed out on stalking you back, didn't I?"

"Oh, I dunno... I wouldn't mind if you made up for lost time. I'd totally be down with that."

"*Elliot! We gotta get going!*" Brünnhilde bellowed from the hallway.

"Whoops, Mommie dearest calls—and at near-operatic levels. See you at school?"

"Where else would I be?"

"Point taken. See you there. Bye, babe."

"Later, sexy."

We rang off.

The ride over was a mess of emotions, partially because Mother dearest tried on several occasions to fish for further info on who my boyfriend was and why couldn't I just introduce him this morning when she dropped me off. Parents can be so random and arbitrary when it's the least convenient.

"Mom, the bell is like seven minutes away. You really think I have time to find him on campus and run his ass back here? Not to mention how many social etiquette rules I'd be breaking. He's a jock and I'm a geek...do I really have to go over this with you? I am fairly positive you had the same social structure when you were in high school. This shit doesn't really change."

"Okay, okay. You're right. I was just trying to short-cut it. I really want to meet him and get to know him, sweetheart. I mean, if he's important to you, then he'd better be to me, right? That's all I'm saying."

"Yeah, fine. I get it, well, we get it. He said to set it up"—she went to open her mouth, but I ran rough-shod right over her—"and it'll have to be next week sometime at the earliest. He's got championship games to deal with. I mean, I'm not even gonna see him all that much over the next couple of weeks. They have a real shot at the championship this year. I don't want to take that away from him, ya know?"

"Well, maybe next weekend? Like for dinner at the house or something? We'll put up a sign saying we're closed for the day due to family issues or something or, hell, maybe your aunt Marsha could cover for us that night. That way we won't have any distractions. See if that will work, okay? I need to know rather soon so we…"

"What? Piss off the random two customers we get a week? I think no one will really fucking care."

"Language, Elliot. He hasn't given you that potty mouth, has he?"

"What? No! Jeez, Mom… I *am* eighteen for fuck sake."

"Okay, I get it. You're all grown up now so fuck my rules then, huh? I mean you're fucking under my roof, so you might as well be saying it out loud then, right?"

"O-M-G, Mom. Wow, I so didn't want to have this conversation with you like… I dunno, forever! Please tell me you won't embarrass me by talking about our sex life when he's here. 'Cause if that's where this is going, I will so not let you meet him until like, you're ninety and on your deathbed."

The pre-class bell rang. I was down to five minutes.

"You better get going. Okay, I won't go there with the sex thing. But I will talk to that boy about safe sex and responsibility."

"We were responsible, *are…we are*…ah, fuck, never mind."

I bolted from the car before it could get any more awkward.

I cast a glance back as I got to the glass door of the school; she was turning out of the senior lot heading to the store. So not the way I wanted my morning to begin. Luckily, I was a creature of habit. As I had mere minutes to make class, I was thanking myself for remembering, in the melee that had been my life as of late, my routine of putting my first-period books in my backpack. All I needed to do was a mad dash up the stairs to Mr. Crowe's English Lit class.

I slid into the room, like Tom Cruise in *Risky Business* only this time fully clothed, just as the bell rang for class to start.

"Nice of you to join us, Mister Donahey. Take your seat, if you please."

I always thought of Mr. Crowe as an experiment of playing against type. For, at least to my mind's eye, he didn't really look like an English Lit teacher, much less a fairly brilliant, educated man. I mean, you think English Lit and you have a picture of someone in their seventies, slim as a rail, with a bird-like snout that kept half-moon spectacles aloft while those eagle eyes did their level best to pierce whatever teenage bravado you'd mastered to get you to participate in class. Mr. Crowe was nothing like that. He was a ruggedly handsome man with a very taut muscular frame that was usually encased, as it was today, in some jewel-toned Ralph Lauren Polo with brilliantly tailored tan or khaki pants down to designer shoes. I mean, what red-blooded American teaching man wears designer men's shoes? As I scooted past a smirking Marco to gain my seat, with a quick whisper from him on my Tom Cruise entrance, I found I was pondering Mr. Crowe in a whole new light. Why today of all days when I'd had him as an English teacher several times throughout my high school years kind of shocked me.

I glanced at his hands as I pulled out my book and MacBook to prepare for the class. They were manly hands. No ring. So he was a bachelor. For a guy who probably was in his late thirties or early forties, though he looked much younger, he was a very handsome man. As he put up on the board the final phase of our midsemester project which was due this Wednesday, I watched the curve of his ass in those fitted pants that flared up to a broad v-shaped back. Fuck me, Mr. Crowe wasn't just some arbitrary male teacher, he was a bona fide stud. I was so latent in my requisite gayboy fantasy department. Marco aside, I should've taken notice of my English teacher long before this. *Wow, was I that much of a shut-in before I met Marco?*

A banner message slipped across my laptop. Marco.

Babe, are you checking out Mr. Crowe?

I glanced at him. His gaze was on Crowe though I spied his eyes darting in my direction for a second, a small curve to his lips, and he knew he had me.

I quickly typed back: *You don't think...?*

"Mmmm-hmmm" was all he said, promptly followed by a small cough to hide it. *Yeah, keep telling yourself that worked, Marco. Wait! Marco has gaydar? When the fuck did that happen?*

I spared a quick glance around the room and found Beau's eyes riveted not to the board but to me. His gaze was hard, foreboding. I quickly looked away. Despite Marco's insistence that things had mellowed, I could see it in Beau's eyes how wrong Marco had been. If anything, the vehemence had only intensified. This guy fucking *hated* me. The fact I was still breathing was a nuisance to him.

As soon as class broke, I walked out with Marco. We were discussing the last few elements we needed to put together for our presentation on Christopher Marlowe's works. He stopped with me at my locker while he worked out the logistics of how we were going to finish with the football schedule looming large as Cindy and Beau ambled by. My eyes darted to them both, catching Marco's gaze. While I didn't openly draw his attention, he was quick to pick up on my line of sight and turned slightly so he could see them eyeing the two of us talking about the project. No doubt, Cindy had shared my little set-to with her just prior to the Homecoming vote. That had to be why Beau was eyeing me with a darker intensity.

They passed us and moved around the corner when I turned back to Marco, his gaze far darker than I'd ever seen him.

"Have you had any trouble with Cindy lately?"

"You're kidding me, right? That bitch has always been a thorn in my side. You'd think she'd be over me by now. But no, I'm still her favorite chew toy of choice."

"Yeah, well, I'm putting an end to that."

"No, you can't."

"Yes, Els, I *can* and I *will*. No one will touch what is mine, babe. No one." He said it softly, but with a very implied big stick. *You go, Teddy.*

"Be careful though. There's a lot of eyes on me right now."

"Who?"

"Well, those two"—I indicated with a backward thrust of my head to where Beau and Cindy had disappeared—"for starters. I know what you said about Beau cooling his jets, but he's doing anything but. I'm telling you, sweet..." I paused as the guy next to my locker came up to grab some books before he headed to class. I waited for a moment until he passed. "Heart, the one thing I get constantly from all of them is that I'm being watched. Far more than I'd like. Trust my gayboy instincts on this. You may know them but not this side of them. You don't have a clue what they're capable of, not really."

He eyed me for a second. When I closed the door to my locker, we moved off down the hall. Several pairs of eyes and muted whispers followed us even though I made sure to put us at a slightly skewed angle with Marco slightly ahead of me, just so I didn't add to the impression that we were in any way a jock and a geek sharing any more than our permitted time together.

I could tell he was finally taking note of how others were viewing our progress down the hall. His demeanor stiffened a bit; his shoulders squared off. No doubt he had the pointed gaze that scared the shit out of everyone else but me. When he aimed it my way I knew it was a completely different goal he was after. I was cool with that. I knew my guy could be scary as hell if he wanted to, and I was oh so thankful he was firmly on my side.

As we rounded the hall leading to American Civics, I noted Beau had completed talking to Cindy and was moving off to wherever jackasses went for second period. Cindy's gaze brightened a bit as Marco approached her. Her facial expression clearly was intended to be genuine, but the pained lengths she went to paint it on her face completely derailed that.

"Hey, Marco, how's your morning going?"

"Just fine, Cindy, thanks." He turned to me as I came up behind him. Cindy's eyes darkened a bit as his focus shifted in my direction. "Elliot, I think I see two seats in the third row. Let's snag 'em before someone else gets in the way."

He turned his gaze back to Cindy with his last words as if to emphasize his point that her presence was not required. I made to move in behind him, and Marco shouldered her into the door and grabbed my sleeve to tug me in after him, leaving her to huff in our wake as the teacher was calling the class to order. We slipped into our seats, leaving Cindy to take the front-row seat next to Cheryl Peterson. I pitied Cheryl. She was a nice enough girl and certainly didn't deserve to put up with Cindy's damage.

Mr. Grant began the class with a discussion on the current stand-off in Congress over the debt ceiling. While it was a topic of interest with me, I felt I was already far too exposed after Friday's spectacle to deal with being out front in the discussion of this timely topic. So, I kept quiet, my head down in my notes, while Grant tried, in vain, to get the students motivated into the vigorous debate he no doubt envisioned we'd have on the subject. While I did believe most of the student body probably did have an opinion on the subject, it was always an effort to get someone to break the ice with a significant enough impact that others would take part in the discussion. Usually that was left to me, so Grant was struggling a bit. Marco turned to me for a beat. No doubt even he was pondering the cause of my newfound withdrawal from the class discussion.

I just shrugged and pressed on with taking notes. He quirked a brow at me but decided to let it go. He picked up the baton I refused, and within minutes the class discussion finally ignited to Mr. Grant's satisfaction. I don't know what the hell had gotten into me. The only thing I could attribute it to was Cindy's dark gaze as Marco yanked me through the door after him.

After class was over Marco lagged behind while I put all of my junk away into my backpack. I looked around as everyone piled out of the classroom.

"People are going to talk the longer you stay near me. My shadow has a very long reach," I muttered to him as new students started to file in while we made our escape. He just shrugged, unconcerned. I already had my Calculus book in my bag, but Marco indicated that he needed to pick his up which was on the same wall as our math class, so I tagged along in his wake. I made sure to at least keep some distance between us to limit the amount of damage I was causing him. He may not care, but I cared enough for the both of us.

The rest of the day went pretty much along those lines. By the time lunch rolled around, I went to grab my lunch sack when Marco came up behind me. Since we hadn't made any plans for an off-site lunch period, I figured I was on my own.

"C'mon, we're putting this whole bullshit to rest once and for all."

I had no idea what he was talking about, but if I knew my guy like I did, this couldn't end well. I tagged along behind him. As we approached the open multilayered courtyard, Marco started to make his way to the upper tier of the layered garden. I sort of stalled out partway up the second tier when he realized I hadn't moved any further. He stopped and turned to me with a pointed gaze that clearly said I needed to follow him. I really didn't want to do this, but it was Marco, and I knew I would.

His social crowd had all gathered at the top of the field, the footballers taking up the majority of the top tier. I couldn't help but acknowledge that I found the whole visual of the jocks taking the topmost tier of the garden courtyard to be rather telling. They were, like the gods of Olympus after all, the top of the social strata at Mercy. As I watched the rest of the layers down to the bottom ground level, it was as if whatever part of the courtyard you inhabited seemed to personify your place in the social mix of the school. Where had I often rated in relation to this multitiered diorama? That was easy. Gayboys were relegated to the stands in the stadium. I didn't even rate the courtyard at all. Best not seen if I wanted to enjoy my lunch. The very fact I was crossing social lines without written permission or even my current vaccinations to ensure I wouldn't contaminate their social realm was causing tongues to wag as I followed Marco to the top tier. I even spied a couple of people with their cameraphones going full tilt, no doubt thinking a thorough beating of the local fag by the football team was today's lunchtime entertainment.

As we cleared the top level, nearly the entire quad had gone to a murmured hush. Jesus, I knew it was a breach of etiquette, but fuck me if I wasn't bowled over that it was the social faux pas of the century. The way these fuckers were reacting even surprised the hell out of me.

"What the fuck he doin' here, Marco?"

"'Cause I say he can, Beau. I've got to work through some project shit we have to do this week. He's with me, so show some muthafuckin' respect and be cool about it."

"Have *you* lost your muthafuckin' mind? We don't need his faggoty ass up here in our shit. We're trying to enjoy our lunch, bro. If you gotta do that shit, then take it to the library or wherever we ain't gotta witness it."

"Marco, it's cool. I can meet up with you later in the library or…" I was trying to extract myself from the wall of pointed glares that were all aimed my direction, not to mention the smartphones also all trained on us. It was way hella too hot water for me to be treading. I needed to get my shit out of there and quick. I knew this was a bad idea. Maybe now Marco would see it for real. Marco rounded on me with a stare that stopped me in midsentence. He didn't say anything; he didn't need to. I knew he'd protect me, but I wasn't so sure I wanted him to just then.

"He stays, and if any of you fuckers got a problem with that, then let's take it up with the coach. Let's have a little discussion about *teamwork* and *sticking together*. Let's discuss how you all need to man up and let a brother get some schoolwork done so I keep my grades up so we don't lose any ground while we go into the championships. He's helped me keep my English Lit class grades up, so if I gotta do some work over lunch, then you all better chill and let a brother get to it. I don't have to hide. As your captain *and* your muthafuckin' quarterback, you all need to own up to your shit and *back me the fuck up*. Now chill and go back to what you were all doing. Elliot, we'll sit over there—" Marco indicated a planter bench where no one was sitting about three feet from where Beau and Stephen were eating lunch with a thoroughly astonished Cindy and Sony. Eyes down and head slightly bent, I started to move slowly to the bench he indicated. Marco looked around with a hard gaze, clearly cocked to pounce if anyone so much as flinched in my direction. No one seemed to meet his gaze.

"Any of you got a problem with that, then let's go see the coach. I'll explain to him how your panty-assed attitudes are going to crimp my style. Fuck all, I may even threaten to pull out. I know you all can smell that championship, it's so muthafuckin' close you can taste it." He held his splayed hand in front of his face, inhaling deeply through his nose to emphasize his point, not that I think he needed it. "Wanna blow your wad on Elliot, hey, be my guest. My stats are third in nationals—where are yours? I'm going on to Stanford to play—practically a given. I'm golden. I don't need the championship to play in my future. But I'm betting you all need my ass to get the little star next to your name that will put you over the top and get you tight with your new college coaches. The choice is yours. Man up, or let's do this." He waited around to see if anyone moved. There were so many smartphones trained on the whole standoff you'd have thought it was on the precipice of war. Maybe it was. Fuck all if I knew how these macho boys played. Beau just threw a dismissive hand in Marco's direction, clearly not taking the bait.

"Yeah, that's what I thought."

With as little fanfare or drama as I could muster, I quietly pulled my PB and J out and took a small bite. It was the best I could do given that the situation had zapped just about any appetite I could muster. I was beside myself, not really seeing much of anything in focus, just a bundle of nerves floating in a sea of nausea. Sure, I had Marco watching over me. But to my way of thinking, gayboy in a very strange land, I thought we'd made a serious tactical error. I just didn't know how to get him to see that. He was so confident about how this was all going to go. And yeah, if I was a girl with less than the social status of a cheerleader or, hell, even the pep squad, this would be far easier to take. As it was, I was the meat in a social stew that was about to boil over. My ass was cooked—well done, I might add.

But Marco didn't see any of it. He sat down next to me and pulled out a roast beef sandwich three times the size of my own paltry meal. My boy sure knew how to eat. In between bites he started to bring up our English project, which we'd already discussed at some length, so I knew this was just for show, to let the guys know what he said was the truth of the matter. Somehow, he gauged that this little performance would guarantee my meteoric, if temporary, rise in the social echelon of our school. No doubt while I slowly, silently chewed my sandwich, the Twitter feeds were lighting up all around us. Thankfully the conversations from the crowds had swelled back to normal levels. I had little hesitation on my part to think that the favored topic of discussion was my eating lunch with Marco and the football team. I tried to subtly glance around the team to see the effects of my being here and what it was costing Marco in football jock cred to pull off what he did.

My phone buzzed in my pocket. I yanked it out. Twitter. Fuck me, like the proverbial carrot I couldn't resist. I clicked the app, and there on my feed within minutes of the event was the tweet with a video link to a YouTube posting by the guy who was the editor of our school's social media titled *gayboy scales football jock mountain*—with the hash tag of #MercyGayboyJock. Insert sarcasm here: *Oh, yay, me! This is all I needed.*

I handed Marco my phone and tried like hell to go back to my meager lunch. Not being able to eat another bite, I crammed it into my bag and held my hand out for my phone. Marco's mouth was a grim line, but he said nothing. Our speech was rather limited with so many of his teammates trying very hard to gauge what this whole new turn of events was about. He handed me my phone. I glanced at it again, and it already had over four hundred hits on the YouTube-linked video. And that was in the span of like ten minutes. I refreshed the link, and it was broaching one thousand hits. There couldn't be that many people interested in this little squabble, could there? Okay, gayboy needs an out on this one. Marco might get pissed off at me, but he'd just have to let me have my say and hopefully it would stick.

"Eh, look, Marco, I just remembered I gotta do something. I'll call you about the project tonight."

I grabbed my shit before he could say anything and bolted from the bench at a near run. Within minutes I was safe—far away from jock mountain, and in the stands of the stadium, choosing to sit on one of the cement steps rather than the comfort of the chairs, not that they were all that comforting.

"You were awfully brave. You know that, right?"

I turned in the direction of the voice, a boy's voice, a nice baritone at that, quiet, timid and understated as mine had certainly been in my freshman year. I didn't know the kid though I'd seen him around. I think we even had Art together, though he kept to himself in the back of the room. He was definitely a freshman by the looks of him. God, he was young. Had *I* ever been that young? I supposed I had at one time, but I couldn't recall it to save my life. I guess I just became inured to how I looked.

As if to clarify it, he held up his iPhone displaying the YouTube-linked video. Just from the walk to the stadium it had already grown to over fifteen hundred views and showed no sign of dwindling. I pulled it up on my phone and scanned through the comments. It seemed to have struck a nerve with the gayboys and their supporters everywhere. What do people do all day, wait around and randomly search oddball video titles? As I looked closer, some of them were even commenting how hot it would be if the hottie jock were my boyfriend. Fuck me, we so didn't need this added to our list of troubles.

I could only thank the stars above that my mother had no working knowledge of Twitter. Facebook alone was confusing to her. Tweeting was a concept I knew she didn't get at all. So I was at least safe there. Unless, of course, one of her girlfriends happened to spy the link and send it her way. The video was grainy enough and far enough away, choosing to focus on Marco rather than me, that unless you really knew me, it could almost be anyone he was talking about. The video pretty much focused on Marco's rant with me staying in the background, sheepishly keeping my head down so my bangs obscured most of my face. Safe enough I supposed—well, except for the homo-aesthetic blond fringe along my bangs. *Fuck me, I'm screwed.* She'd know who it was now.

"Thanks, I guess," I said to the kid. He indicated the space next to me on the stairs, and I shrugged.

"Your funeral, dude. Whatever," I murmured to him as if that warning worked with anyone lately. The irony wasn't lost on me.

"I'm Danny, by the way. Danny Jericho. Just moved here this year from San Francisco."

"Now why the fuck would someone chose to leave the City for this Podunk hick of a town?"

"Didn't have much choice. Dad got an offer to run the local grocery store as the manager. It was a good move for us. A helluva lot cheaper to live and he got a raise in the deal. So, here we are."

"Well, lucky you, I guess. Not that I think you won some damned prize or anything 'cause most of us are trying like hell to figure out how to get out of this crap-assed town."

I watched Danny for a moment. He was a nice enough looking kid, a bit on the thin side like me—though with enough toned musculature to give him the slight body edge on me by comparison. He had fine features that strode the line between male and female, androgynous, a classic sort of beauty. His shoulder-length wavy dark brown hair, complemented by lovely hazel eyes, gave him the appearance of one of those skater kids always on a skateboard going somewhere, though he didn't appear to have a skateboard with him now. He was dressed in some retro faded blue tee hanging loose over his nimble frame to the baggy jeans with frayed ends that were shredded around the heels where the pants were too long and dragged behind him down to his slip-on checkerboard Vans. Like his jeans, they had definitely seen better days. He hiked his legs up and wrapped his arms around his knees, leaning his head to the side as he watched me.

"Is he?"

"He, what?"

"Your boyfriend?"

I didn't respond right away, which I guess was all the confirmation he needed.

"Must be hard, huh?" He said it quiet-like, as if it was suddenly his task to help me protect myself from others finding out.

"It can be. But he's worth it."

He snorted, a smirk playing across his lips. He seemed far wiser than his short years on this earth would've permitted him. A calmness emanated from him, almost a Zen-like peace, a resolve and determination that he was completely comfortable with who he was and how he was going to live his life. Maybe it was gleaned by living in that liberal city to the north. Maybe life was easier to be gay there. Certainly, that was the mystique about the place. It was sort of the gay capital of the United States, wasn't it? At least that was the way the neocons liked to portray it in the media.

"Yeah, I bet it's rough wrapping that around you," he said with a touch more remorse than I'd have imagined, like there was experience there talking, not just some gayboy jealousy.

"You say that like you have first-hand knowledge."

"You could say that. It didn't last. Not because we didn't want it to, but it just didn't."

The sadness from his simple statement was powerful. I may have my troubles, and they were plenty, but whoever this kid was had me beat in the game of love. From the sounds of it, he'd played, played hard, and lost. That couldn't be an easy thing to cope with.

"You a freshman?"

"Junior, actually."

"Fuck, you look like a freshman."

"Yeah, I keep telling myself it'll pay off when I am sixty and look forty-five."

I chuckled softly. "Let me know how that works out for you then."

"You got it." He nudged me in the shoulder with his own.

I smirked, a sideway glance his way, seeing he was watching me, not in the way that said he was checking me out, but just in that way I knew we'd be friends for life, like a switch had been flipped or I turned a corner and there he was and it made me feel like *Oh, there you are. Where've you been all my life?* Like the right arm, I didn't know was missing until it was suddenly there.

"You two gonna come out?"

"You have no idea what a topic of conversation that has been between us. He wants to and I keep telling him no."

"You've got the right of it. Believe me, if I had any way of not knowing the truth of that statement, I'd give just about anything to ensure I didn't."

"He was a football player too?"

He tilted his head. "Captain, varsity lacrosse, no less. Huge son of a bitch. I fuckin' ate up that shit like it was the fruit of the gods, know what I'm sayin'?"

I nodded. My heart sort of broke a little bit for the pain I felt in his words, though he did his best not to show it. I admired him for the calm poise he had when he talked about what had to be one of the most painful things to endure.

"You never get over your first love, you know that, right? Isn't that what they say?"

"Yeah, well, *they* say an awful lot, so I tend to take what *they* say with a grain of salt. No one can be that knowledgeable about everything."

"You might have a point there. But hell, it's not like my story is all that unique, obviously." Again, with the nudge from his shoulder to mine. I laughed softly with him and nudged him back. We already seemed to be at ease with each other, my long-lost friend I forgot I had, or something like that. We fell silent. The breeze from the ocean billowing our hair as it gently glided over us, it was a companionable moment. A newfound friend, someone I could hopefully confide in, someone else to cling to in times when I was in turmoil. I wasn't alone, the lone gay in the village, as it were.

"You wanna talk about it?"

He frowned in the way men and boys do when the offer is upon them to open up about something painful and they're trying like hell to display the irrelevance of their pent-up emotions on the subject, when all they really want to do is cry their fucking eyes out. That was the kind of grim set to his features he had going on just then.

"Maybe some other time."

"I'm glad for that."

"What? That I have a painful story of my own?"

"No." I shook my head and turned to face him so he could see the fuller meaning of my next words. "I'd never wish that on a friend." His smile blossomed at my words. "No, it's just you intimated that there'll be another time."

He smiled with a shadow of warmth mingled with whatever lingering pain he was hiding.

"You don't know how happy it makes me to hear you say that. I was worried though. Actually, once I moved here during the summer, I got wind of your reputation on campus, and I knew at some point we'd have to become good friends."

"Wow, should we be picking out china patterns together?"

"Not with the bohunk of love you got on your backside. Marco looks wicked-assed crazy when he gets pissed. That's not something I'd want aimed in my direction."

I spared a glance at the school courtyard, trying to see if he was there railing against his teammates or if he'd wandered off as pissed as I had been. I couldn't spy him anywhere.

"He stormed off shortly after you did, though I didn't see where he got to."

We both were looking in that direction.

Neither of our gayboy sensibilities were on alert as they should've been. We jumped at the sound of Marco's warm, yet commanding, voice.

"That's because he spotted someone else following what was his."

We both stood as Marco descended the stands from above where we were sitting. He had a smirk on his face, so I knew he wasn't pissed off, not really. But I couldn't resist the opportunity to tease. More than anything my doing so would diffuse any anxiety that either of them might be feeling.

"Yeah, well, I've about had it with your drama, big guy. Thought I'd find me someone a little more quiet-like."

"Hey, I never said I was quiet. You'd be surprised. *I am* from the City after all."

Marco whistled. "A big City boy out here in the sticks where the men are men and the sheep are scared? We must all seem like backward country hicks by comparison."

"Marco, Danny—Danny, Marco." They shook hands. I flushed with jealousy as Danny's eyes flashed when he felt the strength in Marco's big rough paws as they clasped his slender hand.

"Danny."

"Heya."

Thankfully the beat between them passed. Crisis averted, at least the one that fired my overactive imagination.

Danny turned to me as if he could already read my mind. "Not to worry, lover boy. I can tell Marco's heart beats only for you. It makes me happy to see that. You've no idea how much. I sorta need that now, to know love goes on."

He said the last as he tucked his hands into his jean pockets and scrunched his shoulders together in the way guys do when they're trying like hell to be noncommittal about something, like it was no big deal, when it was clearly the opposite.

"Jesus, Danny. He really did a number on you, or what?" It was out of my mouth before I realized I'd said it. My hand immediately went to my face as if I could shove the words back in. Clearly too late, damage done.

"You'll have to learn to live with that, Dan." Marco chuckled. "My boy has a habit of spouting whatever's rolling around in that beautiful head of his. It gets him into more trouble than it's worth sometimes. I take it as a blessing. I never have to wait too long before it'll all come spilling out, one way or another."

"Yeah, that's me, Miss Diarrhea Motor Mouth. Hopefully you'll get used to it and not run for the hills like most of my so-called friends."

"Actually, I find it quite charming," Dan said softly, his eyes going slightly lidded on me. Bedroom eyes?

Marco's eyes flared for a second—wow, zero to sixty on the jealous meter much? Danny was quick to change tactics—hands up in mock surrender. He was already one of us.

"But only in that brother-from-another-mother kind of way," he confessed, whether sincere or not I wasn't sure.

"Yeah, relax, big guy. I'm still all yours," I countered, just to be safe.

He smirked. Yeah, he knew the whole time. Just flexing his boyfriend muscles. *I getcha, Marco; I really do.*

We sat back down again on the steps. I glanced at my phone, and we still had another ten minutes to go for lunch.

"They give you much trouble after I left?"

"No. Beau just sort of smirked until I stared his ass down. But the next time I tell you to stay put, sweetheart, you better fucking stay planted. Your running away did me more damage than your being there in the first place."

Danny sighed softly. "God, I miss that kind of talk." He turned his head back to Marco. "You sure you don't have a teammate or another brother who might be interested in an athletic, sweet, and very attentive boyfriend?"

"You see any of those running around you be sure to point them out to me and I'll see what I can do," Marco replied with an arched brow.

Dan clutched his heart, playing along. "Wow, you don't pull any punches, do you?"

I smiled at Marco until something flashed across his face. It was fleeting, but I spied it just the same. I made a note to ask him about it later.

I held up my phone again to Marco; we were now holding around two thousand hits on our video—that was like 10 percent of the town population. His mouth became a grim line. He just shrugged it all off, like it was so easy to do. "Well, we're out now. Tongues will be wagging even if no one actually said it."

"Yeah, well the comments are chiming in with the whole 'gee, wouldn't it be hot if he was his boyfriend?' thing." I sissied up the last line just to make a point of how overly clichéd I thought the whole thing was. Social media could be a real bitch, and not one you always wanted around as a bestie, either.

Marco just got the biggest shit-eating grin on his face. Danny watched the two of us, a small glistening gilding his eyes. Whatever pain he went through, it was big and deeply felt. I wanted to hug him then, but since we'd only met, I decided to withhold that for another time.

"Oh yeah, Elliot. This one's a keeper," he said, all misty-eyed with a wet chuckle to go along with it. Yeah, he was feeling it deep.

"That's what I keep trying to tell him." Marco knocked the back of his hand against my shoulder. Then to me, "I think I like this guy. Can we keep him?"

"Yeah, well, don't get all over the top on it because I just remembered something..."

Marco was right there for the hand-off. "I said your name, didn't I?"

I nodded and planted my face in my hands.

This only caused Dan to have a thoroughly confused look on his face. "What would that have to do with anything?"

"Well, for starters, my mother. She doesn't know."

"Doesn't know you're gay? Wow, that's like a mindblower..."

"What? No. Even I know that would be near impossible to pull off. No, that Marco's my boyfriend."

The light finally came on. "Oh, wow, that's just as...er, perplexing. I missed that last memo. Why *are* we keeping it from your mother?"

I made note of the *we* in that last question. God, he already was a part of us.

"I know, right? God, I *love* this guy!" Marco was beaming, slapped an arm around Dan's shoulder, and pulled him in close to him. I could see how Marco's masculine exuberance caught him off guard. "I've been trying to get him to put it all out there. He's got this silly idea that it'll ruin me."

"Yeah, well, there is that. He's got a point," Dan conceded.

Hallelujah! The saints be praised...we have another smart boy in the house!

"Ah-ha! *Now* who's on the right side?" I countered. Marco quirked his lips, clearly perturbed with my pressing a point he thought we should be long past.

"No, Elliot. Really, Marco's the one who's right. You shouldn't be hiding this—that never works out in the long run; but you have a valid point. That's what I meant. But what I don't get is how this will be a big ol' sign your mother will get wind of. Is she on Twitter?" I shook my head. He shrugged and then continued, "I don't think this has hit any Facebook or Snapchat yet."

"She won't know how to access those anyway unless one of her nosy girlfriends gets wind of it, though it's rather grainy and I'm in the background. I might've gone unnoticed until handsome over there says my name, thereby removing all doubt who he's talking about, at least from a local standpoint, that is. Thank you, my hunk of a glorious man." Marco just beamed brightly in the glow of my back-handed compliment. "She's not the technical type. Hell, sometimes her mobile phone confuses her, and it's not even a smartphone, if you can imagine."

"Elliot, I think you've let one piece of the puzzle slip from your consideration." Dan suggested.

"What's that?"

"It wasn't the only phone capturing the turn of events. No doubt there will be other postings—one where you might even be the center of focus. If anonymity is what you were after, I don't think you'll be able to secure that for much longer. You'll just have to trust that there really weren't any incriminating statements."

"Incriminating? You make it sound like..."

"I'm not saying anything of the sort." He snorted a bit as he pressed on, "This thing has already gone viral from just the whole 'local gay boy being defended by jock quarterback' perspective. Just wait till the activists in the City get wind of this. I'd imagine HuffPo's San Francisco staff will probably start chasing it down, get someone from their live TV trying to sort it out and figure out where we are. But rest assured, there will be other videos posted, and it may catch the attention of local news as a human-interest story. Star quarterback, defending known gay boy on his own turf. Sort of the stuff that tends to get people all sentimental and gushy—as well as rile those conservative twats we so shouldn't be listening to anyway. Especially with us gay boys making inroads as prom kings and Homecoming..." His eyes sought out Marco rather pointedly. "Well, you get my meaning. By the end of the day, it may be difficult for anyone in town not to know what happened here today. But if, by some random miracle, it escapes your mom, what will you tell her after the fact? She will find out eventually. That's a given. I should think you'd want it to be on your terms."

I shrugged, and Marco huffed in complete exasperation. The pre-class bell rang, signaling that lunch period was winding down and I had to start making my way to Art class. I held out my hand and Marco started to take it. I swatted at his hand and grabbed Danny's. "I'm not going there just yet. We'll wait till it all comes out in the wash. Which it may not."

Danny looked at me with a thoroughly disbelieving gaze. Marco just looked plain hurt. I leaned back and kissed him on the lips, which sort of brightened his mood a teensy bit.

"You're still my guy, babe. Just, Danny's safer at this point. Might even throw some suspicion off your tail—you'll come out smelling like a rose for defending me with no real vested interest for yourself other than being a really great guy, which you are, and for the purpose of our continuing education. It's a win-win, you see?"

I started to pull Danny along. He wasn't buying my ploy either from the looks of it, but I could see he didn't want to make waves so early on in our new friendship. Smart boy, he is.

Marco, on the other hand, wasn't fooled for a second.

"That is until your mother remembers you said he was a football player and not some random boy from the school. She may not know how to work a phone, but I'll bet she's committed to memory every comment you've ever made about me—even in passing."

I let go of Dan's hand and turned around to see him standing there with such a look of supreme confidence, the gorgeous bastard, that he'd had the right of it.

I sighed, turned to Danny, and said, "Mister Jericho, would you do me the honor of escorting me to my Art class?"

"Why *I'd* just *love* to…" That was Marco, doing his best impression of a saccharine-infused Southern belle, complete with a higher-pitched voice that nearly made the three of us laugh outright.

"Oh, babe, don't ever do that again. I think you just gave me a big ol' soft-on."

"Me too, and I'm not even your boyfriend. That was just like sixty-three shades of wrong."

"C'mon, Danny. We gots ourselves some drawin' to do."

"Right with ya, boss."

I turned to Marco who looked rather amused at the way Dan and I seemed to fit together, like long-lost brothers or sisters or something, "Yeah, I think we'll keep him. Where the fuck have you been all my life, Danny?"

"Oh, never you mind about all that, sugah, I'z here now. That's what's impo'ent."

Oh yeah, me and Danny-boy are gonna be real good friends. Like conspiring sistahs in a cathouse, I can just tell…

"Somehow I think this is going to come back and bite me…" was all I heard Marco comment as we left the stadium on our way to class.

By the time we entered the building, the hallways were all abuzz with the lunchtime entertainment. Several students, for whom I had never been a blip on their radar before this afternoon, watched with great curiosity as Dan, Marco, and I moved among them. They parted like our presence alone was strong enough to push them back. I was thankful there seemed to be no hard stares following our progress down the hall, more of a hushed awestruck timbre to it, which was as cool as it was off-putting. Cool in the sense that, for once at least, I was sort of basking in the glow of Marco's aura, even if he was only a few steps behind me, and off-putting because my gayboy sensibilities told me this wouldn't last, that it was the buildup to a humongous downfall. I was just waiting for the other shoe to drop.

Dan stopped at his locker with a quick word to me that he would meet me at our classroom. I nodded and kept moving on with a small glance behind me to see if Marco was still there—he was.

"I got you" was all he intoned softly to me as he walked me to my class. I pulled out my phone and glanced at it—three minutes to the final bell for class to officially begin. As I turned the corner to the hall leading to my Art class, I stopped. Marco nearly ran into me. With a muted smile, followed by words so soft I think Marco had to read my lips to understand me, I told him I'd be fine and he could go to class. He shook his head and nodded in the direction of my classroom. With a gentle nudge of his right hand to the right side of my waist, bringing a new round of whispers and glances our way, Marco followed me to the door of the classroom where I finally turned, rolling my eyes.

"Okay, safe and sound. You didn't have to do this," I whispered through slightly clenched teeth, though my eyes were probably saying how much I loved him for it.

"Are you kidding me? I'm enjoying this immensely. You see the way they're all watching us? How frickin' weird-awesome is that? Like my cred is parting the seas."

"Yeah, but you've no idea how this could just be the calm before the storm. Go on; get to class. I'll see you in Psych."

"You stay here after Art. I'll come and get you."

"Marco...no," I whispered, trying like hell to not make a big scene out of it. But I needed him to understand how dangerous all of this was.

"Els, not an option. You stay; I'll come," he said quietly, with the pointed gaze that said this was the way it was going to be. A ragged sigh broke from my lips. I wanted to kiss him so badly but knew how disastrous that would be. So, I tried to do it with my eyes as inconspicuously as I could. He smiled as Dan rejoined us.

"Ready for some wicked art time, bud?"

Marco nodded to both of us and moved off. I just hoped he'd make it in time for class. I glanced Dan's way for a moment. It still sort of amazed me that Dan had been in my Art class all along and I hadn't really paid much attention. Jesus, this whole boyfriend thing could really throw a gayboy game way off base.

Dan and I shared a desk space on one of the large art tables. When I pulled out what I was working on, I saw it in a whole new light given the day's events. I stared at the multitiered garden area of the school as a landscape drawing in pastels I had going. I had it all fairly roughed in and it was starting to really take shape. Originally, the idea was to put it dead center of a large white paper. Now, I saw it for what it truly was. I was going to recast the work as an allegory to the football team being the gods of Olympus here at our school. I began to slowly rework the original vision into a cloud-like presence, like the terraced gardens rising above the clouds. I set about adding in the framework of a few of the football players fully suited up in their gear in that classic hero V-shaped formation, with Marco at the apex being the only one without a helmet in the role of Zeus/Jupiter, a literal pantheon of champions. As I began to work on Marco's outline of my newly reimagined Olympus, I marveled how I'd come to this point in my life. If you'd have told me this is where I'd be, drawing the footballers as Olympic gods, when I was in school last year, I'd have looked at you like you had sprouted tentacles from your forehead. Nothing could have been more absurd than your suggesting this is what I'd be doing this year for the winter art gallery. Yet, here I was, sketching in my guy in the starring role of my little Romanesque allegory.

Marco.

Marco was a god of sorts, far more than he was to me. I always sort of knew football players were viewed that way at their schools, but this was the closest I'd come to actually experiencing the effects myself. I had trouble keeping my vision clear as I began to mist up a bit at how drastically my life had changed. And it appeared with the recent tweets and comments on the YouTube video that the change still wasn't over. If anything, it had taken on a new life. Viral didn't begin to describe it. I could already feel the shift in the room, eyes darting to me off and on. Far more attention than I'd ever had to deal with before. I chose to ignore it as best I could and go about the business of drawing.

Marco was no doubt fast becoming an internet sensation. One of the videos that concentrated on me had gotten buried with a paltry twenty-four hits. It was the biggest sigh I had ever let out in my life. I was happy with Marco being the star attraction. He carried it well. The oddball thing that came out of it all? He had ample license to stay right by me the entire time. I was sure we were going to became local celebrities. Turns out there's one thing that trumps the tried and true restrictions of the social cliques in school and that's internet celebrity, for whatever reason.

For the next couple of days Marco and I were inseparable. We went together everywhere on campus. This left Cindy fuming, which I found deeply gratifying. In a very weird way, it gave us more of a license for him to stay close to me, out in the open and everything. He was lapping it up, often putting his arm around my shoulder like some big bulldog bodyguard. Well, at least that's what he was going with, though not everyone was excited with the arrangement. Some underclassmen girls gushed as he walked by with me. I almost retched, and Marco found it infinitely charming. He whispered to me once that he wanted to bone me right there in the hallway when I gave a nauseating look at the gushing vag-laden gaggle of freshman girls who practically swooned over him.

The football jocks weren't happy campers, but it seemed there wasn't much they could do. Even the coach, from what Marco had told me later, turned Marco's rant into a big-time pitch for how teamwork was supposed to happen, holding up to the team that Marco's delivery was dead-on in backing each other up. He also said that protecting Elliot showed the team in a really positive light. If the 49ers could do an *It gets better* video, then Marco's little stunt showed how the Avenging Angels could be a part of that. I had to say, I gained a whole new appreciation for Coach Ostrich when Marco told me what he said. Coach Ostrich even acknowledged me with a small smile and a curt nod, almost like I was one of the jocks the next time I saw him at PE. Marco just beamed like the Cheshire Cat.

The team were doing their level best to rally around Marco's battle cry to protect and, more importantly, accept the gayboy on campus. But the good-willed nature of the team, the smiles and good nature they projected, never did quite make it to their eyes. Well, except for Enrique. I knew he was genuine about it. When Marco wasn't looking, when the rest thought no one else was, those happy and supportive faces dissolved to their darker doppelgängers. I wasn't always witness to them, but having spied them once or twice, it didn't take me much to figure out those were their truer selves bubbling to the surface. The smiles and affable demeanors were masking how put-upon they felt.

This newfound openness on campus did allow Marco and me to be together, but I was smart enough to be sure to keep him for the most part at arm's length, choosing to keep our little announcement that he was fairly bursting to tell everyone from the public consciousness. When we sat together, whether at the library or in the quad garden at lunch, I made sure to sit across from him, never side by side. His gaze was always pointed, but he never said anything about it. Once or twice he'd slowly make his way around to me as we talked. I let him have his way about it but did my best not to outwardly respond. I knew he thought it was pointless. He never hid his love for me from his eyes. God, even I could see how clearly he looked at me, the way he laughed whenever I said something absurd or even remotely comical. And people noticed. They did.

Our presentation went off without a hitch in English Lit. Mr. Crowe was quite impressed with our analysis of Marlowe's life and times and how those influences shaped his literary works. Though one pair of eyes held no kindness about them while we gave our report, dark brown eyes, peppered with malice, though they were careful to soften their steely gaze each time Marco looked up from our script to bask in the glow from his fellow students. He was Clark Kent and Superman all rolled into one in their eyes, one of *them*, and something for them to aspire to. I was just the butterfly flitting about the halo that shone all around him.

Game attendance soared to nearly capacity levels. Even my mother got Aunt Marsha to run the shop and she came along with me to the next game. For all of her pestering about my boyfriend, you'd think the local hoopla surrounding Marco would have clued her in, would have given her the impetus to ask if he was "the one." Nada. Zilch. Not even a blip on her radar it seemed. *What the fuck was that about?* Hammer, hammer, hammer, and then nothing? I didn't get it. Maybe she knew. Maybe she just guessed. But you'd think she'd press me for details then, wouldn'tcha? Nope. Not once.

That held true until the following week at breakfast (again)—a meal I was learning to dread in our house. I am so not a morning person, unless it was my boyfriend rousing me to consciousness to relieve the morning wood. Then you could call me Mr. Morning. But if it wasn't his cock, then I didn't really wake up until sometime in the middle of PE. But as I said, she learned to attack at breakfast, when my guard was down. It was too early and I was often too ill-prepared for her pointed questions. Which, in thinking about it, was probably the whole point.

The same morning my mother renewed her *who is your boyfriend and why haven't I met him yet?* attack, Marco skyped. Not that this was anything new as he did it every morning. For some reason with my mom's hovering about me, I found myself a bit more rankled about it. I didn't want to bother him about it, so we talked. He told me how happy he was with how things were going at school, how open we could be about us. Then he berated me for raining on his parade/lovefest when I reminded him not everyone was happy about it and this whole celebrity thing was going to blow over soon and the school rules would go back to being in place again. Our fifteen minutes of fame was fading fast. He argued that with the first championship win the previous Friday the local news media covered it and gave the game a fifteen-second mention due to the story gaining some traction—star quarterback, defender of human rights, was on a winning streak and might look to take their division championship. He then told me about a HuffPo Live Gay Voices interview he did online the previous night that he conveniently forgot to tell me about—probably because he knew I'd go all dramatic queen all over him and he'd just wanted to avoid it. He needn't have worried—I found out anyway. I nearly hit the roof over it, until he gave me the look that said there wasn't any room for me to bitch. What was done was done. He asked if I wanted to see the clip; I said no. I trusted whatever he had to say on the subject. He said good, and the world knows our wedding day is planned for the day after we graduate. I face-planted into the keyboard, severing our Skype call.

He called me on the phone to resume the rest of our morning conversation. Peppered with giggles and so many *I love yous* that I nearly retched again, and he told me I better eat a healthy breakfast and to count on some serious boning at lunch; we may not even have time to eat then. Yay, nooners!

Hell, even Dad had gotten into the picture when he last skyped me, congratulating me on finding someone who stuck up for me because I'd helped him with his grades. I didn't have the heart to tell my dad he was my boyfriend or that Marco was smart enough to get his own good grades and I actually had little to do with it. I definitely didn't say that Marco's rant was little more than a distraction to gain some space we could call for ourselves at the top of Olympus. It was all just too much to go into just then, so I didn't. Ignorance and bliss…what a healthy combination in my book. If I kept them ignorant, then I was in bliss.

After finishing my morning wake-up call, I showered, shaved—as it had been four days and I had like six hairs to show for it, so I broke out the hedge clippers and had at it. I dressed myself in a sort of smart ensemble that Marco had bought for me on a whim—'cause if he was going to be fucking the shit outta me at lunch I at least would make him slow down enough that he didn't rip the clothes he bought me I hadn't gotten around to wearing yet. I ambled, slightly more awake than when I first crawled out of bed, though just barely, into the kitchen and with a zombie-like shuffle to my step. I finally reached the coffee pot when my mother's voice pounced like the predatory leopard she could be from the kitchen table.

"So, I think it's about time I meet your boyfriend now. How did that go with planning it this weekend? Can I pencil us in on that?"

I shrugged, hoping if I committed to it Marco wouldn't have any conflicting plans. I guess I could always reschedule if he did, but Marco would see it as a weakness of some kind in my mother's eyes. He wouldn't be cool with that.

"Great. What does he like to eat?"

"He's a football player, Mom. Protein and veggies for sure. Salad? I dunno. Something like that. Hell, we could just probably order a pizza and he'd be cool with that."

"What? Are you crazy? No, I'll cook something for him. What about that roast chicken dinner you like me to make for you sometimes?"

My mood brightened. A roast chicken dinner was one of the few my mom could whip out and actually was quite tasty. "Yeah, okay, let's go with that."

I inwardly sighed a huge breath of relief. I was a fool to think that was the end of it.

"So, do I get to know his name?"

I shook my head. I didn't know why. "Look, I know it seems weird, all the secrecy about it, but I really am doing it for him. He wants everyone to know about us. He keeps chomping at the bit over it. Not sure why it's such a big deal to get it out there."

"Honey, maybe he just doesn't like hiding. I can see how tiring that would be."

"Yeah, I get that. But you all have to trust me on this. I've been gay my whole life, despite what you or Dad may think that it suddenly came up on me in junior high; I know how deep this shit can reach in and fuck you up." She shot me a warning look. "I know, I know. Language. Sorry. But it doesn't negate what I said. None of you have had to deal with the shi–crap I have. It can cut. While he may have jock status to burn, being out and proud will leech that away to nothing within seconds of it leaving his mouth. I don't want that for him. Not while he's still playing anyway. He seems to think his team will stand by him. I'm not so sure. I've spied things in them that aren't on the up and up."

"Such as?"

I sat down with my coffee and some toast she had out for me, the butter cooling into a speckled creamy mess. I fingered the puddle of congealed butter as I answered her.

"The guys are all smiles and supportive until he, the coach, or, hell, any of the other teachers look away, then a darkness comes over them. They aren't the least bit happy about the way things have gone. There are times I see them when they don't think *I'm* looking and their gazes are hard, unforgiving, but definitely pointed in our direction. I don't think Marco's noticed—or my boyfriend for that matter, but they're there, just the same."

I was hoping a mention of Marco *and* a boyfriend in the same sentence might throw off suspicion on the subject. It was stupid, silly even, to keep his identity from her. She'd have to know sooner or later. Why I was insisting on it being later I wasn't sure. *Maybe it's because I want to keep Marco all to myself for a little while longer.* Maybe there was some stupid reason I hadn't admitted to myself that I liked the whole "down-low" element to our relationship. The danger, or the intrigue? I guessed all the above. I was sort of used to his being solely mine. Not that common knowledge would take any of it away from me, I realized that. I wasn't that much of a lovelorn blithering idiot. I just sort of liked to wear it like my favorite shirt. *Besides, Saturday the full reveal is going to happen, so everyone can just wait until then. So, there.*

"I thought Marco's little argument with his players was rather nice of him to stick up for you. Since you were helping him and all..."

I nodded, chewing my toast, and then shrugged my shoulders in a way that said I didn't want to go there but she generally had the right of it. I sipped my coffee, finally feeling the synapses of my brain really beginning to fire.

"Yeah, he's cool. It worked. For what it was. How'd you find out about it anyway? You never said..."

"I do watch the local news at night, sweetheart. And Marcy has shown me how to do the Tweeter thing."

"Twitter."

"So I've been following the *twits.*"

I giggled slightly at her little Freudian slip, though she wasn't aware she said it. "Tweets."

"No, I *had* it right," she said with a pointed gaze that told me she was onto it the whole time. Mom was a basket of surprises it seemed, far more than I'd given her credit for. Who knew parents could be so intuitive or far-reaching? I sure as hell didn't.

"Well, I'm off. Gotta get to school."

"Want me to drive you in?"

"Nah, you're still in your PJs. I'm good."

I was confident my boyfriend was already at our appointed location. I placed a kiss on her cheek, grabbed my backpack and jacket from the rack at the front door, and was out before she could come up with any sort of retort.

Within a couple of minutes, I cleared our corner, and there was the Impala, her rumble reverberating within me even from the fifteen or so feet where I met the road. It was a very brisk foggy morning, and I was so thankful I could actually ride all the way into the school lot with Marco now our relationship, in whatever form the kids at school thought it was, was sort of out in the open.

As soon as I got in the car I began to rub my hands and blow into them to warm them up a bit. Thankfully, Marco had the car nice and toasty with the heat blasting away. I barely had time to say good morning when his big hand gripped my neck, pulling me to him, and he gifted me with a deliriously wet morning kiss.

"Good morning, beautiful."

"Hey, that's my line..." I chided him playfully.

He just beamed as he pulled the Impala out from the side of the road. "I can't wait until I can just come by your house and pick you up without all this secrecy."

"Yeah, about that... Mom wants to know if we're still on for Saturday." Then I gushed like a racehorse with diarrhea that burst from the gate as if I couldn't wait to get to the horsey bathroom or whatever, "You can totally back out and I can reschedule. I still feel weird about putting you through all that. So, if you want out, *no* problemo..."

He took my hand in his and held it tightly. I could tell he was getting overly emotional. My guy didn't always let himself run away with whatever he was feeling, but in moments like this, the way he would hold me or caress me spoke volumes of what he was going through.

"Nah, we're good. Looking forward to it, actually. Makes us more real, if you know what I mean. I just want to put the hiding away. I'm done with it. So fucking done with it all."

"Light at the end of the tunnel sort of done with it?"

"Totally, babe."

I pulled our entwined hands to my lips and kissed my own. He smiled when I made some big deal of kissing the wrong hand by mistake. As soon as my lips touched the back of his hand, he slipped it from mine and reached out and ruffled my hair before retaking it again.

"I love you, you know that, right?"

"Right back atcha, sexy," I said as I tried to reassemble my fab look from his mussiness.

We drove to school in a companionable silence; just enjoying the crisp foggy morning where the road was completely obscured then would open into a strong patch of blinding sun before lapsing into obscurity again. It was a good morning and we were enjoying each other's company. Boston's "More Than a Feeling" was playing softly in the background. It was our go-to song when we were cruising. A thumb across my palm, gentle but incessant, brought me out of my languishing thoughts.

"Not now, sweetheart. School."

"Always, baby. I always want to."

I smiled, not bothering to hide the lust that colored it. He caught my gaze though it was aimed out of the front window. He pressed his thumb a little more firmly against my palm.

"Always..." he whispered, so softly I felt it was more a confirmation to himself than to me. Not that he needed reminding. I knew we were good there. But it was as if it had always been this way for him. I guess it was that moment when I realized how long his love for me stretched out. It did have a history, a weighted history at that. Weighted in that it was a silent burden he carried, never knowing if it would come to anything, never knowing for sure if I'd choose him over any others.

Like that was never going to happen.

I know I railed against him with Greg. But that was the lonely gayboy railing against all jocks in general. I'd just made Marco the poster boy because he was the most glorious example of a man I had in my world. I didn't care if the hottest male model came bounding into my life, saying he would forsake all others if I would have him. I'd always choose Marco. It would *always* be him.

"Always..." I said softly. My eyes darted to him, his eyes glistening with the shared sentiment between us.

We turned into the senior lot, slowly cruising past Beau's motorcycle and a collection of the team and some leeching cheerleaders who were sucking the prime right out of this studly collection of young men. Marco didn't seem to notice how when they spotted the two of us with other eyes upon them beside our own, they waved and had their carefully painted smiles and goodwill as we cruised by. Only when we'd fully passed and I glanced back in the side mirror did I see them slip back into their darker personas.

As soon as the car slipped into Marco's spot in the lot, I began to gather my things.

"What's with the rush? It's cold out."

I slunk back into the seat again in a pseudo-huff.

"Whoa, what's that all about, babe?"

I turned my head back to where Beau Hopkins was holding court with the other teammates. I felt his steely dark gaze all the way across the lot to where Marco had parked.

"Them."

Marco turned his head around to see where I was looking only to spy the group breaking up and moving onto the school grounds.

"What? Beau? You're still not on about him, are you?"

"Never stopped. You don't see it, Marco. He's not a happy camper. Not at all."

"You're nuts. I've talked to him about it, and he's totally on the level."

"And you're seeing what they want you to see. It changes, Marco. When they think we're not looking. I haven't caught it all the time. But I've seen it. Just like now."

We watched them silently as they glided across the front of the car. Most of them were looking forward, though Beau made it a point to turn our way and wave with a smile across his face. I hoped Marco could discern the painted-on effort Beau had to go through to pull that off. I'd like to think Marco could see through it. But since most of his life had been spent with guys like this, guys who were conditioned to hold their feelings in check, to calculate their every move, I had to wonder if Marco truly saw the deviousness they could descend into, using the long-built trust between them as a viable weapon.

"Huh" was all he maddeningly offered.

I noted while Beau did his best to convince us of his amiability, it was the cheerleader under his arm who didn't bother to hide her scowl as her eyes flitted in our direction: Cindy.

A small rapping on my window made both Marco and me jump out of our skins.

Danny.

I reached around and unlocked the back door for him. He slid in and began to rub his hands and blow into them.

"Fucking chilly morning, huh? Whassup, dudes?"

I glanced at my phone. Eleven minutes to class. The early bell would signal in about six minutes.

"Nada. Just ready for another slugfest through school. You?" Marco said, regarding Danny in the rearview mirror.

I turned myself to lean against the door so I could watch the two of them. I couldn't help the small smile that broke across my face as my boyfriend and my new gay buddy were in the car with me. I was beside myself with the warm fuzzies—for the moment, all thoughts of painted smiles and hard glares seemed to seep away from me.

If my world only included Dan and Marco, I would be content. They were the only two guys I'd ever require. Well, Greg too, I supposed. He did deserve a prominent place in my life—just not the big gay one I could share with these two.

"Hot-assed ride, bro. Totally full-on Jensen Ackles, huh?"

"Dude!" They fist-bumped. Marco had a big ol' shit-eating grin. Yeah, it seemed Dan knew how to push my boy's buttons too. I watched them both. I knew where my boy was with Dan's entrance in our life. I was still his one and only, that much was clear from his expression while he and Dan found common ground. My eyes roved to Dan. He seemed so at ease with the gay thing but was still a guy's guy. Dan's gaze slid over Marco. There was a trace of something. What, I wasn't sure. I didn't think it was lust, but more of an appreciation. There was something else too, a sense of loss. Whoever the guy who broke his heart had been, it was big. Epic, even. Marco was a reminder of what he no longer had, that was all.

A hand clasped my shoulder, shaking me from my thoughts. "You're one lucky guy. This one's solid."

Marco chuckled, his eyes flashing brilliantly as he drank me in. "That's what I keep telling him." I quirked a brow at him and he clarified, "That *I'm* the one who's lucky. Lucky he said yes, lucky he loves me despite my faults."

"Whatever you two, get a room." Dan chuckled lightly.

I looked at Dan, being sure there was no mistaking the look in my eyes. "You're sitting in our room."

"What? Awww, dudes, really?" He scrunched his face for a second, then looked between us. A sparkle twinkled in his eye. "We should so film that sometime." He wiggled his eyebrows at the two of us. Marco just burst out with a wild laugh and high-fived Dan. Within seconds we were all laughing about it when the first bell rang—five minutes to class.

We scrambled out of the car. I looked at Dan as he extracted himself from the back seat, a small smirk on his face as he eyed the seat, as if he were imagining the sex Marco and I had there. *Boy, could I tell him stories.* Not that I would. Well, I didn't think I would. But, fuck me, it's not like I'd ever had a gay BF before. Maybe that's what we did, talk about sex and love and how hot our boyfriends are. I tried to recall the few DVDs or Netflix films I'd watched that were about gay boys, which was about all I had to go on when I thought I was the only gay in the village. Perhaps Dan and I would tell each other our deepest, darkest secrets.

I nudged him gently. "Put your porn director's hat away, Mister Morris."

"Jericho."

"Okay, you need to turn in your gay card. You don't know your porn directors?"

"No, I'd rather make porn than watch it."

The impish twinkle in his eye told me how much sentiment went into that statement. I snickered and wrapped my arm around his shoulder, tugging him away. Marco joined us at the head of the car. We took a few steps silently, a new tiny elephant strolling behind us.

"I wasn't joking. I could totally film you guys. I have a really good eye."

He pulled out his iPhone and flicked through a series of selfies, some clothed and some sort of not, nothing remotely pornographic or totally starkers. But enough that there wasn't too much left to the imagination. He was a very healthy-looking guy. He had the body I wanted, like a dancer's body, lithe, with excellent muscle tone. Dan was beautiful now I really looked at him.

He mistakenly tapped into a couple of photos of a stunningly beautiful warm brown-colored man. And I meant man, Marco's sort of man.

"Who the fuck is that?" It just spilled out of my mouth.

I hoped Marco didn't take it the wrong way. The man was stunning in the signature way South American men held themselves. Marco was my guy, but fuck me if I didn't admit that Brazilians, and especially Argentinians, did it for me. Fucking slayed me every time I saw one.

"Paolo." A strained beat later he softly added, "My ex."

Three small words that carried the weight of the world on his shoulders. Marco and I watched him as he slowly flicked through a couple of them before he couldn't take it anymore. I pulled him close, and without thinking I placed a small kiss on the side of his head. It just seemed the right thing to do. He chuckled and sniffled a bit. I looked over at Marco who was smiling warmly at me. I knew I'd done right, though I could see the wheels in his head turning.

"You wanna take a breather today—seeing how I'm gonna be gone on Thursday. Whaddaya think?"

"Yeah, but we probably shouldn't."

"Hey, I'm down," Dan chimed in, wiping a small tear that had spilled unguarded from his right eye.

"Our parents will know—you realize that, don't you?" I told them, trying desperately to be the voice of reason I knew one of us should be. But I looked into Dan's eyes. He needed this, needed us, probably as much as we were growing to need him.

Marco shook his head like the two of us were hopeless and grabbed Dan's hand and pulled us back to the car.

"C'mon. Free day. If you guys get into trouble, just blame it on me. I'll take the heat. 'Sides, we're eighteen. It's all on us."

"Yeah, but Dan's not. It wouldn't be fair."

"I'm eighteen, just had to repeat a year—long story. But, we don't have to, you know," Dan said.

"Why?" Marco paused, clearly not getting where Dan was going with it.

"Shirley," he said with a small shrug.

It was then I realized how odd it was that most teenage kids didn't have overly massive shoulders and trapezius muscles with all the shrugging we did during our teen years. I giggled a bit with that thought, bringing Dan and Marco out of theirs.

"What?"

"Hmmm? Oh, it's nothing, totally random. Forget it. So, Shirley. Shirley, who?"

"Shirley Crabapple. My gran."

"What?" I broke out in hysterics, on my knees hysterics, beating the grass with my hand hysterics. Marco just got redder and redder as I went on with my fits of hysteria. I was crying. I spared a glance at Dan through my laughter and watery eyes; he looked utterly lost between us. I'd have liked to help him out, but the thought of Marco flirting with Dan's grandmother was just too rich.

"Enough, Els," Marco said through gritted teeth. "I mean it. I will so leave your ass and take Dan off to make some porn fetish flick without you, and we'll see how much you're laughing then."

Okay, that put the skids on my giggle-fest right fucking quick. I went from those percolating chuckles to a grunt faster than a super-charged Tesla.

"Over my dead body!"

"There's my guy!" Marco smiled as he put out a hand. I took it only to be hoisted up onto his shoulder Tarzan style.

"Oh, I so gotta get you two on video" was all Dan said as we made our way back to Marco's car. Thankfully Dan had the foresight to grab my backpack from where I'd dropped it during my laughing fit.

Marco turned to face Dan as he walked backward with me still on his shoulder. "No posting to RedTube, Pornhub, or whatever..."

Dan held his hands up in surrender. "You two will have the only copies. I swear. I'm just doing it for the experience."

A few seconds later, we were pulling out of the senior lot, the rumble from the Impala thundering behind us.

Chapter Six

Danny Jericho, Porn Director

We made a pit stop at the local Denny's in town. It was the only chain diner we had in Mercy. Actually, when you thought upon it, we had all of those Americana chain stores in our town. Baskin-Robbins, the Q, Denny's, the list went on for a bit. Hell, we even had one of the few Der Wienerschnitzels to be found in this part of California. Mercy was the kind of small town where Americana went to die a slow, painful death.

It was a cool calculation on Marco's part. It was only 8:00 a.m. and Mom would still be home. This would keep things clean. So we had a proper breakfast. Well, I had a yogurt with some granola sort of thing they had on their "smart heart" part of the menu. Dan went with the French Toast Slam, a family classic, while my man opted for the whole fucking enchilada: three eggs scrambled omelet style, two sausage links, two strips of bacon, hash browns well-done, side of ham, and a short stack of pancakes and washing it down with a carafe of OJ. And he said he was thinking of something for after.

"Oh, did you all want OJ too? Better make that two carafes then," he advised the waitress who winked at Marco before trundling off to get us our mornin' vittles.

I asked what army he was feeding, and he retorted that if he was going to get a workout today then he needed to bulk up on the rations. Then he and Dan waited for that little bomb to sink in. When it finally dawned on me what he was hinting at, I went so red I wanted the floor to open beneath me and swallow me whole. They just howled before the other people in the restaurant started to turn in our direction. I had to shush them both down while I tried like hell to collect myself. It wasn't easy with the future Jake Jaxson on our hands—Cockyboys.com be damned 'cause Danny already had an eye for it. I guess we *were* starting our own porn studio. An audience of three: the stars, and the burgeoning director. I really didn't think we'd go through with it. It was all talk. Bark with very little bite.

Marco's eyes never seemed to leave me. Flaming infernos, they were. *Fuck me. We're going to do it.* I knew that look. He wanted it. Hell, he always wanted it. I knew it wasn't a far-fetched scheme. Teenage boys were doing it, a lot, and posting it everywhere. In-your-face fucking on an epic scale. I'd even found a cute boyfriend couple from somewhere back east who had a regular vlog of their fucking. You could see the love they had for each other mingled with the lust-laden sex they were having. So yeah, not totally unheard of an idea. I just wasn't sure I was ready to take the plunge. But I knew he wanted to do it. He'd always want to.

"Always…" he said softly to me as if he knew exactly what I was thinking. Dan tried to act like he didn't notice, but I was sure he did.

We spent the first part of the morning chatting about how Dan's life had changed from living in San Francisco to the oppressively quaint stroll we called Mercy. He quirked a brow at how I used the term *oppressive* to describe life in our little town, though before I could reply he had regrouped and said he thought he understood my perspective on it before adding he didn't have that baggage to carry about the town. He was still in the mode of reinventing himself in his new life here.

"Reinventing, why reinvent? Weren't you happy with who you were before?" Marco asked through a mouthful of eggs. I shot him a warning glance to not be rude and talk through his food. He smirked, but I noted that the conversation continued without his masticating through his speech. Inwardly, I was pleased we could be wordlessly in synch.

"It's not that. Not really. More of…" He paused, glancing up to the ceiling as if the word he was looking for were pasted up there. "A shedding of some unneeded skin. Things needed an airing out. Spring cleaning of the soul, so to speak."

I thought Marco would press Dan for particulars, but Marco seemed satisfied with his reply. Probably from years of being around the guys on the team, you just didn't delve into a guy's life too much. That sort of unspoken rule between men is probably what served us in our early days at school. No one asked the deeper questions, even if they were thinking them.

My thoughts wandered over to Beau and Stephen in particular. Both seemed to have quite a lot of pent-up emotions they were carrying but had no outlet for. Marco had me, but I couldn't see Beau or Stephen baring their souls, their deepest anxieties with either Cindy or Sony. Those girls, like the rest of the cheer squad, were toxic. Muffinators who would eat up their men, produce a litter of kids, collect their diamonds, and spit them out the back without a second thought. Beau was a big guy who could most definitely take care of himself, but even I think he doesn't bare it all with any of the women he's been with. And from what I've heard in passing, there's been quite a gaggle of women in that boy's past. Man-slut doesn't begin to cover it. The quintessential preacher's son if there ever were one.

Dan chewed a particularly big bite of his French toast, washing it down with some milk he'd asked for in lieu of the second carafe of OJ Marco had ordered for us.

"Paolo and I had a very intense relationship. Very serious, right from the start."

"Like us," Marco said so matter-of-factly that if you weren't watching him, you might even think it dismissive, when that couldn't be further from the truth. I smiled at him, finishing up my yogurt and sipping on some OJ which sort of clashed with the breakfast I was having. I passed the glass to Marco and picked up my water instead. He just smirked and moved from his finished glass to mine.

"I guess that's what gets me all misty over you two. I can see the fire. It's there."

"Well, if you can, then no doubt everyone else can," I deadpanned.

"Oh, you'd be surprised at how much teenage kids don't see. Or choose not to see. I mean, Paolo and I were fairly obvious we were a couple, even at school. You'd think for a well-known liberal metropolitan city like San Francisco we'd be fairly golden. Left alone, to be in love. Well, even there, we had our detractors. But Paolo was a big guy and totally down with that whole Capoeira stuff. Fucking bad-assed dangerous with it. He was thinking of getting into MMA stuff, but I talked him out of it. But you have to imagine it. He's six four and two hundred sixty-five pounds of solid muscle. He lived and breathed lacrosse. Once he discovered it, it became his passion. Became team captain in his junior year. He was a year ahead of me." His eyes darted between the two of us, watching to see how we'd react to hearing his story. To be honest, I felt like he was making something public that should be held with deep respect; intimate, private. To speak about it in the restaurant seemed too public for me.

"Hey." I reached out and placed my hand on the one he had on the table, moving his thumbnail around a groove in the knife handle as if that simple repetitive action would ease the pent-up emotions I could sense rolling around in there. "We don't have to talk about it here. I mean if you'd like to get back to my house where it's a bit quieter…" My eyes darted to Marco. I could tell he wanted to take Dan's lead but was happy that I'd spoken up about something obviously so tender and fragile to Dan.

"Nah, it's good. It helps to get it out sometimes."

"Yeah, I could see that," Marco said softly. His appetite seemed to have waned a bit as we moved to this topic. I glanced at the plates he had populated into nearly every available space on the table that didn't hold mine or Dan's. My boy could eat.

"Anyway, we were pretty hot and heavy. While some may not have liked how forward we were with each other, no one dared to give us shit about it. You'd have to understand Paolo, see him in action. He commands respect, but he isn't a bully about it. He's actually quite gentle and very kind. Sometimes too kind."

That last was said with a point to it. I knew it was there where their relationship had taken its turn for the worst. Someone had taken advantage of Paolo's kindness, had hurt them both with it.

"I know you think it's odd how I just popped out with the whole 'let's make a porn' thing. But that's Paolo. He was brutally honest when it came to sex, when it came to men's bodies. He was utterly fascinated with our bodies. The way they moved, their strength. The command they could emote. The respect they could carry just by simply being."

"Not that I'm not saying something against you, but, how did you two hook up?" Marco piped in.

"Sweetheart, that's a little bit rude. Hook up? Really? Is that what you'd use to describe how we met and got together?"

I rolled my eyes at him, but he could see I wasn't too put off by how he'd said it. Thankfully, he was smart enough to look respectably sheepish about it.

"Nah, it's okay, Elliot. Really. You'd have to know Paolo. He was quite the character. That was a man truly filled with wonder. It's what drew me to him." His eyes got a little moist from the recollection. "It's what I miss most, actually. That spark and wonder he saw in everything." He sniffled a tiny bit before he continued, "Anyway, so I had no idea he was gay. He doesn't look or act that way, whatever that is, 'cause frankly, living in the City, you get to see all sorts of gay men. Those stereotypes go right out the door after you've been there for a while. The whole your-hairdresser-is-straight-but-your-plumber-is-gay sort of thing." He shook his head at how he found the observation still humorous.

"He saw me dancing one day after school. I was just warming up, you see. My ballet class wasn't for another hour, and my dad wasn't going to get to the school for about a half hour; so I just changed quickly in the boys' locker room and went to our dance room and began to run through my paces to get warmed up. Paolo was heading down to his lacrosse practice when he spotted me working out a particularly difficult sequence of moves I was struggling with. To be honest, I really hadn't noticed he was standing there watching me. I was that into my working through the problem areas. I tend to get tunnel vision when I'm dancing."

"I didn't realize you were a ballet dancer," I said, well, really more mumbled—as if I were trying to picture it.

"Been training for nearly all my young life. Pretty damned good at it. San Francisco Ballet and everything. An up-and-comer. The next great thing. I was being groomed, you see, to become a principal."

Marco's eyes widened and his eyebrows changed residency, relocating themselves somewhere mid-forehead. "That's saying something. I've been to San Francisco Ballet's performances before. Were you in anything I might have seen?"

"Mostly corps, so I doubt you'd notice. I'm still quite young for a shot at the bigger roles. But they were watching me. From both ends, actually."

"Both ends?" Marco seemed rather caught up with the whole thing.

In truth, it had simply never occurred to me that he would attend the Ballet. But then again, they were rich and his parents were all about the way their family presented themselves, so I guess that would include the classical arts—ballet, opera, and the symphony. While San Francisco would be a hell of a drive, I was sure the family made a trip out of it. Hell, they probably had a townhouse in the City for just such occasions.

"Yeah, the production staff are always watching. Always. Constant polling and re-polling of who is where and how are they holding up under the pressure. Plus, you get some of the attitude from the established dancers who think the young kids are constantly nipping at their heels. The men generally last longer in their careers, but that just means the competition is far fiercer because there are fewer spots to go around. It's highly competitive and very hard on the ego. But it's my world." A long pause while he let that last bit out of his system. "*Was* my world."

I could see he needed to change tracks. "So he saw you dancing, and..."

A warm smile lit up his face. His hazel eyes sparkled so brilliantly they looked far more violet. "Yeah, he was watching me. One of the jazz dancers, a girl whose name I still can't remember, partially because she's a girl—I tend to be a militant gay that way. I don't have much use for women, so I don't commit them to memory. They're fleeting in my world. Well, 'cept for my mom, my sister, and your best girl, Marco."

I snorted at that. I couldn't help myself. It still tickled me how much he'd flirted with Dan's gran.

"Keep it up, Els. You're so going to pay for it later."

"Oh yeah, I don't see how."

"We're so gonna do the porn thing, that's how. Even if I have to strip you bare and tie you down." He leaned forward toward me, and I knew this last bit was rather salacious. "And I will bone you within an inch of your life. We are so gonna do it."

"Hardy-har-har. Yeah, we'll see how far that gets ya," I shot back. A look colored his eyes, and I knew I'd pushed him a bit too far. He was right. We were going to do it. Fuck me.

Uh, yeah, that's what you're gonna do.

"C'mon, let's get outta here. We can talk when we get back to your place, Els."

"What's with this 'Els'?"

Marco let a small smile snake across his lips, but I was the one who chimed in. "It's what he's called me from the first day we kissed. I thought it was a bit odd too, but now I can't imagine him calling me anything but."

"Well, except sweetheart or baby, or..."

"Yeah, yeah, we get that you're a lover not a fighter, big guy. Scoot." I shooed him out of the seat so we could get going. He laughed softly at my little embarrassment over his pet names for me.

As I got out of the booth, Dan came up to me and slipped his phone into my hand.

"I don't want you to feel uncomfortable around me. So I thought I'd make the first offering: look at the videos marked 'Paolo.' You might want to put your headphones in though or we're gonna get some really odd stares."

He winked and left me to fumble with the phone and my earbuds as he joined Marco at the cashier stand.

As we left the restaurant, I finally got everything connected. I held up the phone to his locked screen, and he looked at me with a quirked brow and deadpanned, "I figured you for a smarter guy, Els."

Marco shot him a pointed look, and Dan just chuckled and held up his hands in surrender. Marco chuckled, then said, "Okay, maybe it's cool if you call him that too. After all you're gonna film us boning, so I guess the pet name is the least of my worries."

I pondered the lock screen when it hit me: Paolo with zeros. I heard the small click that indicated I'd successfully unlocked the phone and held it out to show Dan I was in. He smiled warmly and pulled me to him, slinking his arm around my waist as we walked to the Impala.

I started to navigate to the videos on his phone when he leaned over and nudged one with his finger other than the one I was pondering.

"I should warn you, Paolo was a very ardent lover. He got into filming our sex scenes so much my room back home was rigged with those little Hero cameras in strategic places. When my parents were out, we'd spend most of the afternoon fucking and the evening editing the damned things. I've got literally hundreds. Some solos, some the two of us, other times we'd play with someone else. It varied. But he never strayed from me. Not once. We had our fun, but he said the sun and moon were under my control in his life. I'd like to think we captured some of that. It's sort of what keeps me going, to watch them and remember. And I do remember, every single one. Everything I felt at the time. Every subtle nuance when we fucked. We got very good at it. That one there." I glanced at the screen. It showed a still frame of some beautiful flowers in a vase with some out of focus shadows in the background. "That one is sort of the culmination of what we could do together. I'm rather proud of it. Being a dancer, I think you'll see why it appeals to me."

We piled into the car, and as soon as I was buckled up, I hit the play button. The film was quite breathtaking. For a couple of teenagers these guys knew how to shoot men having sex. No, it was more than that. It was porn, but fucking erotic and almost over-the-top porn. No storyline, no silliness. Just raw, manly, musky in-your-face unabashedly hot man-love. I found myself getting hard just watching these two lovers go at it. You could see it in Paolo's eyes how much he loved Dan. They were very beautiful together. Paolo with his massive manly frame and Dan with his lithe and limber body. It was almost like a dance in bed, and the fucking was brilliant.

"What're you watching, sweetheart? A music video or something?"

"Or something," I murmured, completely absorbed with Paolo and Dan's masterpiece of porn. It was beautiful to watch but at the same time, very heated, masculine, a battle of love between the two of them. This film was fucking hot. Better than some of the shit I'd seen on the net, that was for fucking sure.

"He's watching Paolo and me fuck. That's all..."

Marco slammed on the brakes, and we all lurched forward. "What? You're kidding, right?" Before I could say anything, Marco reached over to my crotch and felt how hard I'd gotten. "So not fair, lover."

"Don't be mad, Marco. I was gonna show you, too. It only seems fair if we're gonna do this. I just knew Elliot would have a harder time with it, that's all. This was my way of warming him up to it, to show him I don't do trashy shit. It's quality, right, Els?"

I nodded slowly, still so taken with how good it was. "Marco, babe, you gotta see this one. If we could do something like this...holy fuck, I'd watch me!" I turned to Dan. "And that's saying something 'cause I can't stand to see myself in, well, anything."

"Yeah, you should see how hard it is for me just to take a picture with him. I have so very few. He's the most beautiful thing to me and he won't share... Bastard."

"I'm just trying to spare your eyes when you wake up and figure out what you've really got."

"You're not gonna start that shit again, are you?"

I rolled my eyes; no, I was not. I knew better. It'd be easier to saw my way out of shackles with a wooden toothpick than to convince my guy of my absolute banality in the looks department. I guess I should be pleased, but in reality, I was sort of shy about it.

"I'll get you to see it, Els. Not a problem. When I'm through, you'll wanna make love to you."

"Oooh, that'd be hella hot to watch, my baby and a dupe going at it."

"Ah, ewwww, so wouldn't happen."

"Why? Because it's incest or something?" Dan asked as he rolled his eyes and shook his head. "Those rules don't apply. Men can't reproduce, and that's where that shit comes from. Besides, it's not like he's saying it for real. Marco's just expressing how much he loves you when he says that. If he could have more of you, he'd be over the moon about it. Am I right, Marco?"

"Fucking dead-on, bro. I fucking *love* this guy!" Marco beat his hand on the steering wheel and cranked up the classic rock radio when he heard Boston's "More Than A Feeling" come on. "This is where my baby really shines; sing it, babe." I shook my head. Dan ripped the earbuds out of my ear and pointed at my face. "Sing!"

So I did, with Dan and Marco joining in the background. We weren't half bad. I did substitute Marco's name and gender for the character of Maryanne within the song though, something that never failed to get him to smile, beaming brighter than the sun.

When the interlude hit, Dan just gushed, "Dude! Fucking amazing! You're such a good singer! That's hella hot."

"Right?" Marco was smiling so broadly, my heart melted. By the time the vocals came back I gave it my all, bellowing to the four winds as we just rolled the windows down and let the town take us in as that Impala cruised down the road. It coulda been the end of a *Supernatural* episode. Okay, a really gay episode, but I think Jensen might have even smiled at our little remix.

I put some coffee on as the boys settled in. I handed Marco Dan's phone, watching him retreat into the living room to watch Dan's little porn masterpiece. Dan followed me into the kitchen.

"You gonna be okay with this? I don't want you to get all weirded out. It's just our bodies, Els."

"Yeah, I get it. I mean, it's not like we haven't seen the junk before, right?"

"Yeah, and I have. Seen your junk, I mean. Though you and Marco whip through there so fucking fast. Like you gotta get away real quick like...and okay, I'm a fucking idiot for never putting that one together: nooners." He winked an eye and put a finger to his temple. Someone came home to that lit-up house they're always talking about.

"Wait, you're in my PE class?"

"Marco's too, though I guess why I never rated even so much as a glance my way when you've got tall, dark, and gorgeous following you around, huh?"

I smiled. "Yeah, he's aces in my book."

"Ah, come on, he's a helluva lot more than that. I can see it. You are both so in love, you don't even see anyone else, do you?"

I blushed so deeply when he said that.

"Yeah, he's my world. I tell him he's mine and I mean it, but fuck me why he's so into me? I've never understood it."

"Well, it's not for you, is it?"

"That's what he says," I sighed thoughtfully.

"Don't try to figure it out with this." He tapped the side of my head. "It's meant to be felt with this." I knew where he was going with it, but something still stirred inside when he touched upon it. "It's a beautiful thing, Els. Try not to hide it too much. It'll worry him. I made that mistake once; look what it got me."

"Is that why he left you?"

"No, nothing like that. But I loved him so much I was afraid to tell him all the time. I didn't want to smother him. Didn't matter really in the end, but I know I'd take him back in a second if he asked. No hesitation."

"He cheat on you? Is that why?"

"No. Definitely not that. It's a distance thing. Let's leave it at that, 'kay?"

I nodded.

"At least for now. Maybe someday I'll tell you both all about it. It's just too raw right now."

"Hey, we're gonna be friends for life, right?"

"Fuck yeah, if I've got anything to say about it. And believe me, I've got plenty to say."

He was standing in front of me as I leaned against the counter. He had his thumbs tucked into the front belt-loops of his jeans. The way it tugged down on his hips, he was flashing a small part of his lower abdomen I couldn't help but spy. He so had the body I wanted for myself. I reached out and pulled him to me. Without hesitation he gave me a quick chaste kiss on the lips before he fell into a warm hug.

"It hurts sometimes, you know."

"What does?" I asked him as he ran his hands slowly up and down my back, his face tucked into the crook of my neck. I stroked his hair with a free hand.

"Simple contact. I miss it so."

"Well, not anymore. Until you've got your own squeeze boy, or Paolo comes to his senses, then you can always get a hug and cuddle from me or Marco. Deal?"

He sniffled a bit. When he spoke, it was rough; the emotions at play within him were strong. "Thanks. You don't know how much I wished you and Marco would take me in. I've felt so lonely, so disconnected."

"Wow, you sound like you don't have any friends left in the world. What's that all about? You're quite a looker. You'd think at least a gaggle of girls would be following you around."

"Oh, I got me one of them."

"What? A girlfriend?"

He nodded.

"I don't understand. I thought…"

"What? That I'm gay? Yeah, I am. But I've had sex with girls since I was like thirteen. It's just something I do."

"But is that really fair to her? I mean, don't get me wrong. You've completely lost me on the whole girl thing. I just don't get it."

He shrugged. "Yeah, even Paolo didn't. He was really into guys. Thought I was bat-shit crazy when I told him I fucked girls too. Well, at first he laughed his ass off 'cause I can take dick like there's no tomorrow. I fucking rock at it. So, I guess he translated that to being strictly bottom. Which, when I am with a dude and in love? Then, yeah. Totally bottom material here. But I like to fuck too. So there ya are." He pulled back a bit and sort of rolled to stand next to me leaning against the counter. "Sex isn't always so black and white. That's how you can get so many straight guys"—he used his fingers in air quotes when he said *straight guys*—"to have gay sex. They say it's for the money. Yeah, if you get hard and kiss a dude on camera, you're pretty much a bisexual. Money or not, it's not gonna keep it hard if you've got no interest."

"So you're bi?"

"No. The other end of the spectrum. Gay because I love men. There's the difference, Els. I love men. Fall in love with men. Hopelessly fall in love with men, as it turns out. Breaking up with Paolo fucking shredded my heart. It's still painful." I let him have a moment, because he went silent as he contemplated his last words. "But the whole sex thing. Yeah, I fucking get into it, regardless. So guy, girl, it doesn't matter. The difference is I know for a fact I couldn't love a woman. Just don't have the temperament for it, couldn't stomach the drama. My girl right now drives me bat-shit crazy. I told her last weekend after I'd just got done boning her that I was in it for the sex, which to be honest is okay. I've had better. But I miss the contact of another male. I need men in my life. They feed my soul, feed my heart, keep me going."

We lapsed into a contemplative silence. I was really pondering his words.

"Yeah, I can see it now," I said softly, though I was facing forward looking at the *Game of Thrones* calendar my mom had hanging on the wall. It was set to a picture of Kit Harington, who I had fancied as a potential fantasy boyfriend—this was before Marco entered my world though. Marco was far sexier than Kit. *Sorry, Mr. Harington, not even a close second.*

"See what?"

"Why you'd make an excellent porn director. You've got the right mentality for it."

"Artistic as well as a keen business sense." He tapped the side of his noggin to emphasize his point.

I smiled at how he saw things. It was certainly far removed from how I saw them or how I was brought up, the whole Catholic guilt about nearly everything that permeates our lives, though my family were latent Catholic. Religion more in name than in practice, going through the motions with a half-hearted attempt. Hell, sometimes the lights never made it onto the house at Christmas. That's how latent we were with the whole spiritual aspect of our lives. So, it wasn't as if I was traumatized over opening up about my sexuality. From what Dan had said, he and Paolo were definitely in love and very committed to each other. Hell, they'd documented it on a very intimate level. And quite well from the looks of the one video I'd seen. Speaking of which...

"I'd better check on my bohunk to see what he's got *up* to."

"I'll get the coffee for us, if you'd like a moment..."

I smiled and nudged him for being so considerate. I reached around him and pulled the drawer to his left that held the spoons and pointed to the cupboard where he'd find the coffee cups.

"Milk's in the fridge, and the sugar bowl is there on the counter. Help yourself. I take mine straight up."

I meandered back to the living room where my boy was sitting, semi-stretched out on the sofa with one leg on it and the other on the floor, his legs splayed out a bit, leaving little doubt as to his aroused state. His python of a cock was fully erect as it coursed around his hip. A very succulent vision if I'd ever spied one.

"You're awfully quiet, babe," I cooed to him.

Then I realized he couldn't possibly hear me with the earbuds on while Paolo and Dan moaned and writhed on the small phone screen in front of him. I knelt beside him and ran the side of my cheek along his hardened cock, nudging it with my face. He purred; a soft satisfied rumble coursed through his body as he ran a free hand through my hair.

He whispered, "This is fucking hot. I so want to do this sort of thing with you."

I nodded, making sure my face gave the right amount of pressure he could lean into. He moaned softly that I had the right idea. I slowly turned my face so I could run my lips over his cock.

"Aw, baby. You feel so good," he murmured, pressing himself into my mouth, the fabric of his jeans gently but incessantly rubbing against my teeth. I nipped lightly, making sure the pressure would be just enough to drive him wild. His breathing became ragged—it was working.

A soft cough broke our actions.

"Enough fluffing, Elliot. Or he'll blow his wad before we can get started." Dan came further into the room as Marco quickly scooted up into a sitting position on the couch, a slight color taking to his cheeks at our being caught. He sheepishly turned off the video and pulled the earbuds out of his ears. I sat down next to him. We both took the offered cups.

"I didn't know if you wanted milk or sugar, so I'll be back with those."

"I'm good," I said to him.

"Yeah, I'd like some," Marco said with a slight husk to his voice. I snickered and he nudged me slightly, though he was careful not to do it too much or I'd spill the hot coffee all over myself—which so wouldn't look pretty on a video.

"I take it you liked?" I indicated the phone on the coffee table when he took the cup from Dan.

He nodded, wiggling his eyebrows while he sipped the black goodness. He winced. "Eck, so needs cream and sugar. How can you drink it straight?"

"It's the only thing I take straight, big guy."

He chortled as Dan came back with his own coffee and some milk and sugar on a large platter he found somewhere in the kitchen. Lord knows where, because I could barely find what I needed in there. My mother's sorting logic often escaped me. Probably why I'd never bothered learning how to cook—I'd have spent more time just trying to find shit to cook with than actually making anything of use. Dad was the major cook in the house but, yeah, well…so much for that.

Dan took a seat on the coffee table to face us. I was thankful it was one of those old sturdy numbers from the early to mid-1960s and not one of the flimsy Ikea crap Mom and Dad had favored as of late.

"So, the veil's been pulled back. Any thoughts?" He quirked a brow as he sipped his coffee, watching both of us with an analytic eye.

I piped up only because I was fairly itching to comment on this whole proposed escapade since it came up. I mean, I knew Marco had hinted at it for a while now, but with it looming large like it was, I needed to get this off my chest.

"Well, I'm sort of reeling with the whole I've-only-known-you-for-a-couple-of-days-and-now-I've-watched-you-fuck-your-ex-boyfriend, which, by the way, fucking over-the-top brilliant. If you do porn, you gotta at least do it like you two did. I can't imagine how you planned it all. But I'm getting off track." I sighed and regrouped. "I'm sort of a bit off-kilter on how intimate we've become so quickly. I mean, I don't know you, not really. And that's not a personal judgment against you or anything like that. I feel really close to you, but hell, I mean you could be a full-on sociopath—an Andrew Cunanan in the making, ya know? I have no real way to know that."

"Sure, you do," he offered.

"What? You mean my gayboy survival instinct?" He nodded. "Yeah, well, that and a dollar fifty-nine will get me a coffee at the local 7-Eleven, thank you very much."

"Really? I'd think your survival skills would've been properly honed living in a small town where everyone knows your shit."

"Sure, but it's the unknowns, like you'd get in the big city, that would make you a better judge of character."

"You'd think so, but for the most part I think while it gives you a peripheral appreciation in surviving, you miss the more subtle changes in a person. It's too impersonal in a big city. What do you think, Marco? You've been awfully silent."

"Marco lives in a very insular world. I'm his first gay anything. No, wait, that's not true, is it?"

Marco shot me a pointed look, probably because I was spilling his shit before he could. I needed to keep a lock on my tongue when it came to his past. It was *his* after all.

"Well, Els is right. I don't really have the experience you all have. And given I'm fairly well known in this town I don't know that it'll change terribly much when they do find out."

"Tsk." That came from me. "You are so naive to say that, sweetheart. Yeah, some people will be shocked at first and then come to accept it because they'll realize it's still the you they've always known, that nothing, as far as they're concerned, has changed in their interacting with you. But there are others."

"You mean Beau, don't you?"

"And Stephen Lowry."

"Stephen Lowry's giving you shit?" Dan asked, suddenly taking an interest in where the conversation went.

"Yeah, he used to be my best friend till I came out to him in the seventh grade. Asked him to be my boyfriend back then. He thought about it for like two seconds before saying no and leaving. We never did talk again after that."

"I didn't know that," Marco said, astonished.

"Why, the little two-faced prick," Dan said as he set his coffee mug down on the table next to him.

"What? Why two-faced? How do you know him?"

"Because he's my fucking second cousin on my mom's side. She's a Lowry. And let me tell you somethin', El, that boy has had gay sex. Make no mistake about it."

"Wow, how would you know?"

"'Cause it was with me, that's why. He'd come up to the City during the summer break for a couple of weeks. This was before Paolo last year, mind you. All we did was practically fuck the entire time we were alone. He knows his way around a dick, that's all I can tell you. Don't let him make you think otherwise."

"Huh. That explains it, then."

"Explains what?" Marco asked as he set his finished coffee on the end table next to him.

"Oh, it's nothing I haven't handled before. Just he, Cindy, and Sony cornered me in an empty classroom just before the Homecoming fiasco and threatened me about taking Cindy's precious crown away from her. *As if...*"

"What? Why didn't you tell me?" he exclaimed—his look of surprise mingled with a rising tide of anger that was threatening to overtake the conversation. I patted his knee to calm him a bit.

"Calm down. I handled it. But it did leave me wondering about a certain look that crossed his face when that day back in the seventh grade came up again. Like I'd spied something in him in that moment, and he was panicked about it. I didn't know what the hell it could be until just now when you said all that. Who'da fucking thought?"

"I'm gonna kill the son of a bitch! That boy can swing on a pole better than some chicks I've done. Hell, he *has* no gag reflex. I banged the back of that shit—fucking skull-fucked his faggoty mouth. Arrrgh! Fuck!" Dan got up and started to pace back and forth in front of us, biting his thumbnail.

I held out a hand to stop him in his next pass by me. He glared for a moment. "Dude, breathe. Jesus, you're fucking scaring me more than he ever could. Hell, I know how to deal with Stevie. We don't talk much, but when we do, I've got his number."

"Yeah, well. I'm still gonna give him shit about it. Someone's getting a call tonight, that's for fucking sure."

"No! Dan, you can't!"

"Why the fuck not, babe?" Marco startled me by jumping in.

"Because, lover boy, he'll go crying to Beau, that's why."

"Oh! We're not on with that again, are we?"

"What the fuck does that mean?"

"Whoa, whoa, whoa!" Dan put his hands up between Marco and my sudden flare-up. "He's so not worth getting into an argument over. Kiss and make up."

"What?" I turned to Dan like he'd just farted on me.

"Do it! I can't have my stars getting upset over my fucktard of a cousin."

Before I could say anything else, Marco gripped the back of my neck and we kissed. Within seconds I melted into it. When we broke, Marco smiled gently. "He's right. He's so not worth getting upset about. I just hate for anyone to take advantage or hurt what's mine."

I nodded.

"Good. Crisis averted," Dan said as he retook his seat on the coffee table.

Marco gazed directly into my eyes, the lust building like a raging back-burning fire. I glanced sideway at Dan. "So, what would this filming involve?"

Dan smiled warmly. "Nothing you wouldn't be comfortable doing. I want you both to stop thinking of it as porn. I know we throw that word around, but really, think of it more that I'll be documenting the love you feel for each other."

I looked back at Marco. He was just radiant, his eyes never leaving me. I could feel them on my skin like fingers touching my body. The arousal it caused in me made my stomach flip like a million little butterflies had taken roost there.

"Does it have to involve sex?" I was a little nervous about my body on camera.

"Babe." Marco's voice, warm and encouraging me closer to him, magnet and steel as the song goes. "This is just for us. Right, Dan?" he asked Dan, but his eyes never left mine. That same soul-penetrating gaze held me in its spell as it always did.

"That's right. On your phones, you'd have the only copy. We could edit it all at my house later if you'd like. But that's after. The only copies would be in your possession. Well, Marco's if we use his phone."

"See, it's just for me. And I've seen you. Please do this for me, sweetheart. I love you so much. If I could have this little thing all to myself..." I coughed a little, and he changed course. "Well, ourselves, then why not? It's not like you or I would want to post this, right?"

I shrugged. "It's just..."

"You're nervous about being naked on camera?"

I shrugged again. Why weren't my shoulders bigger? I fucking shrugged a helluva lot. I should look like the fucking Hulk from all that action.

Dan put a hand on my knee.

"We won't do anything you don't want to. Right, Marco?"

Marco nodded. He looked a little disappointed, and I knew he'd get what he wanted. I'd always cave. With him, always.

"Always..." I said softly.

"Always..." he echoed.

Chapter Seven

Keeping Score

I'd like to relive the video we made together. But in truth it went so fucking smoothly (pun intended) I barely knew Dan was there. I mean, I *knew* he was there. I wasn't blind. But Dan was such an incredible director, gently telling either Marco or me what would look great on film, that the whole affair seemed effortless. It was slightly staged but still comfortable and intimately familiar. At the start I felt my nerves creeping up on me. Marco just caught my chin with a finger and pulled my gaze to his.

"Stay right here, sweetheart. I'll never let you fall. I've got you. I love you, baby. You've no idea how much my heart beats for you and you alone. You're my world"—he kissed me softly—"my life"—another caress of lips on mine—"my love." After that it all lapsed into a languishing lovemaking session where I'd only peripherally noticed Dan was in the room whenever he whispered some sort of direction to us or when he was standing on the bed next to us as we fucked.

Marco varied it up. We ran the gamut, slow to fast and furious to slow and grinding. By then Marco was in the groove of the whole filming thing. He got Dan to capture the thing I evidently do with the pointing of my toes that drives Marco bat-shit crazy with lust as he's screwing the daylights out of me. For Dan's part, he was very supportive and nearly nonintrusive. Being naked around him got to be fairly normal. There were times he'd reach into the shot to move an arm, or a slight turn of the face, but they were few and far between.

After we came and wrapped up the whole thing Dan said he thought we looked amazing. He said there were a couple of rough spots he knew he didn't get right, but those would be easy enough to edit. He got really excited about one sequence he said he had to show us. He climbed up on the bed and scooted in between naked Marco and me. I sort of snaked myself across Dan. Marco raised a brow at that, but he could see it was partially because I was still sort of shy about being totally exposed. Wrapping myself around Dan's frame provided a modicum of modesty. He rolled his eyes and leaned in so we could watch Dan as he slid his finger quickly along the timeline.

"Look at this part. It's fucking over-the-top brilliant."

He cranked the volume up a bit so we could hear ourselves writhing in passion. I was shocked to discover that Marco spoke to me softly in Italian as we fucked. Why hadn't I ever noticed? Too trapped within his gaze, I suppose. Marco was like that. I was just as caught by his spell over me as he was by mine.

Two stars caught in a dance...locked together, inseparable. Angelo's words took on a deeper meaning now.

Dan had taken to the side of the bed where the light came through my bedroom window, softly diffused through the gauze-like curtains, softening it. I was on my back as Marco was slowly driving into me. We were completely in shadow. I had to admit, it looked very sexy, partially because it could almost be anyone. The features were sort of lost. You could hear Marco and me softly moan into each other. The shadow play of his hellacious cock driving into me was very erotic. Even I thought it looked rather beautiful.

"Paolo and I tried this many times and I never quite got it right. *This* is what we were after. You guys fucking nailed it on our first shoot. You both are so fucking beautiful when you make love. It fucking turned me on. You so have to let me keep making these for you."

Marco gazed over Dan's head at me. I had my head on Dan's chest as I watched it, nibbling on my thumb. I glanced up at him and smirked. He knew I was in.

"Thanks, Dan. You've made a dream come true for me."

He kissed the top of Dan's head. I sensed Dan blush a bit over what we were all feeling. I wasn't sure what my feelings were on Marco's openness with his feelings around another guy. I mean, it was Dan and I felt close to him as well. It was hard to explain. Dan just engendered that. You wanted to get close. There was most definitely an aura radiating about him and all the things he did. Perhaps it had to do with his ballet training. I wasn't sure. But he always seemed to be "on" but not in a my-life-is-one-grand-stage sort of way. He walked through life as if paparazzi were on his trail all the time and he could live with it. I pondered that about him. There was a magic there. Was I attracted to him? In a way, yeah, I was. Certainly not in any way that would suggest I could replace Marco with him. It wasn't anything like that. But I did know there were many conflicting feelings I had about Dan. It wasn't a bad thing, just new and needed to be sorted.

"That's a hell of a porn cock you got there, Marco. You could so make bank with that."

"Yeah, that'll never happen. It's Els's and no one else's. I am completely happy with our arrangement. I *only want* him."

I blushed openly and unabashedly at the emphasis he put on those words.

"I can definitely see that, and that's what makes this work. It really does. This, my boys, isn't porn. It's art." I looked up at him. He shrugged. "Well, not Matisse, mind you, but a form of art, nonetheless."

He handed Marco the phone and slapped the leg I'd snaked over his jean-clad one. "C'mon. You two get cleaned up. Then it's off to my house. Video games and film editing while enjoying pizza and beer. What could be more American?"

He didn't have to ask twice. Marco and I hit the shower while Dan caught a little TV in my room. We didn't bother hiding our lovemaking in the shower, though Dan was kind enough to let us have our time alone together. I thought I'd never say this, but thank god for the Q. I couldn't imagine if we had to do this with the threat of my mom coming home in the middle of it. That would so not be the way to introduce my porn star boyfriend.

Okay, so we felt rather guilty around lunchtime. What did that say about us? Big breakfast, a little porn filming, then video gaming, pizza, and sodas. What was there to feel guilty about?

We all decided that we'd go to our last set of classes for the afternoon. So around 11:00 a.m. Dan flipped the pizza into the oven and we opted for ginger ale instead of beer since school was on our horizon. Marco and I played *Assassin's Creed 3* on his hellacious sixty-inch flat-screen TV as the smell from the baking pizza waffled about the room. A smidge past noon we decided to pack it in and head back to my place since I'd left my backpack in my room.

By the time we rolled into the senior lot, lunch was in full swing. Dan said he had to swing by his locker for some art supplies and he'd catch up with me later in Art. That left Marco and me to wander around. We decided to take a walk around the track, have a little quality time. We set our backpacks next to the bench the guys used during the games, and we started our stroll. Nothing fast, just a lingering pace.

"So, you okay with what we did this morning?"

"What? The sex or the filming of it?"

"Well, I think we've got the whole sex thing down. You seem to like what I do, well, what we do."

"Yeah." I stretched, raising my hands up above my head. Just thinking about our fucking caused that sort of reaction in me, a sudden surge of pent-up energy requiring release. His eyes roved over my torso as I stretched. So much love and desire there, I still wasn't used to it. Didn't know if I ever would be. "We're definitely good there. No, I guess I am okay with it. Still sort of can't believe we did it, to tell you the truth."

"Yeah, but it's sort of freeing at the same time, though, right? I dunno. Dan sort of made it a lot easier than even I thought it'd be."

"Yeah, there's something about him, isn't there."

"What? That whole Rainbow-child hippyish free-love sort of vibe going on?"

"*That's* what that is! I had so much trouble putting my finger on it. But now you say it out loud, yeah. That's totally it."

"I'd say his grandmother's name was probably Starchild or something groovy like that, but we know who it is."

"Speaking of which, how is your girlfriend these days?"

"I'll tell her you send her your love, next time I see her."

"You do that...*stud*."

He nudged me. I nudged back.

"I love that we can do this, you know," he murmured, his eyes on the horizon.

"What? The quiet times together? Walking just like this?"

He hummed in his pleasant singsongy kind of way that spoke volumes for how content he was. I was glad I could give that to him.

"I know you've been worried about the guys though. I get it, Els. I really do. But I think you put way too much stock in that whole gayboy red alert status you've got going on. I know it's served you in the past, and I'm thankful for that; I really am. I shudder to think if you weren't a major part of my world. You've no idea how you ground me. You keep me so sane and safe, even if I haven't always deserved it."

"Hey, we said we'd work through the whole Cindy thing, didn't we?"

"You did. You're so amazing to take it like you did."

"Well, it wasn't easy. I struggled with it. I did. But ultimately there was one thing I couldn't get past. One thing that held strong in the hurricane of hurt I hurled at it."

"What's that?"

"You've never given me a single moment where you weren't completely devoted to me. And I know Cindy. I get her better than she knows herself, actually. It was definitely her scheming that got you in the mess we're in."

"Yeah, well, don't go discounting my mother's involvement in it. I wouldn't be surprised if she had knowledge of it."

"What? That she knew you were coerced through some sort of intoxicant?"

"No. Not that. Well, I don't think so. I dunno, she can be quite calculating. I know she loves, uh, me, but she loves my father more. That much has been made abundantly clear on many occasions in our home."

"Wow, even if he threatened you?"

"Even so. Dad is her world. She'll fiercely protect that, protect the image of his family to the town, to its people. If I didn't have control of my trust fund, I'd be really worried about now, what with you and me. She won't understand it, won't get why it's you."

"Yeah, well, I'm right there with her on that one." But I was quick to surrender the point; I knew better. "And I get that it's not for me...yada, yada, yada."

He nudged me with that powerful shoulder of his, nearly toppling me over. His hands were quick as always, grabbing me by the torso to keep me upright. They lingered for a few seconds before taking a respectable distance from me again.

By now we had successfully made one circuit around the track. We'd lapsed into an uneasy quiet between us. I knew it was because there was something on his mind that he wasn't saying.

I stopped walking and sighed, "Okay, out with it."

"Wha? Out with what?"

"What are you simmering up there in that head of yours that you're not telling me?"

He stopped, his head down, staring at the track. His hands on his hips made the letterman's jacket bow outward, emphasizing the expanse of his chest and taut eight-pack of his stomach. God, he was fucking beautiful. The way the wind was blowing about him, very romantic stuff. I pulled my phone out quickly and snapped a photo of him. That was going to be my new wallpaper, for sure. He looked so serious in the pic. My mythic Olympian god regarding something very deep, very important.

"This whole thing has pointed out to me that maybe I'm not enough for you."

I walked up to him. His eyes were still cast down, not looking at me. I realized what that contemplative look was all about: shame.

"What? Are you fucking kidding me? Why would I ever consider that?"

"Well, you almost did. And, well, I did."

"It was a mistake, one that cut deeply, I won't deny it. But it wasn't your fault."

"Yeah, maybe. But it didn't preclude it from happening."

"Yeah and we both said we weren't going there again, Marco. Not for a fucking second."

"Still points out how lax we'd become in our relationship, babe."

"Why? Because you slipped and I almost totally gave up the goods? So what? Not that I'm giving you license to fuck around. That will never happen as long as you're with me. I don't play that way."

"Well, good, 'cause I'm never putting myself in that situation again. So we're safe there."

"Then it's settled."

"No, it's not. It's still not right."

"Babe, I'm not going to go and have sex with someone till we blow a wad just so you can feel like we're even. It wasn't your fault."

"Yeah, but you'll hold it over me for the rest of our lives. I can't have that."

I chuckled a little at how he was reasoning it out.

"So you want me to finish what I started with Angelo, is that it?"

"What? *No!* Christ, I don't *want* you to do that. I think *we* need to do this, to keep things on an even keel."

"It's not a contest. There's no score here. At least not from me."

"But it's killing me how badly I've hurt you. I need to hurt too. It isn't right."

"Yeah, well, okay. I get what you're saying."

"Okay? So...uh, who, then?"

"I dunno."

"Dan?"

"He's beautiful and fun, but I don't think so. And *no*, not Stevie, either. So you see, we're fresh out of boys, and I don't think Angelo should be in the mix again. So, how 'bout this... I'll table that 'affair thing' until I'm like seventy-five and I'm utterly tired of your old bones and I'll find some sexy sixtysomething I can have a one-nighter with... Will that satisfy you? I'll take a rain check."

He groaned loudly at that; I'd just frustrated the hell out of him. Honestly, I couldn't figure out why it was such a big deal. I was moving past it all. Why were we even talking about this?

"You're killing me, Smalls...seriously, killing me!"

"Well, that's the best I can do, lover. It's all I got. You're just going to have to figure out a way to live with that. Rain check or nothing."

He looked at me with a dark penetrating gaze. He wanted to fuck again. I could tell. That wasn't happening. I don't care if he dragged me to the car and tried to bone me in the senior lot. It so wasn't going to happen. He could just be frustrated. Maybe I was going to lord it over him. That wasn't my intent. I didn't want to go there. I really was trying to put it behind us.

"Ai-right...I getcha. You're gonna make me pay for it."

"That's not it at all, babe. I know you got some sort of competitive spirit and that going on because of your football training and all, but... "

"It ain't got dick to do with that. It's just hard to live with the shame of what happened, of what's still potentially out there."

"So you wanna put me in the same fucking hole as you? Is that what this is about? I thought we were above this. I thought what we felt for each other was far more important. I thought Cindy wasn't supposed to get to us, that we're stronger than all of that. I know it is for me. I thought it was for you too. I guess I was wrong about that."

"No. No, you weren't wrong. I just, I dunno. I don't know how to feel about it."

"That's because you were a victim in the whole thing. Just let it go; just put it down. I'm tired of carrying it too, sweetheart. She's gonna bring more rain soon. I can feel it. It is far from over. But for now, just let it go. 'Kay? There's just us. There's just you, wanting skinny ol' scrawny me. Just us, okay?"

He nodded, his eyes still on the field in front of him. He turned his head to look down the field at the quad courtyard where everyone was finishing up their lunches before he turned back to me. "Yeah, you're right. You are. I'm just, I dunno. Going crazy with how I've let you down. That's all."

"Baby, I know that. Believe me, if I could, I'd take it all away from you. I don't like your feeling this way either, you know. It's not just all about you. I got cut by it too, but you don't see me wallowing around in it. It's in its place, tucked away. I'll deal with it when it comes up again, when we have to deal with it. Ya know?"

He nodded. "I love you so much, Els. So fucking much. It hurts sometimes 'cause it's so big for me. And I just…"

He got frustrated again and growled a bit at the air around him, his arms bowed in the pent-up anger he was feeling about himself, like those big he-men do when they're frustrated or getting their alpha on. His fingers curled into claws, wanting to tear, to rip, to rend something they can't bear to witness any longer. Though I couldn't see it as the letterman's jacket was covering them, I knew his muscles were taut with the anguish and rage he had for himself and however he felt about causing me any degree of pain. I don't know why it was, but it was. I knew at that moment how very real his love for me was, how deep it ran, how all-consuming it was for him. Marco always carried a degree of control, a poise that garnered respect and attention. He was a man very much at ease and confident in his own skin. Many men and boys play like they are, trying like hell to exude the air of machismo, the confidence, the swagger to profess to anyone who'd take notice that they are a man, someone to be reckoned with. With Marco it was effortless. It was passionate. It was all-consuming. And it was because of me.

He turned and walked right up to me, put his hands on either side of my face, and kissed me with a fierceness that made my knees weak. Each time I tried to break the kiss he pulled me into him. After a few intense moments of that kiss, he slowly broke it.

"Baby, I don't think you shoulda done that," I panted at him, still a bit delirious from it all.

"I don't care anymore. I'm through. You're *mine*, dammit." Tears were falling from his eyes, silently, painfully. "I will no longer deny what's mine."

"Baby, you can't. You just can't. Not now. We're so close."

"Dammit, Els! I'm over it! Fucking beyond over it! The world can go fuck itself! I don't fucking need their approval. All I need is yours. Not my parents', not your parents', not the team. None of it. All I need, all I want in life is to be with you. If I can have that, if that is mine, then the world can take whatever else they want."

He started pacing back and forth, his eyes darting to the quad. I didn't think anyone had spied us. We were rather far away. Someone would have had to be looking and at the right angle to pick up on it. So far, from what I could tell as I glanced over his shoulder at the lunch crew, our little suck-face session had slipped by unnoticed. Or so it seemed. Time would be the final arbiter in that little drama.

He came up to me and fiddled with the buttons on my pale pink button-down shirt I'd put on after we made the little video.

"Just you, babe. Only was ever going to be you."

I couldn't help teasing him when he got serious like this; it's a twisted quirk of mine. And I do it partially to take the mickey out of his being so serious about something.

"And what if I were straight and had a girlfriend? Then what would you have done? Answer me that."

"Simple, I'd have converted you."

The devilish gleam returned to his eyes, the color back to his cheeks. The first bell rang to indicate lunch was officially over.

"C'mon, you dork," I teased him, pulling on his jacket sleeve to get us moving toward the classrooms.

"Still your dork, though."

"Yeah. Still mine, big guy."

I scooped up both our backpacks and handed his to him. We had to pick up the pace if we were going to make it to class on time.

"I don't know if you should go to school tomorrow."

I heard the pensive tone to his voice. The sudden realization that he wasn't going to be there to watch over me was eating away at him. His breathing wavered into the phone. I had to soothe that.

"Sweetheart, it's not like I didn't go to school before we were together. I think I can handle one day without your being there. I'll lay low. 'Sides, I got Danny around, not like I'll be totally by my lonesome, ya know? And there's Greg if I get desperate."

He sighed. He still didn't feel good about it.

"Baby, I just worry."

"Oh, sure, *now* you bring it up. Not like I haven't been grumbling about your boys going evil-eye on me at every turn. Now it's suddenly an issue?"

"No, not suddenly. Always. I always listen to you. I may not react immediately to what you say. But it's not that I don't think about it, reexamine it. Understand it. And I take care of it in my own way. I've cornered Beau, Stevie, Willem, and Mackenzie. Yeah, you weren't so clued in on the other two, were you? Yeah, well, I overheard them talking to Stephen at the Pizza Hut when I stopped in to pick up a pre-practice snack. I confronted them on their little talk. So yeah, I deal with it. More than you realize. But, baby, I gotta be there to make sure they don't go off the rails with you. That's why I say you gotta play sick or something."

I slapped the dryer shut after putting the last of the clothes from the washing machine in it.

"Yeah, well, I think I'm gonna be fine. 'Sides, I got hell for the half-day hooky you talked us into, and that was only a couple of days ago. So I really can't go off taking another breather from school. I'll get nailed for that. Restriction kind of nailed."

"Yeah, well, at least I'll know where you are. I'll know you're safe."

I rolled my eyes.

"FaceTime?"

He sighed. "Yeah, okay."

As I schlepped my way back to my room, I punched the button on my phone to switch it to FaceTime. His amazingly beautiful face, covered in a sheen of sweat (he'd just finished his workout), glowed softly from my phone as I flopped onto my bed.

"Yeah, but I'll be trapped here at home. School, work—that'll be my life for the next several weeks if I skip tomorrow. It won't be easy to see you if that happens."

"I can still sneak in."

"Okay, let's look at this. I do this, get caught, get put on restriction—which, fuck me, at eighteen and *on restriction*. That's like seven kinds of wrong. I'm a fucking adult in the eyes of the law, but not to my mom."

He opened his mouth as if he had anything to contribute at this point. Silly boy. I ran right over him.

"So not done with my point, big guy. Then you come over for dinner on Saturday, because, even if I'm in the doghouse with my mom, she isn't about to renege on the whole dinner-with-my-boyfriend gig. So there'll be that and it will be pleasant—though I gotta remind you the whole not-using-a-condom-during-sex will surely be a topic of conversation for us. So we're gonna have other battles to fight that night. My being on restriction will not help us. Do you think for a moment that if I am on restriction, I won't be able to see you? Even if you sneak in at night? Don't you think she'll be in on that? It'll be the first thing on her mind. Hell, she knows it's happened already. You don't think she'll be looking out for it? So, no, I don't think it'll be a good idea for me to skip school tomorrow."

He sighed and tried to work through the Donahey logic of things. He might as well give up. Hell, it didn't often make sense to me, but I'd lived through it enough times to know how it will play out. It was something he had better start getting used to if he was going to be the permanence in my life he wanted to be.

"Okay. I don't get it."

"You're not supposed to. It's just how my life goes. You think it makes sense to me? Silly boy. Eighteen and on restriction?" I snorted. "There is no sense to be made of that, no matter how you slice it. It's gonna be a part of your world too, so you better get used to it. It's often that none of it makes any sense. But that's Kayla. She cares; she loves me. But she'll never really understand me. Not that she doesn't try. But it'll never be. And Dad, yeah, well. My being gay is what drove him all the way to Alaska. Isn't that rich? They say they love me, but he couldn't handle the big reveal. And it's not like it was a huge *ta-da* moment, either. For fuck sake, it wasn't like I was the raging hetero-thug boy growing up, the picture of masculinity he'd secretly hoped for."

"Honey, I'm sure he loves you."

"Oh, he does. He makes sure to say that every week when we skype, but it's not the same. There's no hug; they're just words. Words are cheap. They have power but only what I choose to give them. Right now, I want a little action from them both. They've been woefully short on that as of late. It's just words. That's all I get from them now."

"I didn't realize..."

"What? That it's so bad?" I smirked sardonically. "It's not."

His brows furrowed a bit. "I don't understand."

"I mean that they mean well. They love me, I'm sure of it. But they'll never get me. Or us. They'll try. They'll say they're making an effort, and maybe they will. But I know it's just not within them to really see why I am the way I am."

"Are you getting all teen angst on me?"

I laughed. "No, not really. I'm sorta beyond all that. I've resigned myself to what it is. A distant but loving father who prefers the wilds of Alaska and the rigors of an oil-rig life surrounded by the big burly he-men he knows his son will never be. And a mother who finds it's easier to let me slip into adult obscurity with my new lover than to actually deal with the fact they have a gay son, someone to be seen at Christmas and Thanksgiving. That sort of thing."

"Fuck, baby. That's some kind of fucked up. Are you sure you aren't just getting all angsty? I thought your family life was a hell of a lot more normal than mine."

I shrugged. "Look, I know it sounds dark. Maybe it's just the mood I'm in. It's a bit more pointed than usual. But it doesn't make it less true. And it probably is more normal for gayboys like me than we know."

"I guess. So, you're going to school."

"Check."

"Even if, you know, I'll be worried the whole time I'm away?"

"Even if...it's just how it has to be. You can't be everywhere at once, you know. I mean, even if I get into Stanford or even Monterey Peninsula College, I will have different classes than you. I'll have to be away from you sometimes. So I do what I gotta do."

He didn't look remotely happy about that, but he knew it was the truth. "Yeah, I know. It's just..."

"I'm your everything. Yeah, I get it, and right back atcha. Okay, so we'll be apart for one day. I'll still get you back in the evening, right? I mean, you're coming by the house after, right?"

"Oh yeah. It's our future, babe. I gotta check in with my guy to make sure he's happy with what's going on."

I smiled; so did he. It was our life we were planning. Our life together. Fuck me, I really never thought this would ever be in the cards for me, much less that it was that way now.

"Rugrats and nannies?" I ventured.

"Rugrats and nannies." His confirmation started a new round of blood rushing to my nether regions.

"No museum?"

"Fuck no, no *goddamned* museum. I want us to have a house filled to the rafters with love. Love you bring into my life. I want to be immersed in it. Pull it around me like the warm blanket it is."

I heard my mother's car pull up into the driveway. I glanced at the time in the corner of my phone. Yup, she was right on schedule—9:45.

"Mom just pulled up. Guess I better check in with her. Want to call me in about an hour or so while I get ready for bed?"

"I'm gonna have to pass, babe. Long drive and all tomorrow morning, remember? I gotta turn in early."

"Oh, yeah. Love you, baby." I blew him a kiss.

He kissed me back. I flushed with warmth every time he did that. It never failed me. Never.

"Night, lover. I'll see you tomorrow night," he cooed softly. I could tell he didn't want to let me go yet.

"Elliot?" she called from the front door.

"Be there in a sec," I hollered back. "Gotta run. See you tomorrow. Drive safe, and sweet dreams."

"I always drive safe, and they're always sweet if you're in them. Love you."

"Love you too. Night."

"Night." Another quick round of blowing kisses to each other and we rang off. I had to fight the urge to call him right back. Somehow, I knew he was struggling with the same thing.

The morning was as gloomy as I felt. Just knowing Marco was slipping farther away from me made my stomach flip. Why I said I could handle this was totally beyond me now. I'd grown weaker with my survival skills, if anything. He'd been my protector. My senses had grown dull since he'd entered my life. I supposed that was bound to happen. He was always there when he could be. I was safe when he was around, even when we weren't in the same room. I knew he was protecting me just then. But now, now I'd be going in alone.

The phone rattled on the sink counter.

I spit out the toothpaste and rinsed as I saw Dan's face light up my phone. I slid the answer button and pressed the speaker icon. "Hey, my man Dan, 'sup?"

"Heya, E-man. Howzit hangin', bro?"

"You're such a straight-sounding gayboy. Did anyone ever tell you that? Way too Keanu Reeves."

"Well, if anyone would know, it'd be him. But between you and me, while I'll bone a pussy every now and then..." I wrinkled my nose that he could do that. I didn't get it. Never would. But to each his own, I guess. "I'll always take a cock over a cunt any day. It's just my thing. Like you and Marco—all googly-eyed and everything for each other. Speaking of which, I'm supposed to check in with you and see if you want me to pick you up on the way into school."

"Yeah, I guess so. Though I'll never understand your draw to the poontang 'cause that's just eight flavors of fish and I so can't go there. But that aside, I gotta ask, did Marco put you up to this?"

He chuckled. No doubt I tickled him about his predilection for fucking girls despite his professing a love of men over the ladies.

"Yeah, he did. But you so can't tell him I told you. He'd be wicked angry. He made me like swear like a million times that I wouldn't say anything. We spent nearly an hour last night after you two had talked just so he could go over how I was to keep an eye on you. Totally upside down because I got only like those two classes with you. But he got to Gran and she gave him my schedule. I swear he could charm the skin off a snake if he tried."

"Yeah, he's pretty tight with his girl in the front office."

"Huh?"

"That's why I cracked up so hard when you told us she was your grandmother. Turns out that was who Marco'd been charming to gain intel on me while he was in his stalker phase."

"Oh." Then he let go with a short round of hard laughing.

"I know, right?" I chuckled.

"Totally. Oh, we so gotta ride him about that. Too fucking hilarious. I wondered why you lost it then. You never said."

"Yeah, well, I didn't want to rub his nose in it too much."

"Oh, but this is too sweet. We just gotta..."

"Yeah. But hey, why'd he call you last night? I mean, really, why?"

"Wow, jealous much?"

"What? No way..." I made some sort of *tsking* sound with my tongue.

"Fuck me. You *are* jealous. Ah, man, you ain't gotta be. I mean, yeah, he's hot as shit and all. But I would never do that to you, bro. Not ever.

'Sides, I ain't got a chance in hell. He's all into you in a way no one could ever break. Anyway, my eye has roved elsewhere."

"Yeah, okay," I said sheepishly.

"I mean, the whole time we talked he was giving me the straight rundown of how today was gonna go. He'd worked out where my classes were and how I was gonna reroute my day to ensure that I could walk with you between classes, just so he would know you'd be covered or at least there'd be a witness to anything that could possibly happen."

"Wow, that's sort of, *weird*, isn't it? I mean, do you think it's weird?"

"He just loves you. It's really sweet, Els. You should definitely be happy 'bout that."

The second line on my phone was beeping.

Marco.

"Hey, that's him. You gonna be by soon?"

"Yeah, like twenty minutes. Is that cool?"

"Yeah, okay. Gotta go or I'll lose him."

"Okay, but don't tell him—"

I hung up to take Marco's call.

"Hey, sexy!" he called out as if he was on hands-free or something. Was that new? He was always sort of gadgety, but I didn't remember the Impala having any of that.

"Hey, babe. Where are you now?"

"'Bout a quarter of the way there. If all goes well, I should make the appointment a bit early. Which is probably a good thing because it's the first time I'll have driven there myself."

"When were you there last?"

"Dad drove me. We were looking into it as a potential college for me. That was before you and I got together though. Actually, about a week before the last week of school last year. Why?"

"Oh, nothing. So Dan just called and said he was gonna be picking me up. Did you have anything to do with that?"

"Yeah." He sounded so fucking cute that I sort of caught him in his little ploy, even if I didn't come right out and accuse him of colluding with Dan to have me watched throughout my day.

"Uh-huh. Okay, out with it. Is Dan my chaperone? What did you do, Marco?" I started attacking the frenzied mop that was my head while we talked.

"Damn, baby. You sure went down that dark alley all of a sudden. Did he call and say something?"

"What? No! He just called to tell me he was picking me up, he'd promised you something about a ride to and from school. It's nice, but he didn't have to. I could've walked, you know. I've actually done it before. It's not that foreign a concept to me that I'd get lost on my way in."

"I know. I just...worry. That's all."

"Yeah, okay. I promise not to ride you too much on it. I know it's 'cause you luuuve me."

"Yeah, yeah. You're all that. Always have been."

"Always?"

"Always."

"'Kay."

Some silence as I made my way from the bathroom to my room. It wasn't unusual. Sometimes we just let ourselves go silent while we did stuff, just to know the other one was there while we took care of the banalities of life. This was one of those times. I knew he needed it more than I did right now.

"Whatcha wearin'?"

"Are you kidding me? I'm so not going down that road with you now."

"What? No, I didn't mean it like... Look, I just wanted to know what you're wearing so I can get a picture of it in my mind. That's all."

"Uh-huh. Just so you can undress me with those same eyes. I know how you work, Sforza; it's never that simple with you. You know I know that, don't you?"

A moment of silence. He was trying to sort out if he was going to be honest or come up with some witty diversionary tactic to change the subject.

"Yeah, I like how you can do that. It makes me feel good. It shows you care."

"Just like you calling and talking for an hour with Dan to sort out the commonalities between my schedule and his so he can completely reroute his day to walk me to classes?"

"Why, that little bitch boy. I am gonna kick his ass! I knew he'd buckle."

"Yeah, you did. And you are secretly loving it that I found out. I know you, Marco. You'd never plan something like that and leave it to Dan keeping his trap shut. That's not like you. You knew he'd tell me. It was your way of letting me know you were watching over me. Not subtly but beat me over the head with the fact you love me and will do whatever you need to to let me know you were still there. I love you for that."

"Yeah, okay. You're right. I knew Dan would blab. He sorta loves you too, you know?"

"Yeah, I like him too."

"No, Elliot. I mean he has a thing for you."

"Okay, you need to pull over to the side of the road, 'cause I know you're too tired to drive."

"Ha, ha. Yeah, you think I'm fucking with you. But it's true. He's sort of attracted to you. I don't think he'd ever cross me on it. But he does have a small sort of thing for you, like a crush or something."

"We've only known him for like a couple of days. That's just way off base. Okay, now I know you're making it up."

"Okay, sure, have it your way. But I'm telling you he does. When I started to talk to him about it yesterday, he was the one who came up with where he was in relation to you on campus. Seems he knew your schedule by heart already."

"What? He said you chatted your girlfriend up in the front office to get the info on his class schedule in relation to mine."

"I never got around to it, and he said he had it covered. So, you tell me why he knew that."

"Well, he did tell me when he moved here, he somehow found out about me and my reputation; said he knew he had to seek me out so we could become fast friends."

"Well, what took him so long to chat you up? I mean, it's not like he didn't know who you were. Hell, he has the same Art class with you."

"PE too, it turns out."

"See? He had ample opportunity."

"Yeah, but you were there."

"Exactly."

"Exactly? What exactly?"

"He was watching you but knew there was something between us. I mean, you're sorta right; we aren't that great at hiding ourselves—partly why I think if we did just come out it wouldn't matter. I think they all sort of know, especially for someone who is looking for the connection."

"You're off your rocker, Sforza. You know that, right?"
"Whatever, babe. We'll soon see."
The ambient sounds from his car phone were starting to cut out.
"Are you still there?"
"Yeah but you…king…call back later…"
"Okay!" I said a little too loudly, like the volume of my voice would somehow bridge the gap. I don't know why we humans think that. But it's almost automatic. Something's not being understood—say it louder! Yeah, that never really works, and yet it's exactly what I just did with Marco.
The signal cut.
Ah, well. I'd catch up with him later.

Danny picked me up in his parents' Jetta. It was a nice enough car. He said it was the family's spare car. He got to use it on occasions. I tried to act like everything was normal, but I had Marco's comments about Dan's supposed feelings for me roiling around up there in my head. I'm sure it'd make my conversation a bit stilted if we were talking. We weren't.

Though he did keep looking at me. Was he checking me out? Oh, god. I wish Marco hadn't said anything. Now it was just weird.
"What?"
"What, what?" I said back.
"Dude, what's wrong? You seem all weirded out."
"Nothing."
Silence. A beat longer.
"Were you just checking me out?"
He quirked an eyebrow at me but said nothing. *Fuck!*
"You're far prettier than you realize, Els."
So not the answer I was hoping for.
"Great, now I'm a princess," I deadpanned, choosing to look outside the window at the houses passing by rather than at him.
"No, Elliot. Not pretty as in a girl. Pretty as in a very beautiful man."
A beat longer. All I could hear were Marco's words echoing over and over in my head. I so didn't want that. I truly liked Dan. I wanted a gay BFF in the worst way. I just didn't want to have to deal with his having a crush on me. I hoped I could get him over that—as completely misguided as his feelings were for me. I let my mind wander onto other things. I needed the break.

As the houses zoomed by while we drove down the road, one caught my attention—giving me the mental break I desperately needed. *Oh, shit. It appears Mrs. Columbine is gonna need her grass trimmed again.* She was an elderly lady whose lawn I helped take care of because she lost her husband the same year my grandfather died and all of her family was back east somewhere. I just realized I hadn't called her about it for a while now. And yes, I knew I was avoiding Dan's comment.

We pulled into the main parking lot of the school since Dan wasn't a senior yet. I waited to say anything else while he pulled into a spot to park. We were still fairly early, so we were able to park up close to the school. He cut the engine and turned to face me, forcing me to do the same. Our chat, it seemed, wasn't over.

"That make you nervous?"

"Why do you have to be so damned open and literal all the time?" I groused at him. Yeah, I said groused. I was in a grousey mood all of a sudden.

"Because you appreciate honesty far more than you want to admit. You just haven't had a lot of it in your life. Though I can imagine Marco's tried like hell to get you to hear it. You're just stubborn about how people feel about you. Or how *you think* they feel about you. Can't I appreciate how beautiful you are without having it mean anything deeper?"

I shrugged. "It's just...awkward."

"Why? Because you think your thing with Marco is some sort of fluke? Because I'll tell you straight up, Els, it's not, you know. He just got there first, that's all. Smart guy, he is."

I shrugged again. I wished we could just move on to some other, more mundane topic.

"You're not used to compliments, are you?"

"No, as a matter of record, I'm not." And okay, that came out far more surly than I intended. He didn't seem to mind my poor attitude. Maybe he did know me better. I mean there was my beloved Marco, and Angelo, and now it appeared Dan. Then there was that strange flicker of something across Stevie's eyes. And according to Dan, Stevie liked dick far more than he let on. Maybe he really had considered my offer to be something more back then and it still haunted him? That haul between them all wasn't too bad considering I didn't have any of them just a few months ago. Maybe there was something to me after all? *Huh, who woulda thunk?* Like my Marco, Dan seemed to glean what I was thinking without my having to divulge anything in the process. It was like he too could hear my thoughts.

"There are many boys, er, uh, *men*—I'll say men, because you're at that age now, Els. Those men would find you very attractive. You're the type of guy who should be loved by as many men who would flock to you. Not that I am saying you have to break your exclusivity with Marco. I just mean men who love other men are going to circle around you. Men of all types. Big daddies, artistic types, businessmen, jocks like your boy Marco. Yes, even them too. Might already be that way and you just don't know it."

I shook my head like he was crazier than using rice paper to wipe his ass. He just arched a brow at me, clearly not buying my bullshit.

"Don't believe me? You'll see, Elliot, you'll see. You're coming into yourself now. Marco's got it exactly right. You are a light. A very, very bright light. The men who notice you will want to stay close. There's just a magic there. Part of its charm I suppose is that you don't see it. *That's* deeply alluring. It's the ambivalence to your nature that attracts, that binds men to you. You'll see."

"I don't see why. There's nothing remotely interesting about me."

"Oh, just nothing like beautiful bone structure, flawless skin, ice-blue eyes, and raven-black hair. That and the soft and sweet light about you. You should be told how beautiful you are. On you, it's natural, like breathing. Not like the rest of us poor slobs who have to really work at it."

"Well, the skin may be flawless, but it's stretched over my rail-thin bag-o'-bones body. It all just screams faggot to these guys." I motioned with my hand to the schoolyard, turning our gaze from the main parking lot.

"Yeah, well, these guys are mostly morons. Some cute-as-hell morons, but pussy-whipped cute stupid morons. Besides, you are not skinny, Elliot; I wish you'd get over that. I should know. Dancer, remember? Fuck, if Marco wasn't around, I would so be gunning for you."

I chuckled—choosing to ignore the other part of his statement. "Stupid morons...sort of overkill, isn't it?"

He smiled, not missing for a moment that I'd skipped over the last half of what he'd said. Like Marco, he never missed a beat.

"You're not gonna get all weird on me now, are you?"

"No. I'll deal. I love you too much."

"Glad to hear it. And Marco's right, ya know. I'd so swoop in on you. Just so we're clear. But I respect the big guy—what you two have. It'll never happen as long as you're happy. Okay?"

I nodded and shrugged. "I guess."

"I can't help the way I feel, Els. But I can keep how I express it in check if it makes you feel weirded out. Marco and I discussed it."

"Yeah, he said you were the one who came up with chaperoning me around campus today, not him."

He at least had the sense to look sheepish about it.

"Yeah, okay, so I stretched the truth a bit there. I just realized how awkward I was gonna make it for you if I said I'd come up with the idea. But he bought into it. We came to an understanding about it. He knows I care."

"Ya know what I find weird is I haven't known you for that long and now you're all into me."

"Well, I just took a page out of Marco's book without realizing it. I chose to stalk you a bit before I approached you. That's all. I know he got there first, so I respect that. And besides, I'm still reeling from Paolo, so it wouldn't be fair to you anyway, which is why I am boning Ashley in the meantime. I just can't hurt some pretty boy like you while I am still hurting a bit myself."

"Yeah, but that's so not fair to her, though. Is it?"

He shrugged, unconcerned. "It's just a body thing. I need to fuck. It relieves the tension; plus, I like the feel of it. Besides, it's not like she isn't getting something out of it. I've got a decent cock; you've seen it."

I nodded. It was a very nice cock. He continued like talking about cocks was the most normal thing to do at 7:46 a.m. "Not porn-king size like Marco, but not too far off."

"Yeah, I know. I've seen it—*I remember*."

He smiled a wickedly impish grin. "Yeah, I really sort of got off on that. Your watching me have sex, that was a very sexy thing. Though not nearly as sexy as watching you being pleasured by that massive dong Marco bones you with. *That* was hella hot. I thought I was pretty good handling Paolo. But you can definitely take some dick. That's a real talent."

I smiled and blushed. Not really the compliment I thought I'd ever hear from someone other than Marco.

"We don't have to be afraid of our sexuality, Elliot. That's one of the most freeing things about being gay. We get to write our own rules. Marriage is fine and all, and I am well aware you and Marco are already planning it for yourselves. But even in that, you don't have to be exclusive. Marriage can mean a great many things. I mean, you and Marco aren't religious or anything, are you?"

I shook my head with widened eyes. The very thought of bringing god (big G or little g) into it scared the bejeezus out of me. I didn't think Marco had any religious convictions, but now Dan had mentioned it, I realized I didn't know where he stood on it.

"Okay, then. You and Marco can write whatever rules you want in the relationship. Monogamous, open, something in between. The important thing is that you and Marco never lose sight of each other, that your love will always burn hottest for him and he for you."

I watched him for a bit as we waited for the early bell to sound off.

"You like doing that to me, don't you?" I asked as I ran a finger along the beading, or weather strip thing that runs around the pane of glass on a car door. I needed to do something other than meet his pointed gaze.

"Yes." There was no qualm or question in the way he answered that. "You're gonna have to get used to that too, if you wanna be around me. I'll always tell you what you need to hear—straight out truth. I don't want to hide anything from you, Elliot. You're too smart, and too special to fuck around with that."

"You don't even really know me."

"I've seen you have sex with your boyfriend. I'd say I know you rather intimately. It was a threesome whether you want to admit it or not. Marco realized that. We talked about it a bit. He said he was cool with it because the actual sex was still between the two of you. Marco's very possessive about you, as he probably should be. At least until you both are solid with what you feel about each other, that is."

"Just watching me have sex doesn't mean you know everything about me."

"I should hope not. You seem to be a far deeper person than just your sexual proclivities."

"Why does everything have to revolve around sex?"

He shrugged, that impish grin making itself known again.

"Because it's what boys like us are preoccupied with. We love to nut, and there's nothing wrong with that. But we have to own it. That was the first thing I learned about being with Paolo. He was unabashedly open about both his sexuality and the way he fucking owned his manliness. And make no mistake, his being gay didn't emasculate him by any means. I mean, you saw the guy...would you have thought he was a big ol' fairy?"

I frowned. "Normally, I'd say no. But knowing what I have with Marco, I'm not so sure anymore."

"I wouldn't be the least surprised if there were a couple of the jocks who are a bit jealous of Marco being with you."

"Now I know you're stretching it. Those guys? Not a fucking chance."

"You'd be surprised how many of them were checking you out in the shower. And not in the 'how do I measure up against the faggot?' way either. I know; I was there. Even if I didn't measure up to gaining your attention, I was watching them watching you."

"Psssht." I raspberried him, not buying that line for a g-d minute. "You're higher than a kite, Jericho."

"Not as high as I could be." He wiggled his eyebrows. The bell rang.

"Finally!" I cried.

I immediately started to grab my shit when Dan leaned toward me and put a hand onto my arm to stall me.

"Elliot, I'm sorry if what I said bothered you. I just don't want to hide anything from you. I mean, I'll keep those other things in check. I'll do that because you asked me to, but it doesn't mean I won't still be feeling them. I made my peace with Marco on it. We're cool. I just wouldn't want anything to fuck up what's happening between us. I've grown to love you too much to let something like my wayward crush on you fuck us up. I'm cool with keeping my distance. But I won't lie to you, Els. I can't. Are you cool with that? Are you cool with me holding onto you?"

I looked down at his hand on my arm, and he had very lovely hands. My eyes followed it up to his face. There was love there. Why, I didn't know. It was all too surreal for me to comprehend. Humor was about the only way out I could see to diffuse the situation.

"Well, if you gotta, I guess you gotta. Whatever, Jericho. We're good."

Before I could do anything, he pulled me into a hug and kissed my lips briefly.

"You're the best BFF a gay guy could have."

"Yeah," I started as I pulled the handle to the car to extract myself from the cabin. "Well, you're the best *bisexual* BFF a gayboy could have.

Whether he wants to admit he's bi or not. Seems to me like you got issues you need to work through there."

"No issues," he replied as he got out and came around to meet me at the front of the car. He beeped the alarm, and we started to walk, mingling with others as they made their way to the main building. "Like I said, I fuck liberally, but who I choose to love, that's strictly confined to the male of the species. My heart is very, very gay."

He said the last part a bit loud, and some of the underclass girls I didn't know because I may be gay but I was a senior and, well, I just didn't bother to commit girls to memory on principle, got a look of shock and awe at our conversation. I turned to them, with their stifled giggles.

"Yeah, but he's fucked more girls than I ever will. So, I'd watch yourselves around this one." I thumbed his direction, and we slipped into the main building.

He had his first class books on him, but he insisted that he walk me at least upstairs to watch me make my way down to the English Lit class before he trotted back downstairs to whatever class he had. I didn't have the heart to tell him that getting to class wasn't the issue. For the first time in a couple of months I wouldn't have Marco as a safety net in the classroom I had to share first thing in the morning with Fag-o-nator Hopkins. It was way too early to deal with this shit alone. I knew I shoulda took the coffee my mom offered.

I waved Dan off before the second bell rang so he could have time to sprint downstairs while I meandered over to my usual spot. However, now I seemed so naked without the wall that was my boyfriend. There was no rock for me to hide under. I was painfully aware at this moment of how exposed to Beau I was. I took my usual seat, longing for my boyfriend to take the one next to me. I feared that not even the ghost of Marco past would be enough to keep Herr Schwarzen-Hopkins from doing his worst to me today.

As if right on cue, Beau whispered something to Cindy, and they passed a knowing smirk between them before she placed a kiss on his cheek and moved off to wherever it was sluts went to work on their mattress-backed ways. Beau strode in, walking the cocky walk that even I had to admit he had the body and school cred to carry off and then some, but instead of taking the back of the bus seat that was his usual haunt, I found him slipping right into Marco's.

What.

The.

Fuck?

He turned his head casually to see how I was reacting to his little change of seating arrangements. I wasn't about to give him an inch on this. I just hoped Marco would be pleased with how it was going—this stand-off between the two halves of his world. I chose to turn myself so I could watch the courtyard as the last few students raced to wherever it was they needed to be before the bell would ring again in less than twenty-three seconds. Marcy Wannamaker was gonna have to waddle a bit faster if she was gonna make it to the girls' changing room for PE. Yeah, this is what I descended into—anything to put off acknowledging Beau's occupying Marco's hallowed seat. Even if it meant the migratory patterns of heavyset girls chubbying it along to their most hated class in school.

"It isn't a good idea to ignore me, Donahey. I'm making an effort here. I really don't have to, you know."

Okay, first off, I was surprised how well-spoken he could be. I didn't mean that to come off because he was black or anything like that. Because, if you knew me, race has so very little to do with it in my life. If you're human, you pass. From the second planet circling Alpha Centauri? Then, we'll talk. No, it was because of what I guessed I'd been prejudiced regarding the mental capacities of jocks in general. Plus the whole way Beau treated the girls in his life, like they were Kleenex or something. I got what Dan said about fucking girls, but hey, at least he was up front about it. I didn't think Beau was anything like that. I think he actually treated them like trash. So yeah, his eloquence was rather disarming. He certainly didn't go out of his way to converse with me last year in Chemistry. Verbal abuse was more to his liking. He was a hetero-thug dick, straight up and simple. The loathing between us went both ways. He just had the muscle to back it up—whereas my muscle was currently somewhere on the outskirts of Cupertino as he wended his way toward the Stanford campus.

"I'm not ignoring you. I just see no reason to engage in conversation when it's clear there is nothing I have to say that would remotely interest you."

He chuckled and shook his head slightly as the bell rang to start class.

"Speaking of which, where's Crowe? Class is starting."

"Yeah, he's a bit busy at the moment, which will give me a couple of minutes to talk." He looked at the door to the classroom just to be sure we still had time to do whatever it was we were going to do. "You have lunch plans with the guys on the team."

I snickered with a bit more sarcastic edge than I think Beau would allow.

"This isn't a request, Elliot. Your boyfriend's health depends upon it."

"But I have lunch plans with Dan..."

"Already being taken care of. He'll find himself preoccupied around that time and won't be able to make your little fag date."

His tones had become far more hushed, though they lost none of their point, as the other students were all filing in and taking their seats with a little more animation than usual given Mr. Crowe's continued absence.

"Really? Huh. That's interesting in and of itself. You can see into the future. Wow, who knew, Beau?" I knew I was being cheeky, but hell, way I figured it, if I was going down at least I could be snarky about it. "So, what does your crystal ball say about my boyfriend. Like who is he?"

"Don't be insulting. I'm not stupid, despite your prejudice against me."

"That's really rich, coming from a guy who verbally assaulted me all last semester during Chem lab."

He smiled like I'd gifted him with a coupon for a free hooker.

"Yeah, that was a great semester," he practically sang. I was seething but was smart enough not to let him see it. I didn't want him to have the satisfaction.

"So, what happens to Marco if I don't choose to make this little date of yours?"

His smile turned dark; his eyes bordered on outright evil. He didn't bother to hide the malicious tone of his next words. "It could be very, *very* bad for him at next Friday's game. That's all I'll say for now. I'll see you at lunch."

Before I could say anything, he got up and moved back to his own seat just as Mr. Crowe came bounding in with a thousand and one apologies for being late to class.

I don't remember what we covered in class. Thankfully, Mr. Crowe's flustered entrance kept him so off-balance for most of the class that he hadn't even bothered to notice my non-participation today. When the bell rang, I got up along with everyone else, my mind still playing out what Beau's words meant. I should call Marco. But I didn't want to interrupt his meeting thing with his new coach and team. It was a really great opportunity with an excellent school. While he said he was okay without football in his future, I knew he loved to play the game. And he was good at it, very, very good at it. I couldn't do something to jeopardize that. No, Beau was right. If I held the key to Marco's continued happiness in playing the game, along with whatever threat Beau was proposing against Marco should I not have lunch up with the team? Then I needed to man up and do this. *I can't crumble just because Marco's not here. Like I told him before, I'll have to be apart from him when we're going to college.* I needed to start making those decisions for us as much as he does. If we were going to be partners, then I needed to own up to my responsibility to see these things through—even if it cost me. I'd have to do it for Marco, as much as for myself.

"See you at lunch then?" Beau's voice broke me out of my thoughts.

He was standing there, all six foot four of him. He was a massive guy, and his smoldering good looks didn't hurt to take in as well. But the dark intent behind those eyes scared me the most. He was definitely gunning for me. But he was smart enough to school his features so that anyone looking our way, and there were a few who noticed Beau was speaking to me—hey, the kids can't help it—wouldn't see the point to his stare. When one of the jock gods addresses someone, if you're nearby you take notice for fear their steely gaze would search you out next. I couldn't really blame them. It was survival, plain and simple. My eyes darted to a couple of them who were watching the two of us with renewed interest. I just had to hope no one was capturing it for episode two of Jocks vs. Elliot on their YouTube channel. We so didn't need that kind of attention again.

I didn't trust my voice to work properly under his gaze. So, I paused in collecting my things and let my eyes dart to his tranquil face, so peaceful—just not reaching his eyes. I simply nodded once very curtly to let him know I'd be there.

"Good," he beamed. And his smile was radiant, and I knew at that moment how he lured girls to him. When he smiled, he looked every bit like the boy who just came down from his bedroom to find Santa had left him a bounty of presents. Though his voice was soft and gentle, I could almost smell the malice within it. "See, you're learning already. I think it'll be a good lunch for us both. I'll see you then." And he moved off.

My hands were trembling, I was so shaken by how things were going. Thankfully I had my Civics book with me, so I didn't need to go to my locker. Dan walked in as he passed Beau in the doorway.

"Heya," was all he said. He too was smiling, though it faded quickly as he took in how shaken I was. "Okay, wow, what happened?"

"Nothing. Uh, we better get going. I don't want you to be late for class."

"Eh, don't worry about it. Free study period in the library. I was ahead in units when I came to this school, so I am taking a lighter load this semester. You ready?"

I nodded as I zipped up my backpack and moved beyond the table to join him.

Chapter Eight

Dan the Wingman
or My Lunch with the God of War

Dan carried a weighted concern for me throughout the morning. I tried to keep it light, but damn him, he had that Marco thing going on where I wasn't fooling him in the least. By the time PE rolled around, he was really adamant about knowing what was going on. I just couldn't go there. Beau had threatened that Dan was going to be "preoccupied" during lunch. I couldn't even begin to guess what he meant. Since Marco wasn't around, I had to find another partner for tennis. I paired up with Larry Culpeper who was a decent enough player and a fellow geek. He was a tallish lanky fellow with a shock of ginger hair buzzed military style but sort of longish on top. If he had some meat on his bones, he could be hella hot—for a geek. We weren't really into playing today, so we sort of batted the ball back and forth without much effort on either of our parts.

In the distance I saw a scramble of guys on the soccer field. A group of them were huddled around someone on the ground. I let the next volley from Larry swoosh past me as my gaze was held by the melee on the field. One of the PE coaches had trotted his overweight self out there. Larry turned to see what had preoccupied my attention rather than our lackadaisical tennis match. I slowly walked up to the net as did he. I am sure we looked like two geeks witnessing an impending alien invasion. You know, one of those moments where some horrific event has you transfixed on the horizon because your mind just can't process it. Then there is a blink, and everyone is running and shoving, people falling to the ground in a mad dash to escape Godzilla or Mothra—you know, that kind of a moment. Well, just now that was Larry and me.

"Someone get hurt?" he asked, eying the crowd in the distance.

"I guess..."

In the pit of my stomach a knot began to form. I realized Dan had said he had soccer for this period. I wanted to run out onto that field. Beau's words were ringing in my ear. So, this was how they were going to preoccupy Dan. *Fuck me.* My bestest BFF was probably on the ground and in serious pain.

"Hey, isn't that..."

I nodded and finished Larry's thought for him. "Dan Jericho. Yeah."

A sickening feeling came over me. This whole thing felt orchestrated. They somehow knew about Marco being out today. How that was, I couldn't begin to fathom. Or maybe Marco had said something to them. Hell, I wasn't privy to that sort of jock boy exchange, so I had no way of knowing. And now there was what had happened to Danny. Something was rotten in the outer banks of Copenhagen, and I was starting to feel a bit worried about my little lunch date with Beau.

"We better finish up or the coach will say something..." Larry murmured, still a quizzical lilt to his voice in that he spoke up out of necessity, not because he really wanted to break away from our lookie-loo status.

"Yeah..." I said with an equal amount of renewed interest in our lack of game. "I suppose we should."

"Nothing you can do for him now, Elliot."

That got my attention. In a flash I rounded on Larry, startling him.

"What did you say?"

"What?"

"What did you mean about doing something for him now?"

He shrugged and frowned. "Well, it's not like you're an unknown entity around here. Marco's video sorta elevated your status at school. Actually, the rest of us are sort of glad. I mean, in one way you shine a big ol' spotlight on all of geekdom here at school. But it's not a bad thing because all of that light is focused squarely on you. So, we all notice who you talk to. It was clear that Jericho is in your inner circle now, where before it had only been Greg. Kinda odd, 'cause Dan-O's made quite a few friends for being here for only a few months. Though it would seem he's settled on you and Marco for the moment. I haven't noticed him around his usual haunts since you've both entered his life. But he fixates like that."

"Wait, you all think there's something between the three of us?"

"Like?"

"I dunno. You tell me..."

He shrugged again, though I noted he couldn't look me in the eye just now. What the fuck was going on around me? *Have I had my head in the sand?* Maybe Marco had been right all along. Did the geeks sort of have our backs?

"Well, it's really no secret about you and Marco. I mean, it's all out there."

There, it was out. In one fell swoop, my world was turned upside down. Cheryl's words were pinging around in my ear—haunting me. *Well, fuck me running,* as my boyfriend often said.

"What do you mean, 'it's all out there'?"

"Dude, it's cool. Actually, I'm fairly happy for you. I mean, it's not my thing, but hey, you broke through the geek/jock barrier. That's huge—gay or not. So yeah, I'm with you there. A lot of the kids are—well, at least among ourselves."

"Do you all talk about us?"

He smirked. Clearly, he thought I was fishing, which I guess I sorta was.

"No, Elliot, you two are not the topic of every conversation. We do have lives outside of your teen scandal drama, if that's what you're asking."

I chuckled, though it had very little mirth. This shit was really turning me around on what I thought I understood about life at Mercy High. *Who the fuck knew it could go down like this?* I sure as hell didn't. Well, there was someone I'd had a conversation just like this with. It appears Cheryl wasn't so far off the mark with her assessment. I knew I'd have to tell Marco, and there'd be a serious round of eating crow over his *I told you so*s.

I guess I'd fished enough from Larry, so I nudged him back to our game, though I kept an eye on Danny as he was being led off the field, nursing an ankle very gingerly. The coach and one other guy were finally helping him get off the field faster by each taking an arm to assist him back to the school nurse.

By the time we were called back to the locker room to shower and change, I was ready to toss my cookies all over the lawn. I knew Dan's fate, of sorts. I'd probably hear the particulars on the way home with him. I stopped dead in my tracks as I headed to the shower. It occurred to me that I might have to drive Dan's car back if he couldn't do it. Or worse yet, walk back home. Normally, this wouldn't concern me. But hey, I was really worried about it now what with Marco being gone, Dan's mysteriously *scheduled* injury, and who knows what else I was going to run into at this ominous lunch date I had with the straight boy-slut fullback from Marco's team? Hey, I'm amazed I remembered to keep walking to the shower, take my shower, and make it back to dress without passing out somewhere in between. I mean, even I realized how cliché it would be to have a gayboy pass out in the shower. I mean it would just send out the wrong kind of message, wouldn't it? *Prison gang rape, anyone? Yeah, so not going there.* I was glad I could hold it together until I made my exit and that slow walk to have lunch with the gods.

Unfortunately, I really didn't know what I was walking into. I did get a sense of what it must be like to be a death row inmate walking the last mile to your doom. There was no mistaking the feeling now. There may as well have been a gas chamber or electric chair up there, fully installed so my fellow students could gather around with their lunches and watch the public execution that was about to take place.

I had my lunch in my backpack, but I just knew that eating was *not* on the menu for me today, which was a pisser because my mom had prepared a deconstructed BLT with cheddar on sourdough. Deconstructed because the tomatoes would make everything soggy by the time lunch rolled around, so I had all the fixings in separate little bags. I just had to put it all together. It was the least healthy thing she would do for me. It meant she knew I was under some sort of stress and she wanted me to know she cared. I was looking forward to eating my sandwich. But there was no way that was going to happen, not when I knew it'd only be coming right back up with the way I was feeling.

As I cleared the PE area, I took in the long walk to the terraced garden. The other students were already starting to mill about and collect into the acceptable lunch groupings. The social strata to Olympus was already forming before me. My eyes slowly scaled the garden. Normally it wasn't nearly as threatening as it appeared now. God, it looked monumental—oppressive almost. My head got a bit woozy just from standing there. How the hell was I going to put one foot in front of the other and climb the damned thing?

A firm hand grasped my shoulder. Beau.

Fuck. Me. Really?

"Glad you could make it." He flashed those brilliantly white, perfectly aligned teeth. He was in complete command of the situation, and he knew it. I was about to have lunch with a god: Mars. And it wasn't lost on me at all that I was at war.

In a flash of brooding brown eyes that looked as if they'd swallow me up into their murky depths, he grinned warmly—like a leopard to its prey. "Shall we?"

The firm grip on my shoulder guided me up the different levels of the garden. I'd seen sketches of the Hanging Gardens of Babylon from around the time of Alexander the Great. The similarity of that and the ascension to the apex of the garden landscape here at Mercy High wasn't lost on me at all. Unfortunately for me, my Alexander the Great was still occupying his time at Stanford. I knew he was looking to our future, but fuck me, if I was gonna make it through today so we'd have one.

I glanced around and saw other students whispering among themselves as Beau and I ascended to the Jock plateau that was their domain. Beau didn't guide so much as pulled me gently but forcibly along. His hand had moved to the other shoulder with his arm across my back, as if we were buddies from way back. I wasn't stupid; I knew when the villain played nice, your fucking number was almost up. They only got nice when they were assured victory. With my hero more than a hundred miles away and with Danny tucked squarely on the nurse's bed, I had virtually no one with whom to fortify myself. I was the Christian walking right into the gladiatorial arena. I stumbled a bit as I reached the final steps to the top; Beau was there in a flash, his arm moving from my shoulder to my waist, with his other one coming around to my sternum. An embrace of sorts. I almost vomited all over him. He was all man, and I was a boy in a man's world. I was fodder for them to play with, a mouse among the big cats.

He smiled warmly, with such concern painted on his face. "Careful now, we wouldn't want you to get hurt. Marco wouldn't approve, now would he?"

I righted myself and nodded just once curtly, not sure if I was even allowed to talk at this point. He released me and pointed to where Stephen, Willem, and Mack were all sitting. Cindy was there as well, but as soon as she laid out Beau's lunch, she retreated one level down with the other cheer sluts of Mercy High. No doubt she had the popcorn and her iPhone out, ready to capture the whole thing.

I sat down where Beau indicated; he sat about a foot or so away from me on the grass. He casually went through the lunch Cindy had brought up for him. It looked like it had a hell of a lot of carbs in that meal. But then he was a very athletic man. I guess he could afford to have such a high intake of pasta. He laid out a napkin on his lap and popped the top off of the Snapple that was part of his lunch.

He smiled warmly again. "Aren't you going to have anything to eat? I see you brought your lunch."

I glanced at my backpack, which was partially unzipped, my lunch sack peeking out from the top. I looked at it and then shook my head. "Don't have much of an appetite."

"You misunderstand me, Elliot. I'm not here to threaten you. I think you're a smart kid. No, strike that, I know you're a smart kid."

I know it sounded like a compliment, but I noted that he said "kid" instead of "guy" or "student" or whatever. He was still, in his own jock way, ensuring that I stayed one down with him.

"I'm the same age as you, Beau. I don't think you'd fancy being called a kid. Why should I?"

Mackenzie stopped mid-bite of his apple, and Will's gaze moved slowly to watch Beau's next move. Stevie just shook his head and snorted softly—obviously, my mouth was going to get me into trouble here.

"Point taken," Beau said quietly, resuming eating his ravioli, followed by a bite of his garlic bread. "I didn't mean to insult you."

"Now you *are* insulting me. You just said I was smart, yet you didn't think I'd pick up on your calling me a kid, nor did you expect that I'd say something to you about it. Look, Beau. I get what you're trying to do here..."

"Do you, now?" His face was calm and placid, though his eyes were as pointed as ever.

"Yeah, this is about my staying the fuck away from my *boyfriend*, Marco." I made sure I made eye contact with each of them as I emphasized my status with Marco. "I get it. I get why you're all scared. If Marco comes out as queer, then it casts a different light on all of you. After all, you've been tight with him for the past two years—working your way up to where you are now, right on the cusp of yet another championship to add to your already perfect athletic record."

Their eyes flickered to one another. I'd hit it squarely on the head. Beau finished swallowing and wiped his mouth with his napkin.

Mackenzie started to edge closer, but Beau shot him a look, his eyes darting around, like a tiger scoping its prey, wanting to see if there was anyone watching us just now. Well, yeah, everyone was; I was smart enough to keep my voice down so that only the five of us could hear each other. I think Beau realized this. But our body language had to remain cool. In a way, they were just as trapped as I was. I think this was slowly starting to dawn on all of them.

My phone rang. They all looked at me as we heard it continue to ring. I reached into my backpack to retrieve it.

Marco.

"Heya, babe."

I knew I was pushing it, but fuck me, at this point I probably wasn't going to get another chance to rub their noses in it. If I was going to go down, I wanted Marco to be aware of it.

The guys all turned their attention away from my little phone call. All of them, that is, except Beau. His dark brown eyes seemed to somehow get darker. But he was clever enough to school his features so no one but the five of us knew what was going down.

"Yeah, it's lunch. How's it going? Uh-huh. Wow, that's really great."

I pulled the phone away from my mouth and spoke to Beau directly. I think he actually blanched at my bringing him into the conversation.

"He's meeting with the head coach at Stanford for lunch. They're heading out now to some swanky restaurant."

Back to Marco, but I noted that Beau's gaze had faltered. It was clear he hadn't planned on Marco's eavesdropping on our little conversation.

"Me? Oh, I'm just having lunch with Beau, Willem, Mackenzie, and Stephen. Yeah, *I* was surprised they asked me, too. It seems you were right about them after all. Who knew, right? Yeah, I guess you did kinda tell me so." I arched a brow at them all; their eyes were riveted to me and this little unplanned twist of events.

"Oh, Beau just wanted to have a chat and get acquainted, since the team means so much to you and I wouldn't do anything to jeopardize that." I was praying like hell that Beau and the boys could grab a clue about what I was really trying to tell them. "Yeah, I think they're getting it."

I pulled up my feet and wrapped an arm around my knees, leaning my face against them facing Beau. While I sounded cheerful, I knew he could see my gaze was anything but. I don't think he was prepared for how much I would push back or that I wasn't even a pushover anymore.

"Mmmm, okay." I pulled the phone away from my ear and held it out to Beau. "He wants to talk to you."

Beau arched a brow but set his lunch aside and took my phone. The guys were silently watching how this was all going to play out.

"Yeah, Marco, 'sup?"

A beat while Marco was no doubt relating how happy Beau's effort had made him. Inwardly, I was a bit saddened that Marco hadn't picked up on my clue that the guys wanted to have me hang around with them when all I'd been telling him was how they would look at me whenever I happened to glance their way when they thought Marco or I weren't looking. I wish he'd gotten how odd it was that all of a sudden I was "one of the guys." It should have struck him funny. But he was distracted. It appeared Stanford was extremely interested in his coming to play for them. He babbled on a blue streak about it all, most of which sailed right by me. I'd have to suss out the details later. He was simply too jazzed by what was going on. I got that. I was happy for him, but it didn't help my situation out, or his for that matter. I just didn't see a way to say it covertly enough that I wouldn't make my situation worse.

"Of course. Wow, glad to hear it. Sounds like a great opportunity," Beau said gently.

Marco chatting again.

"Yeah, sure. We just figured Elliot was going to be rather lonely today, so we thought we could keep him company till you got back. We got you on this. No, really. Not a problem at all."

A beat while Marco no doubt did some more babbling. He had to be over the fucking moon about whatever was going on at Stanford because Marco was not a babbler by nature. Beau's gaze changed slightly. I could tell the other guys picked up on it too.

"Yeah, uh, well, we'll have to see about that. Maybe. No, I know it doesn't change a thing. I never said it did."

I sorta wished Beau would put the damned thing on speaker and was secretly berating myself for not thinking of it earlier. This half a conversation was starting to get real old, especially with my life undoubtedly in the balance. I didn't think that to be any stretch of the imagination here, either. I mean, look what they'd done to not only corner me at lunch but to take out Danny quite effectively. I shouldn't underestimate the value of teamwork. These boys had it in spades.

My eyes darted in Stevie's direction. I found his gaze cold, guarded. That didn't bode well. Even if Stevie had gone over to the dark side, I knew he was a pole dancer from way back according to his cousin. He just didn't want to swing on my pole, it seemed. No, he wanted incestuous dick—*whatever, freak*. As if my thoughts had bridged the distance between us, his eyes widened, and he abruptly found the grass to be of major interest.

"All right, yeah, I'll put him back on. Oh, and, Marco, you might want to touch base with Cindy when you get the chance."

He was watching me intently, seeing if I had any idea to what he was hinting. I can't deny it was indeed a sucker punch I wasn't expecting. Only one thing would make Beau make that particular request of Marco—Cindy had to be pregnant.

Fuck me running.

"Just the same. I think you two need to have a talk. Okay, I hear ya. I'll put him back on now. Have a good trip, buddy. Right, later."

I glanced at the other guys. Their faces seemed impassive enough, but I saw it there in their eyes—particularly Stevie's. It seems the years and physical separation did little to help him keep his thoughts from me. Smiling, Beau passed me the phone. He shook his head slightly to the other guys as he ran his tongue along the side of his mouth as if he found something rather distasteful and needed to clear it out. His eyes held none of the lightness his voice had conveyed. Yeah, I was not mistaken. I wasn't in a very good place at all.

"Hey," I said softly to Marco.

With his being so far away, I didn't want him to worry. The lunch period would soon be over, and he had other things to deal with. Not like I couldn't handle this drama by myself. I mean, I'd been the target of a little jock boy angst before. So I'd get a little roughed up at worst, or at best, just a good dressing down, reminding me of how the rules applied—that sorta stuff. No, I could handle this. I had to. I didn't want him to deal with any of it.

"Heya, sweetheart. See, I told you the guys would come around. Beau seemed pleasant enough. I told him we could double up or something the next time the guys went out with their girls. Don't know if he's quite there or not. But gotta start the conversation sometime, right?"

He sounded so happy, like everything was clicking for him. I couldn't do anything to take that away from him. I just couldn't.

"Yeah, I guess it had to sometime. Hey..." I had to clear my throat because my emotions were getting the better of me.

"Yeah?"

"Sometime soon, remind me all about this so I don't forget how happy you are right now, 'kay?"

"Mmmm-kay. You all right, babe?"

"Yeah, I'm cool."

I watched Beau's eyes. He was listening to every word, every nuance to what I said, trying to glean what Marco was telling me by the way I responded. *Yeah, good luck with that, Beau.* I had no intention of tipping our hand. He could stew in his half-spoken conversation the way I had just a moment ago. Turnabout's fair play.

"'Kay...well, I should be home around eight or nine tonight. Want me to stop by the store and pick you up?"

My eyes were starting to mist up. There was no way I could let Beau or the guys see they were beginning to break me, to break us.

"Uh-huh. I'll be home tonight. I'll stay up until you get there. I'm sure I've got homework or something to do to keep busy, 'kay?"

"Okay. I'll see you then. I can't wait to tell you all about it. This is gonna be so great; you'll see."

"'Kay."

"Well, look, uh, I gotta run. I'm sorta late catching up with the coach and a few of the guys on the team and staff. Sort of another meet and greet, I think. I wish you were here."

"Me too." *And how.*

"But you'd just be bored—we talk about nothing other than football and statistics, plays and stuff. Guy shit."

"Yeah, and I'd know nothing about that."

I watched Beau's eyes as he continued his lunch, though his pointed gaze never left mine. I watched the other three around us, and they'd resumed their on-edge manner. I needed to wrap this up, better to get whatever this was over and done with.

"You know what I mean, sweetheart."

"Yeah. Okay. Well, I'll see you later on tonight. Drive safe. Don't let them drag you off to a stripper joint."

"As if. 'Sides, it's a bit hard for me. Just eighteen, you know?"

"Yeah, like they'd never set up some sort of private little party with some hookers or strippers or something. I'm not completely daft, you know."

I saw the boys share a knowing look between them. Yeah, it was all about the sex, and in particular, a very particular type of sex.

Marco just chuckled at my not letting the whole macho straight guy go like a pitbull with a new chew toy. He may be my guy, and a pole dancer himself, but I also knew the pressures to be a part of their world. Seeing the predicament, I found myself in now, how much more pointed and pressured would the whole football thing get for us? I mean, if high school presented this much drama, what were we going to face once he was playing college ball? Say nothing if he progressed and was signed into the pro leagues? I realized my meandering thoughts had consumed me, so I completely missed what he'd just finished saying.

"What was that? I'm sorry, I got distracted over here."

"It was nothing. I'll tell you all about it later."

"No, really... I'm sorry I missed it."

"Just that I think I'm not the only one on the team, if you know what I mean."

Okay, that wasn't a nothing. I was glad I fished it out of him again. Well, not glad. The last thing you want to hear is that your hunk of a boyfriend's gaydar just went off the rails over some teammate—closeted or not.

"Uh-huh, see what I told you?"

"Told me nothing. He's hot, I'll give him that. Bet he could get just about any guy he wanted, just not this one. I'm spoken for."

"But he's hot."

That caused the guys around me to perk up. Like the big red candy button to signal the mother lode of all alerts, my little teasing of Marco had rattled the homophobic cage. Yeah, I was still dead-on with my little assessment. There was no extending of the olive branch from this crew.

"I'm not gonna lie to you, Els. He is. He's a ginger too. Never knew that was something in my scope of interest. But it'll never happen. Not as long as I am yours and you're mine. I just didn't want to lie about it 'cause when you meet him, you'd definitely hold it against me that I was hiding it. I'm so not gonna fall into that trap. And hey, he's the first I've ever seen outside of you I've even thought was a possibility. So, you're right. I'm sure there'll be others. But I swear to you, it's you, babe. It'll always be you. I just won't get into the whole does he/doesn't he thing. If I see it, I'll say it and move on. I'm not gonna hide anything from you. I saw where that got me before. I've learned my lesson." I heard some commotion on his side of the conversation. "Hey, the guys are all here. I think we're heading out. Will talk later. 'Kay?" The movement on the other side dissipated as if whoever they were had moved beyond him. "I love you, babe. I can see our future so clearly now. You have no idea how badly I want that with you. You'll see, babe. I'm putting things in motion here that are gonna set us up for at least our college years. You'll see."

"Okay." I hated that he was going now. I knew it had to happen; I wasn't so sure how I'd been able to get away with chatting this long with him. Beau checked his watch and ran his finger in a sideway circle, signaling I needed to wrap it up. Holding a single index finger up I nodded, silently asking him for another minute. "Look, I gotta go too. I'm being very rude to Beau and the guys here."

"'Kay. Love you, babe. You'll never know how much, but I'll make you feel it every day from now on. I promise you that."

"'Kay, I know you will. Love you too."

My eyes darted to the guys who all were watching me the way those nasty Orcs eyed a doe-eyed Frodo before they hauled his pretty boy self up to the tower to torture. Dark looks, menacing. My stomach started to knot up again.

"'Kay, gotta run. See you tonight."

"Yeah, see you tonight."

I pulled the phone from my face to watch the screen flip, feeling nauseous as Marco slipped away from me. I knew I'd see him later. I glanced at Beau and the others.

"That was, uh, awkward," Beau said as he finished his Snapple, put the cap back on, and set it next to his nearly licked-clean container of ravioli.

"So what now? Are we at the point where you guys rough me up, or give me a talking-to about how I need to stay away from Marco?"

"The latter rather than the former. I know what you think of me, Elliot. I won't say you're totally off base there. I've roughed up quite a few guys before. I'm not averse to it. I just don't run to it first. Way I figure it, you're a smart *guy*." He arched a brow to acknowledge he'd elevated my status from being a kid after my earlier remark.

"And..."

"And because of that I'm going to lay it out for you and let you come to your own decision about it. I think, in the end, you'll do what's right by Marco. You do love him, right?"

"More than you'll ever realize."

"Good. That's what I'm counting on here."

I didn't like where this was heading. It was way too cordial, way too "let's play nice." I'd almost prefer the roughing up to this. This was too close to my way of thinking. I certainly didn't expect it from Beau. I knew he was crafty. He had to be with banging just about every girl who'd shown him interest and still get away with it. I couldn't underestimate that. That would be lethal in my world.

He was watching me closely; I was definitely the prey here. I understood that. But I had a few of my own cards to play as well.

"So, what, you think Marco and I haven't discussed what happened at Homecoming and the potential fallout from his fucking Cindy?"

Beau's eyes widened slightly with that. Not in some huge *muthafucking what* kinda way, but I spied it, nonetheless. He hadn't planned on my being so well-informed.

"We have talked about it. Yeah, he told me how it went down. Way I figure it either you, Cindy"—I spared a glance at the other three guys—"or one of your lackeys here, slipped Marco some vitamin K or something like that along with a Viagra or Cialis type drug to get him all worked up and hard for it. 'Cause, god knows Marco wouldn't bang that loose hole willingly."

Beau's eyes hardened. They were daggers that wanted to cut. I didn't care. At this point I had to be all in or I was dead meat. Fuck, I was probably dead meat anyway. I might as well go down swinging. I looked at the other guys again. They all were looking everywhere but at Beau or me. Beau watched me for a moment. Without looking at the other three his next words were for them.

"Gentlemen..."

At that singular word they all promptly got up and not only put some distance between us so Beau and I could have some privacy, but they actually left the top plateau altogether. Beau and I were completely alone—Jock and Gaybait. Two worlds that should rarely, if ever, combine. Yet they had in Marco and me. And what we had was glorious. It was potent; it was powerful. But, ultimately, was it enough? Looking at the dark intent within Beau's eyes, there was no room for interpretation. He meant to remove me from their world once and for all.

"Look, Elliot. I get that you feel something strong for Marco. That's understandable. But you have to see that what you're doing is pulling focus from how great a man he can be. You're pulling away how bright he shines. Don't you see that?"

Angelo's words were ringing in my ears. I remembered them well. A single tear escaped my eye; I moved quickly to swipe it away, acting like I had to suddenly scratch along my temple and brushed my cheek as I did. I hoped he hadn't seen it as it was definitely what I never wanted the enemy to see. And Beau was definitely that—an enemy. There just wasn't any other way to see him.

"No, I really don't," I lied.

Angelo had as much as told me so. Hell, Marco had alluded to it one way or another. But there was no way in hell I was handing that kind of ammo over to Beau.

"The way I see it, and here's where you really don't have any room to argue so you'll just have to take me at my word, I'm the one who's been intimate with Marco in ways that ho-bag Cindy—and don't raise a brow about her to me, you don't get that position while I'm making my case. I'd fucking say the same damned thing to her face."

He snorted at that, but clearly he was surprised at my cheek. I think he had a newfound respect for me. Just a little bit.

"In those private moments, only *I* know what's in his heart, what his dreams are, what I mean to him. And I'm not sharing that with you. It's private. I would never betray that trust. But I'll guarantee you this: Marco and I are well into the triple digits of how many times we've been together since July. I know where his heart is, what I am to him. That is unwavering. So, whatever you think you might be navigating here to separate us, think again."

I found his text to me from several weeks ago when the whole Homecoming fiasco happened. *I'll fight for you.* I smiled broadly, turned the phone so Beau could see it.

"That is what he texted me when I tried to send him away after I found out about Cindy's little tryst with Marco. So you see, I've been where you're trying to take me. Been there, done that. We're stronger."

He pursed his lips and handed me back the phone.

"That's a pretty good case. I have to admit, you know how to swing and swing hard. I get what you're saying about what you and Marco share." I raised my chin a bit; that was a very big admission on his part. The win was too easy. There had to be more. I frowned. He didn't seem to be too worried about what I'd said, though. *Not good.* I wondered what he had up his sleeve.

"But there is one thing you haven't considered. Well, I should be clear because you've already figured it out, though Marco is in denial."

"The kid."

He nodded. I shrugged.

"Really? That heartless, are you?"

"Not at all. I feel for the kid. I really do. Believe me, I know what it's like to be one down. But let's be honest, shall we? Can you be entirely certain it's his? I mean, even I know that slut gets around and has been passed around far more than she likes to let on."

He tensed up with what I'd said. I was lying through my fucking teeth, but it wasn't like he needed to know that. And with the way his body language had changed, I knew I wasn't far off the mark with my assessment.

"Don't bother denying it, either. Because *that would* be insulting."

"Wow, Elliot, look at you. You seem to have grown a pair since Chemistry last year."

"Being with Marco has been a revelatory experience. Don't get me wrong, Beau. I may not come out on top of this. As you said, I'm a smart guy. But one thing I can tell you, even if I tried to push him away, he'd come after me. It's not me who needs convincing. You saw the text message. Those were his words, not mine."

His turn to shrug. "You could've easily grabbed his phone and texted them to yourself."

"That's really stretching it. I mean for what possible reason?"

"Still could've happened."

"Okay, sure. I'll concede that. But it won't change the outcome."

"I'm not trying to change anything. I am just hoping you love him enough to see to his long-term safety and good health, that's all."

"Is that a threat, Beau?"

He shook his head slowly, his eyes pointed, like stilettos.

"I wouldn't go so far as that. You know as well as I do that accidents on the field can happen. We face them every time we go out there. While we try to defend Marco as much as we can, guys do slip through."

There it was. I was sure he saw my eyes widen with the possibilities of what he was speaking to. Clever, clever man that he was. It was an admission that they weren't the perfect defense for Marco. In his admission he'd layered his threat to our well-being. A soft, knowing smile snaked across his lips. Like a viper he slithered away into the darkness, the damage was done.

"You'd do that to another guy on your team?"

"What are you talking about?"

"Now you *are* trying to insult my intelligence. You know very well you were implying that Marco could get hurt, purposefully."

"Not purposefully, but we can't be everywhere at once, can we? We're not perfect. Shit happens."

I crossed my arms and leaned into myself a bit. The sucker punch to Marco's safety had signaled something that was far beyond my control. Beau was a smooth one; from the phone conversation he'd had with Marco, there was no way any signal from me would make Marco believe he was in danger from his own guys, that they'd let him get sacked, and badly too from what Beau was hinting at.

"So, what? You want me to give him up so you guys will continue to protect him?"

"I want Marco to become the man he should be."

"Who are you to say what that is? I think he'd have definite ideas on that topic, seeing how it's *his* life we're talking about here. You know what fascinates me about all of you?"

He nudged his chin up as if my next words were of complete interest to him. He probably thought, *Oh this is going to be good—fagboy has an opinion.*

"That everyone in this fucking town has Marco's plans all laid out for him. All he has to do is show up and walk through the role where he has no voice. I mean, who'd want that sort of life? Would you?"

"You may have a point. But you and I both know *a* Marco. You may have had him for the past few months. Intense months, I'll grant you. You've seen a Marco none of us have. I get that. I know what a good piece of ass is. The way you've got Marco all captivated means he likes what he's getting from you. So I gotta give you props for that. Marco's definitely a catch."

"I'm not in it for the money, or the Sforza name. Hell, I fought the *us* he was proposing when he came to me. And let's be clear about it, Beau, *he* pursued me. I sure as hell didn't think I stood a chance at that. In fact, I thought it was a complete setup. Jock boy taunting the gaybait so he and his buddies could jump the fag. So, you see, been there, considered that."

"Yeah, well, like I said, I've had a good piece of ass a time or two."

"More like three or four hundred by the sounds of it."

"You been following my sexual exploits, Donahey?"

"Intelligent, remember, Hopkins? I hear things. I have eyes. I'm *not* stupid."

He nodded.

"So, I get why Marco'd tap that." My eyes widened, and he continued, "Not that it's my cup of tea, but I get it. You gotta be doing something right or he wouldn't keep coming back."

"What's the matter, Beau? You curious about what a gayboy like me could do for you?" I knew I was way out of line with what I'd said to him. Flirting with him was not something I'd ever picture myself doing. But I was curious enough to poke at it to see what sort of response I'd get out of him. Way I figured it, with his rampant homophobia, he might just have an unrequited interest in some gay piece of ass that he was trying to suppress. Wouldn't be the first case of that by a long shot.

"Marco know you flirt that hard with other boys? I didn't take him for the open relationship type."

"Purely an academic question. I was just curious if you were standard closet fare or not. You there with all that brash homophobic edge coming from a secret desire to beat a gayboy into submitting to his baser desires. Shit only another man would truly understand. Mean sex. Rough sex. Messy sex. You know what I'm talking about, Beau. You can school your features all you want. But none of those girls have ever really given in to what you want to really do to them, have they? They just aren't built to take the sort of grueling fucking you want to put out. As you can see, I'm not a girl. And I can *take it* like a man—there's something to be said for that, Beau. Hell, I have had it rough on occasion. Begged for it, even. You have no idea how accommodating I can be. So yeah, maybe, *just maybe*, what Marco and I have is a *very* good thing from his perspective."

I thought better of that and quickly regrouped to protect my guy's reputation. I was getting into deep troubled waters here, and I needed to get out before I found myself drowning in the deception.

"Marco isn't my only sexual experience, either. There've been others."

Yeah, now that was a bold-faced lie—what was it about lying today? I'd certainly had enough sex since Marco, and I'd gotten together that I could swap a face or two and make it believable—so not a total lie there. Not that Beau'd ask for particulars. At least, I didn't think he would. With the look of curiosity buried in his stare though, I wasn't entirely positive of that. I decided on a different tactic. Best not to poke this tiger too much.

"I'm sure Daddy would be very shocked at his son's rougher edge when it comes to sex."

Beau's eyes darkened; his features became pointed, harsh lines and dark shadows. He was definitely menacing. Why I wanted to go there was really sort of stupid. I mean, I knew he could beat the crap out of me for saying these things to him. Hell, he could beat me senseless just for breathing the same air as him. He had the jock status; no one would begrudge him that action. He might catch some flak for it, but hell, I was a fag, easy fodder to mess up and then move on. Hell, he'd probably get a few people in town who'd thank him for bashing the local gay kid.

"Does your daddy know about your rougher side? Or that he's being banged by the local quarterback?"

I knew he thought he'd turned that around on me. Did he really think my parents didn't know I was gay?

"He knows I have a boyfriend. So does my mom. They don't know who it is." I held a finger up to stall his next words. "And that's not because I'm ashamed or anything. We just thought we'd be low key so the team's performance wouldn't suffer. So, you see, Beau, whether you choose to accept it or not, I do have you and the team in mind throughout all of this. I get how important football is to Marco and you all. I want to help protect that, if I can. It hasn't been easy. Marco wanted it all out there. Hell, I'd won the damned title of Homecoming Queen—knew it before the event was called. The school board had to meet to discuss how it was all going to go down. They wanted to make sure I was safe. They are the ones who took that away from me, said it was to protect me from any bullying. Marco wanted to use the whole thing as our coming out. Can you imagine the looks on all of your faces if *that* had taken place? And it very nearly did. It was so close to happening. Marco wanted it. Badly. I've been fighting him every step of the way to keep things quiet. It was our plan to lay low until the football season was over. So you see, Beau, I do have your interests in mind. I want what you all want. And I want it for you. I get nothing out of the deal. But it doesn't matter to me. I'd still want it for you all."

He sat there, his gaze never truly letting the brooding clouds slip away from him. An uncomfortable beat later he glanced at his watch and began to gather his things. I don't think he was fully prepared for squaring off with me like this. I think, like Cindy, he thought I was the same acquiescent kid who'd simply go along with whatever they told me to do. Yeah, after Marco, I sorta did grow a pair and was finally putting a voice to my own convictions, rather than let them die in the back of my throat. It was liberating, as it was completely terrifying.

"We're done here. Think about what I've said, Elliot. I hear what you had to say. You made some points I hadn't considered. But there's still the baby. There's Marco's future. Two truths that aren't so easy to dismiss as you'd like them to be."

"Maybe not. But that's something Marco and I have to discuss together. He and I will decide what's best."

He stood up and I followed. We regarded each other for a moment. The other students had noticed we were about to part ways. I'd nearly forgotten all about my audience at the top of Olympus with Mars. It was time for this mortal to return to my own realm.

"I'll say this for Marco; he knows how to pick them." Beau's eyes almost had a mild admiration for me. Almost. There just was too much uncertainty and malice floating around in there to let me breathe any easier. Beau was still very much the enemy. I started to go when he reached out and pressed a finger to my right bicep, stalling my taking leave of him.

"And for future reference, it's not a good thing to poke at a jock with your gay ways. You just might not like what's at the other end of that stick you keep trying to use. You couldn't handle what someone like me would throw at you."

"You'd be surprised, Beau. I've a fairly suppressed wicked streak in me. But, as you say, it's not your cup of tea and I'm with Marco, so you'll just have to take my word for it."

"How is it you can be so forward with me? You don't think I'll bring it up to Marco?"

"Really? You think he'd believe you over me? Then you really don't have a clue as to how our relationship works. Everything I do, I do it to protect him, protect us, as best I can. If it means I gotta lay low..."

"Or leave him altogether?"

"That'll never happen, but okay, even that. Then that's what I'll do. He means that much to me."

"Just think about what I said, Donahey. Let him become the man he's supposed to be. Quit stealing his light."

I raised an eyebrow, but he released his finger-pointed hold of me and moved off to the trash cans at the bottom of the quad garden. It was just me, the lone mortal at the top of Olympus. All the gods had departed. A stiff breeze billowed around me, emphasizing the barren emptiness surrounding me. I scanned the quad. Several pairs of eyes were on me. *So, this is what it means to be at the top?* I pondered Marco's world from here, tried to see the world the way they saw it, through their eyes. Only one thing came to mind, just then. They hadn't lied about it.

It *was* lonely at the top.

Chapter Nine

Isolation in the Wake of Mars

I stood there alone with only the stiff breeze as my companion. Little consolation in that.

With the exception of everyone else around me, I had a sinking feeling like I was the only man left on Earth. You probably don't get what I'm saying seeing how there were so many more people in my life than before the summer vacation, but I gotta tell you, that was the prevailing feeling. I was utterly alone, with my thoughts, with my feelings, with just about everything I had left in my arsenal for survival—which, given the day I'd just had, wasn't much. No boyfriend, no gay best friend, no Dad. Nothing like being a gayboy with all the men in your life who make you feel safe not being there when you need them most. Being the gay kid often meant you didn't have men around you so much. I suppose I could've tried to skype my father. I knew he'd make the time if he could. But I also didn't want to bother him. Not like he could really do anything about it being so far away. I didn't want to be a nuisance. *I'm eighteen, for Chrissake. I should be able to handle this, shouldn't I?*

The football team had each other to lean on. A brotherhood. I know I shouldn't be so wound up about it. I should be used to being alone. Only being with Marco had changed all of that. I'd gotten used to having someone else in my corner. And I knew he was. I knew that—but at this moment, with him so far away, I felt very much alone.

The clouds had begun to roll in. What had once been a delightful morning had now descended into a gloomy overcast afternoon. My gaze moved toward the ocean. The clouds looked even darker in that direction. Great, rain probably. While I didn't mind the wet weather, I didn't fancy Marco having to trek in the forested area behind my house in the rain if it started. He was right about that, keeping things secret was costing us.

Oh well, after this weekend with my mother and Marco, all will be out in the open. We'll move forward then—no more secrets. After all, it's only a couple of days from now. My Scarlett O'Hara way of thinking was getting to me again: *I'll just think about it tomorrow.* Somehow, like Scarlett, I didn't believe it would be helpful this time around. That whole "tomorrow is another day" was not the right foundation to build a healthy life. I needed to get my head out of my ass and agree with my man what we should do, what he'd been saying we should do. *God, I am such a fucking idiot!*

I looked at my iPhone: five minutes left before first bell would ring ending the lunch period. I had just enough time to check in on Dan.

I scrambled down from Olympus and into the main building at a fast enough clip. I wanted to have a few minutes to chat with him. Of course, I was concerned for his health. He was my new bestie after all. If it hadn't been at Beau's insistence, I would have been more than happy to eat my now useless deconstructed BLT with him. Well, not totally useless. I supposed I could salvage what I could when I got home.

Home.

That's where I wanted to be right now. I needed to sit in my room, collect my thoughts. I resisted the urge to call Marco. He had big things going on for us. I couldn't interrupt that. I mean, we were just looking to going and starting our lives there after all this high school drama wrapped itself up. I glanced up the hallway as I rounded the corner. The nurse's office door was still open. I dashed in between people, trying not to collide with anyone. I was fairly successful. I was nearly there when I slammed into a brick shithouse of a guy: Willem Hawthorne. This was followed by Mackenzie Thompson walking up to where we were. *Fuck me, I never seem to get a break today.*

"You better watch yourself, faggot," he hissed at me.

Mack just smirked. It's what wingmen did, I guess.

I spun around and glided right by them and moved on, not really caring what their drama was all about nor giving Will the opportunity to explain it. I am sure he thought to give chase, but I'd already made it into the nurse's office. *Yeah, good luck with pursuing that, Will.*

"Slow down, Mister Donahey. This is a place where we heal accidents, not create them," Nurse Ratched called out; and yeah, that's not her real last name, but she looked like Louise Fletcher from *One Flew Over the Cuckoo's Nest* and her last name was really Hatchet—something else I thought was ironic for a nurse's last name, so my rename sorta stuck. I just had to be sure to school my mouth and not let that one drop accidentally—something I wasn't always too successful with.

"Sorry, eh, Nurse *Ha*-tchet." Fuck, I was gonna have to do better than that or she'd think I was having a seizure or something. "Is, uh, Dan Jericho here?"

"Yes, he is. His grandmother is about to take him to see Doctor Sforza to get properly checked out," she said very matter-of-factly.

Really, woman? My newly acquired bestest friend was just waylaid by some homo-fearing thugs from the football team and the best you can do is be perfunctory in your explanation? The way these boys threw the testosterone around, it isn't entirely out of the realm of possibilities that Dan could have been seriously hurt. Oh! My! God! His ankle! Dancer...fuck me!

"I wanna see him. Would that be okay?"

My anxiety level was no doubt evident now. Her eyes widened with the sudden alarm flare-up I had stoking in the furnace.

"I don't know. It's not normal procedure. I mean, you aren't family."

"He is to me."

Danny. Fuck me if I wasn't the happiest person on Earth to see him balancing on one foot holding on to the wall.

"Hey, how are you?"

"Come here, pretty boy. Keep me company before Gran descends and the family antics ensue, will ya?"

Nurse Ratched quirked an eyebrow over Dan's supposedly new nickname for me. I wasn't so sure I wanted to go with that.

"Pretty boy? Really? That's the best you can do?"

"Well, Marco's the stud so yeah, to complete my *fairy* tale, that only leaves the pretty one. Which is fitting." He held out his hand. "Now come here so you can help me get back onto the bed to rest. I'll need it before the family wackiness starts up. That'll tie me up for hours."

Nurse Ratched seemed to have recovered from her awkward bemusement over Dan's affections for me. Hey, I was right there with her on that one. I still wasn't used to it. Even Beau seemed to consider my flirtation for a nanosecond before he staunchly declined. *Or had he declined?* I couldn't remember how that went down now. I must have pursed my brow or something because a look of trepidation crept across Dan's face. My eyes took him in fully. He was really a very handsome man. For a moment, albeit brief, I considered what it'd be like in a relationship with him. Probably closer to what I ever imagined I would end up with—some artistic sort of guy.

"Are you just going to stand there holding my hand, or are you gonna help a brother back to the bed?"

"Huh? Oh! Shit, sorry."

I wrapped his arm across my shoulder with mine snaking around his waist. He snuggled in a bit closer than was necessary. I made a point of thinking I was going to have to watch his playful touches going forward. I didn't think Marco would mind necessarily as he and Dan seemed to have come to some sort of understanding about it. Which, of course, only brought me to another point: why were there understandings about me now? When the fuck had I crossed over into salacious man-meat material that everyone needed to have agreements and understandings about? I mean, it's just me I stared back at in the mirror. What's all the fuss about? 'Cause seriously, I just don't fucking get it. Now, Marco and Dan—they were bona fide stud material. No question about it.

Me? I was just plain scrawny, and likely to stay that way if Marco had his way about things, and Marco generally had his way about things. He said I liked it that he ran the show, and he was right about that. I liked that he loved calling the shots about us, made it easier for me. He cleared the cobwebs over silly shit and let me think about the important things, like why do we give a shit what the Kardashian sibs do with their meaningless lives? And really, do we need another American Idol? Hadn't that worn out its fifteen seconds of fame back when, I dunno, like the first season some forty-five years ago? Ya know, impo'tent shit like that, thoughts that preoccupied me and allowed me to keep my gayboy status firmly intact.

Dan's next words snapped me right out of my meandering thoughts. "Christ, set me down. This fucking ankle is killing me." I gingerly set him down.

Before I could occupy the rolling stool across from him, he yanked me down next to him. Without even a question or thought on his part he just leaned his head onto my shoulder and laced his fingers with mine. He sighed as contentedly as his swollen ankle would allow.

"So, uh, what about your dancing?"

"Yeah, well, that's off for a while. I don't think he fucked it up too bad. I think it's just twisted. But even that can carry a price. Probably will upset any long-term dancing plans I may have down the road."

"Really?"

"Oh yeah, the guys generally have a longer career in dance but something like this? Can easily be turned into a debilitating issue when I get older."

I pursed my lips because I guess I could see that, but from what I knew most dancers' careers were wrapping themselves up in their early thirties. It didn't leave a whole lot of room for arthritis to set in that early, did it?

"What?"

"I dunno, just seems unfair that my shit has eked across into yours. I'd hate to think I was the cause of an early retirement in your dancing career."

He chuckled softly. "Yeah, well there's not much of a career while I am wasting away here in Bum-fucked Mercy. It's not necessarily the bastion of the ballet world, ya know. The longer I blow my wad here, the harder it will be to get back in the competition. Who knows, it may have already passed me by."

"Shit. This is all my fault. I hate that."

His brows stitched together on that one. "How the fuck do you figure that?"

Nurse Ratched walked in when he said that. "Language, Mister Jericho. I don't think your grandmother would appreciate you using language like that."

"You obviously don't know the gran I do. She says shit that'll make a sailor blush. Hell, I blush, and I've been hearing it my whole life."

"Damn straight too. I won't have any nancy boy softy on my team!" his gran said from the curtained-off area we were all sitting around. I rolled my eyes and she recovered. "Oh yeah, 'cept you are a nancy boy so that blows the fuck outta that one!" She cackled loudly—years of smoking coloring her laugh. Nurse Ratched (I needed to stop thinking of her that way—I could smell trouble coming a mile away) was visibly shocked at Shirley's cranky outburst.

"That's my gran!" Dan said.

"Well, what the fuck d'you do now?"

"Stephen."

"That pole dancer? Am I gonna have to call Tessa again?"

Dan just shrugged. The bell rang. Shit. And I didn't even get to explain anything.

"Look, I gotta get to class."

"Yeah, obviously I can't drive you home. You gonna be okay getting there? I guess I'm gonna be tied up for a bit this afternoon."

I didn't think anyone would jump me between now and the end of school, but hey, I could be wrong about my chances. Time with Marco had dulled my warning system considerably it seemed. I was off my game.

"Yeah, I think so. Hell, maybe I'll cut out now and go home. Wait for you-know-who to come back."

"Marco?" Shirley asked, a slight twinkle in her eye.

"How'd you know that?"

"It's best not to second-guess Gran's ESP; she's never off base," Dan warned me with a coy look coloring his eye.

"Oh, it's not like there's voodoo involved. That boy's been so into you for a while now. I've been fairly itching to see it all finally play out." She eyed me with the riveting glare of an owl spying a tasty mouse morsel. The morsel being me, of course.

"Huh? Wait, did Marco say?"

"No. He didn't need to, Elliot. Jesus, you two really are as delusional as Dan says. Guess it has to be love," she said plainly.

"Marco said everyone sort of knows anyway."

"Probably. It's already gone through the grapevine. So I'd say it's fairly common knowledge."

"But how? Marco and I did our best to keep things low key."

"Sonny, you two were just short of dropping trou and going at it no matter where you were. It was sorta sickening as it was cute as hell to watch. And lord, can that boy flirt. Christ, you hooked a good one in him. Tell me..." She leaned in closer to us both, giving a glance over her shoulder to check that Ratched had returned to her desk. She had. Satisfied, she continued, "Is he as great a lay as I think he is?"

My eyes widened. Dan snorted and shrugged like "what can I do?" and I sorta got that.

"Yeah, he is. Els can't get enough of it. I can't blame him though; that boy's huge," Dan deadpanned. I didn't know where to look between them. Could the floor just give out from underneath me?

"Oh, I bet he is," she said, her eyes gleefully imagining it.

"Are you two for real?" My voice came out all screechy with how embarrassed I was over this topic of conversation.

"You're right, Dan. He is cute as hell when he blushes. Must be what keeps Marco coming back for more."

"Oh. My. God! *Really?*" I got up from the bed. Dan nearly fell onto his side by how fast I extracted myself from him. "We are not having this conversation any longer!"

"See, I particularly like how his lips quirk up at the ends, so you know he is secretly loving the attention but just doesn't know what to do with all that extra energy."

They were both side by side on the bed while I stammered and huffed. I needed to leave. I so couldn't take any more of the latest episode of "Weird Town Population 1." These two were freaking me the fuck out!

"I gotta go. Look, I'll call you later if that's okay?"

"You don't have my number," Shirley said as if that were the most obvious point I'd been missing.

"That was for *him*."

"Oh, you don't want to call me too?"

"Aren't you in on the school gossip grapevine? I'm sure you'll hear about it all through those channels."

"Where do you think that whole grapevine thing starts?" Dan offered in a matter-of-fact way like it was common knowledge and where the hell had I been?

"What?"

Dan just shrugged and nodded. "Gran's a gossip girl from way back before they had a name for it. She's addicted to gossip; it's like porn to her."

"No, not really. If I can get it, I'd rather have the real porn. There's just so many free sites out there now."

"Oh, we are so not going down that lonely dark alley." I turned to go. "I'll call you later. And you..."

She perked right up, her eyes a brilliant flash of violet. That was the first time I'd noticed it. "Start being a grandmother or whatever. You're scaring the bejeezus outta me. So just stop it. Go put on a housecoat or something."

They looked at me, blinking in some sort of invasion-of-the-body-snatchers kind of way, very creepy and highly effective, before turning to look at each other at the exact same time and then howling and high-fiving themselves for embarrassing me.

"Whatever, freaks. I'm outta here."

"You could tag along, you know," Dan called out to me. His eyes were bright and hopeful despite how much pain I was sure he was in. That put a stop in my step. Dan just hiked a thumb toward his gran. *Oh, yeah. She takes care of school attendance.*

"You both promise to quit with the salacious talking and ribbing of me if I go?"

They looked at each other, shrugged, then turned to me and in perfect unison, as if they'd rehearsed it for just such an occasion, chorused, "Hell, no."

I pinched the bridge of my nose and squinched my eyes in frustration. *Fuck me, I'm going to do this.*

"Fine."

Twenty-five minutes and several shades of red later, we pulled into the parking lot of Dr. Sforza's office. I popped out of the car before Shirley had the thing in park to help Dan out.

"You know, Dan, if this Marco character finally sees the light and ditches Elliot for the comfort of an older woman's arms, then you two should hook up. You both look cute as hell together."

It was Dan's turn to blush. I huffed slightly—saying nothing, choosing instead to let them continue to have their fun at my expense.

"Yeah, don't think I haven't given that a lot of thinking too."

She watched us as we made our way to the front of the car where she joined us. Her mood seemed a bit more somber, less the wild Bohemian than she had been a few short seconds before.

"You boys have it tough enough. I just want you all to be happy. Life's too fucked up as it is without all the love you can get—no matter where it comes from. I'm just glad my Danny found you, Elliot. He needs someone like you right now. So, don't let that go for nuttin'—ya hear me?" That last had some serious bite to it; I didn't think she'd go lightly on me if I did.

"Yes, ma'am" was all I could think of to say.

She glanced around as if she were scoping out who I was referring to. "Oh! Was that high fa-lutin' phraseology you just employed aimed at lil' ol' me?"

She batted her eyelashes that had to have about thirteen coats of mascara on them if they had one. Not quite Tammy Faye Bakker but pretty damned close. I needed to talk to her about that at some point. Shirley was a fairly nice-looking woman for someone's grandmother. But she was caught in the mid-'80s with the way she applied her makeup. I mean I wasn't any Kevyn Aucoin—then again, who was anymore? But I knew enough to know when a woman went too far with the eyebrow pencil or looked like she lost the battle with a mascara brush. The only thing I had to wrestle with was how to break it to Shirley that she was just an application away from challenging Tammy Faye for the queen bee prize in clumpy eyes.

 I helped Dan through the front lobby and deposited him gently into the chair nearest the door, mostly because I didn't want him to struggle any further. Luckily, there didn't seem to be too many people waiting around, which was kind of okay. My gaze darted to the receptionist desk. It was empty at the moment, so Shirley had to hang out until someone came back. I secretly hoped Francesca was on deck today. I hadn't seen her in quite a while, and that time had involved personal family drama.

 A few seconds later and I heard the lovely contralto voice that had a musical quality to it, her Italian accent only serving to add to her allure. Damn, was I turning into a straight boy for her? She came gliding around the corner—a wisp of everything females aspired to, this girl had in spades. The thing with Francesca was that she made it all seem so effortless, as if breathing took more concentration than the upkeep of her ethereal beauty. Her brilliant green eyes, so striking in the Sforza line, caught mine. She smiled warmly but tended to business first. She took in Shirley's explanation of why we were there. Her eyes darted to mine when the subject of Dan's accident during PE came up. I stared blankly back at her, unable to discern with any accuracy what her gaze could possibly mean for me.

 She informed Shirley, and us by extension, that the good doctor would be with us in a moment. Shirley collected her things and came over to sit with us. Francesca busied herself with receptionisty things, her eyes flitting to me while she wrapped up whatever paperwork was preoccupying her time. I don't know why, but I was utterly fascinated by her. Perhaps it was that she moved with the supreme air of a Sforza, but that wasn't everything by a long shot. Then I pondered that some qualities seemed intimately familiar to me because they were elements Marco possessed as well. I guess the whole Kinsey scale thing was really true. There were females out there who would captivate even a fairly solid gayboy like me. Who the fuck knew? That memo had surely slipped by me. I was going with the whole she-was-a-female-version-of-Marco and that's what had my juices flowing. Yeah, I'll stick with that.

She finished whatever she was doing and got up from her desk to once more disappear around the frosted glass wall that only now, after coming here for as long as I had, I realized had a very faint acid wash so that if you caught the light just right it had the face of what had to be Venus or Juno or one of the other Roman goddesses. I chose Venus because it seemed to suit this family. A beat later and the door to the lobby opened and she did that runway-walk I am totally exaggerating here, but I was flummoxed by her beauty. Everything she did just exuded how glamorous she was and how not I was every time I was around her. She walked right up to me, to the shocked expressions that were painted on Shirley's, Dan's, and my face.

"So what? You show up after weeks of nothing and I don't rate a kiss? We're family now. It's automatic. Do I need to explain everything?"

The words sounded terse, but she had the pouty playfulness I saw in Marco whenever he was trying like hell to get me to let him bone me. Not that he had to work much at it. Hell, I gave up the goods for him whenever he wanted. Probably would do the same with her if she pressed it.

I stammered as I got up. She pulled me into a fierce embrace and left the customary kiss on each cheek. Very European and completely scary how far I was now entrenched in my future family. For Francesca, there was no question; I was in.

"There." She smiled and my heart melted. No matter what had happened today, her smile was worth it. Fuck me, these Sforzas were a deadly bunch. I was fucking screwed with this crew. "That's better. But you gotta remember the rules. Okay?" She leveled a look at me that if she said strip, I'd just do it despite the embarrassment it'd cause me. Her wrath would be a hell of a lot worse. I could tell. But now she was all smiles and my heart was full. She turned to Dan and Shirley.

"I'm going to steal him for a bit. Family stuff. You understand. Vincenzo will see you in a minute. You need an ice pack?"

Dan and Shirley just sat there with glazed looks on their faces. Yeah, I got how the Sforza thing worked its mojo. It scared the bejeezus out of me, and fuck me, I was in with this clan. They could at least escape their aura once the doctor visit was over. I, on the other hand, was knee-deep in the Sforza goo and sinking fast. They sort of nodded in that wide-eyed vegetative state. Shirley kept blinking like she thought the magical mirage of Francesca would dissipate with each successive blink of her eyes. Twice her mascara clumps got stuck so one of her eyes just looked twitchy. I rolled my eyes at them and shrugged like "What can you do? We're family..." sort of thing.

Francesca took my hand and tugged me along to the door that led to a thousand examining rooms. I remembered mine was something like number 426 or something. Marco had even tried to convince me to come back here with him so he could bone me on that same damned examining table. I flat-out refused. I ended up sucking him off twice in the car just to keep the edge off his request. There was no way I was going to end up on some secret security camera boning the heir apparent to the Sforza dynasty as a way of my coming out to his parents. That so wouldn't help me make a good first impression. Though, given that volatile exchange I'd had with my mother the last time I was here, it certainly wouldn't warm up Vincenzo and Sofia to my side.

We cleared the door, and Francesca stopped by the nurse's station. "I need a cigarette break. Can you cover for me?"

The nurse there, a lovely woman of Caribbean or Creole descent, looked up and smiled at Francesca. "Sure, honey, you got it. He's a hell of a cutie. Where'd you score that one? I want me one too."

I looked behind me, thinking someone had walked up. Then I realized she meant me. *What the fuck?* I thought better to say anything. Women confused me a bit. I know I was supposed to be all in with the female crowd, being the perennial gayboy, but the truth of the matter is, I just can't seem to engage them very well, which makes the whole I'm-relegated-to-the-sex-I-desire-but-they-often-won't-talk-to-me-because-I'm-a-fag sort of an impediment to my having anyone to talk to. Which is why the whole Marco-moving-in-to-lay-claim-to-me was such the boon to my social life I thought was never going to happen with me.

"He's Marco's."

"Oh, he's the one. Pretty eyes."

Francesca smiled and held a finger to her lips.

"Oh, I remember, completely DL." She winked at us, our secret apparently secured from the elder Sforza.

"Thanks, Bree." And with that Francesca tugged me along toward the back door of the office.

We burst out of the back door, and rather than some crappy backside of a building with an over-worn access road, it was a nicely sculpted garden area with redwood benches on four sides and enormously sprawling red and green Japanese maples in gigantic ceramic pots. A patina bronze statue of Venus (who else?) graced the middle of a large fountain grotto recessed along the sloping hill that gently rolled to the back of the medical office. I wandered ahead of her, instantly regretting the moment I pulled my hand from hers. There was something magical about the Sforza touch. It crackled along my skin. Amazing how that happened. Made me wonder if it'd be the same way with Marco's parents. I tried like hell to remember how it felt every time the good doctor had seen to me during my appointments. Besides the fact that Vincenzo was the personification of what I knew Marco would evolve into, coupled with his papa being one fucking stud muffin of an older man...and now, holy shit, it seemed I had a thing for my doctor and future father-in-law. Crap, could this day get any weirder? Marco can't go away any more. My day goes out the g-d window whenever he isn't around.

"Wow, this is really beautiful. Remind me the next time I come here for an appointment to ask if I can wait out here."

I heard the click of her e-cigarette as she inhaled before she spoke. "Okay, but you're family now. When you come here, you won't have that long to wait. I see to that."

She floated in the goddess-like way that was part of her magic to a bench and patted the area next to her, motioning me to sit down.

"Marco's been making big plans, you know."

I nodded, leaning back into its backrest. "Yeah, he calls all the shots for us. I'm used to it. It makes him happy, and it keeps the daily crap out of my life so I can do other things. I'm good with that."

She nodded, but an arch to her brow told me there were other things on her mind as well. I waited. Patience was a necessary quality to have when you hung out with this family. Several months of being with Marco had schooled me enough in that. I laced my fingers together and rested them across my chest with one elbow on the armrest and the other along the back. I scooted into the corner of the bench and just looked pleasantly back at her.

"You're a tough one to crack."

"Crack? Why is there any cracking going on?"

"No, I mean, I know why Marco is into you. *Tu sei assolutamente il suo mondo.*" She puffed again on her e-cig before blowing out the water vapor from it. I wasn't a smoker, other than the occasional joint when I could score one, but on her it did add to the allure. She was deeply sophisticated in that old-world way. "What I can't quite figure out is, why him?"

I shook my head like she'd asked why I had tentacles instead of testicles or something equally as idiotic. "Are you fucking kidding me?" I stammered. "Aside from the fact that he's—no, that the *entire* family, present company included, are fucking gorgeous beyond anything, it's really his heart I love the most. Marco is—" I sighed. I couldn't help myself. Marco just did that to me. I happened to sigh a lot these days. Well, at least since he entered my life as my boyfriend. "Marco is the most amazing man I have ever met. Everyone pales in comparison. He has no equal."

She pursed her lips, puffed on the cig again. "So it's not about the money then?"

"What? No! Why would it ever be about that?"

"But you do know about it?"

"He said something about it around the time of the Homecoming dance. To be honest, I didn't pay much attention to it. I'd marry him if we were penniless and were living out of his car. I'd say *my* car, but hell, I'm too broke to have one of those, so all I'd be able to offer is a cardboard box I could scrounge up."

She tilted her head, considering my words. "Let's forget about that loud-ass car he's got for a moment."

I snorted. Obviously, she just didn't get the whole Impala and Dean Winchester thing. Silly girls. She barreled right on.

"So, if he was broke, and only had his heart to give you—you'd still take him?"

"In a New York minute." Not that I had any real clue what that actually meant. I just knew it meant I'd do it quickly.

"So, it isn't the money then?"

"So what? So, he's got a couple thousand dollars. Great, that'll make things easier as we begin our lives. College will mean we won't be living on Cup-A-Noodles or Top Ramen and there'll be fewer peanut butter sandwiches, so that'll be cool." I unlaced my hands and began to run my thumbnail into a small crevice in the wood along the backrest. I didn't want to talk about his money. It was his. I certainly didn't think I shared in any of that.

"A couple of thousand? That's what he told you?"

"No. He didn't say much other than he had some money and that we could leave and GED out of school and begin our lives together now if I wanted us to. He told me to say the word and we'd do it. But I can't ask him to do that. For one, it wouldn't be fair to him. He needs football. Even I'm not too gay to realize that. It's like his lifeblood or something. So I told him that no, we'd stick it out through high school, graduate, and then make our move to wherever, which I guess is Stanford though I haven't heard back from them yet. I did get my acceptance at Berkeley, but I don't want to be that far away from Marco, so I stashed the envelope away so my mom wouldn't see it. It's where my dad went, so they're kind of gunning for me to go there."

She puffed on her ciggy again. She was so fucking cool in that spy-movie-vixen kind of way, the way she sat, the elegant but sophisticated skirted suits she favored in the office, to the nearly ridiculous high-heeled *come fuck me* stilettos that completed the *fuck with me at your own risk* sort of look. A dichotomy of allure and danger. She was the kind of woman studly manly men wanted to fuck and dominate. Somehow, I didn't see her letting that happen. I mean, sure, she'd bag a big strappin' sexy man 'cause that's just how the Sforzas did it—not that I was manly, but I wasn't necessarily a screaming girl (most of the time) either. No, if she scored some hot strapping tatted-up stud, he'd have to make the cut. Big muscles, colorful but tasteful tattoos that screamed bad boy, but he'd have to have a heart of gold, and the most requisite piece would be that he'd have to have an enormous cock. I could tell Francesca and I shared that certain proclivity. We understood cock. We both knew how to please men. I knew Francesca was picky, but I also was well aware she was no virgin—whatever story she played to her aunt and uncle.

"Well, he should have been a bit more honest with you. It isn't just a few thousand dollars he's got."

"So it's a little more. Just means we can go out from time to time," I shrugged. It really didn't matter all that much to me. Like I said, it was *his* money.

"Try one hundred and fifty million on for size and that's just the liquid assets—cash in hand sorta stuff. We aren't even considering his holdings that are invested. That puts him in a completely different financial stratosphere as in another comma to that amount. It just keeps growing—the family's got great financial advisers." Her eyes narrowed a bit. I knew this was the tipping point and okay, inwardly I was freaking out. *My man is a fucking millionaire! How out of this fucking world is that?* But instead I pulled that gayboy mask of indifference and cooled my features a bit. "It started out as like sixteen million when the boys were young. The investments and property gains have been good to them, even through the whole financial crisis that hit in '08. And it's all his now. As soon as he turned eighteen."

"That's pretty fucking amazing, but it doesn't mean that much to me. It's his money, *not* mine."

"Either you're the most incredibly principled person I've ever met or you're naive as hell. Either way, I can see why he wants to marry you. And make no mistake, he'll get what he wants. Marco always does. It's a talent of his. Easy, like breathing."

I shrugged and sighed—again with the sighing when I thought of Marco. The two went hand in hand—well, like me and Marco.

"Yeah, well, that's why I don't argue with the big guy. It's easier and a hell of a lot quicker if I just let him do what he's gonna do. I just have to be there for him any time he wants. But that's when I really score." I wiggled my eyebrows to let her know exactly what I got out of the deal.

She laughed a big throaty laugh that was like sunshine and a Rossini melody all wrapped up in one—giddy and memorable. She slapped the flat of her left hand on her crossed knee to emphasize how much she knew exactly what I was saying and she was thoroughly happy that we were of one mind on that score. Well, not her and Marco, 'cause that'd be so many kinds of an Italian *Gone With The Wind* wrong between cousins and all. It was the one thing about *GWTW* that still never failed to creep me out—cousins marrying cousins. So wrong. Setting *that* aside for later ponderings, I smiled. Two cock-hungry kindred spirits, that's what we were. She smirked in the Marco way that went right to my dangly bits. Now it got dangerous. This whole fucking family was like some sort of psychotropic sexual stimulant drug. They were fucking Fae for all I knew. I mean they were beyond magical. *She's a woman for Chrissake!* And here I was, completely clueless in the ways of women and sex, and yet, when she smirked like that, all I could think of was I wanted to kiss her mouth. And maybe do a little bit more. I could just tell she'd make it fun trying.

"Okay, we need to stop because you're about to cross a line you don't want to."

"Huh?"

"You look like you wanted to kiss me. I get it, but you're Marco's."

"I wasn't going to..."

She quirked her brow again, damn her. It seemed gleaning thoughts from my head wasn't just limited to Marco. Did all the Sforzas possess this extra-sensory gift? As if this family needed one more jewel to put in their treasure box. I mean, seriously, they had to be otherworldly. No family can be this golden.

"Okay." I looked at her sheepishly. "It's just that your mouth looked like Marco's—it was too familiar. Well, except for the lipstick. But that, well, argh!"

She giggled a bit at my frustration. "You poor boy. I get it. Yeah, you're not the first to get confused around us. I don't know what it is; it just is. Sometimes it drives me crazy that I have some men who won't give it up...you know? Leave me alone when I say so."

Yeah, I guess I could see that. I wish I had that problem.

"But I know why Marco is in love with you. I could fall for a boy like you too."

I needed to get back to what was important. "So, am I supposed to say something to my multimillionaire boyfriend that I know?"

She shrugged. "It all depends if he brings it up. But he'll know you know, so you may as well confess. It's the curse. We just know these things. I know he hates it as much as I do. But it is what it is."

An hour and a foot binding later (turned out all Dan had was a badly sprained ankle—nothing was broken, thank goodness) they dropped me off at home. By the time we rounded the corner to my house, a light mist had started to fall. I glanced out of the back window and noted that those far-off dark clouds were now truly upon us, only now the clouds had small flashes of lightning. The day had been sorta warm up until lunchtime, so I could get how we'd be heading for a lightning storm. I assured Dan I'd check in with him later as I popped open the door to Shirley's car. I waved them off as I gathered the mail from the mailbox and began to plow through the utility bills, some of which looked like second notices. Dammit, I hoped we got some cash infusion soon, or things were really going to get rough. And I wasn't about to tell Marco about it. Rich boyfriend or not, I simply wasn't going to go there.

Then my heart stopped.

The letter from Stanford had floated its way to the top of the pile. Panicked, my hands trembling, I slowly turned it over and sat down on the front porch of the house—not the swinging bench either but the actual porch floor.

I didn't know what to do. Part of me didn't want to know. The other part, the part that needed to let Marco know as quickly as I knew the answer, was pressing its advantage within me. I took a deep breath and ripped open the envelope.

I pulled the paper out so quickly I gave myself a paper cut. I hissed and licked the side of my left index finger where I'd sliced myself while my eyes scanned the contents of the form letter. *Why aren't those letters making any sense? Why is my brain misfiring? I'm having a stroke. That's what it is. Christ, leave it to me to have a brain aneurysm burst or something equally catastrophic suddenly take over and end my life on the precipice of my everlasting happiness. Really? Am I Elizabeth Bennett pondering my options of my affections for Mr. Darcy now? Get your head out of the clouds, concentrate, and read the fucking letter already!*

Then I got to the line that indicated their determination of my application. Yes! I was accepted! I sighed very loudly and kissed the fucking letter.

"Thank the fucking maker!"

I pulled out my phone and stared at Marco's smiling face that graced my wallpaper. He was going to be so happy to hear this. I paused, my thumb just above the passcode screen to unlock my phone. He was still doing the meet and greet thing. Maybe I should wait until he got home? No, surely, he'd want to know straight away, right? I got up and started pacing on the porch, before realizing how silly that must look to anyone who might be passing. But then we're at the end of the block, and who the hell would be watching our house all of a sudden? But I already had an answer to that, for I knew Marco had spent a great deal of time watching this house, watching me.

Marco.

I pawed my keys out of my pocket, bolted inside, and headed directly to my room, taking only a brief moment to toss the other useless mail onto the coffee table and not caring a jot that most of it skidded right off onto the floor. I had other things to worry about.

I tossed the backpack onto my writing desk, toed my shoes off, and plopped onto the bed still clutching the letter from Stanford. I knew Marco had no doubts as to whether I'd make it in, but I was really beginning to worry that I hadn't seen anything from them, even if it was nothing more than a "thanks but no thanks" sort of letter. This was way better than that. For a moment I really allowed myself to ponder what my life with Marco would be like once we were out of this Podunk town.

I picked up my phone from where I'd tossed it onto the bed. I scanned through some of the photos I had taken of Marco. There were a few of us together, but mostly they were just him in all his masculine and studly beauty. Fuck, he was truly the most beautiful man I'd ever beheld. And he loved me. Me, of all people. I still didn't get it. I shook my head at how the world worked and how random and nonsensical it could be. It didn't make sense. It had no kind of logic I could apply, but Marco was mine and I was his. And now, with this letter, this precious, precious letter, I had a path to our future in front of me.

The phone rang, startling me. I very nearly dropped it as I was lost in the captured gaze of my future husband.

Dan.

"Heya, stud..." he said as soon as we were connected.

"Howzit hanging?" I shot back, wiggling my toes into the comforter of my bed.

"When you're around, never is, stud."

I chose not to rise to that bait. Instead, I left him hanging. He never hung around for long.

"So you seemed like you wanted to talk to me about something when you came in the nurse's office. 'Sup?"

I bit my lip. Should I tell him? I mean, I really didn't have any way of confirming my suspicions on the subject. Beau had only hinted that they were somehow involved but not directly. I didn't know if I should worry Dan about any of it since I had nothing other than my suspicions to go on. I guess my stalling was enough of a warning shot across his bow.

"Out with it, Els. Marco will have my ass, and not in a good and sexy kind of way, if something happens to you on my watch."

"Fuck..." I blurted in a hoarse whisper. I hated it when I got all gayboy warning flag on them. They always seemed to think I was overreacting. I guess I was the drama queen in this clique.

"We can see to your needs later. Now, out with it."

"It's probably nothing."

"Let me be the judge of that. Marco and I came up with a pretty extensive list of what should happen where if you felt threatened."

"So you're like, what? My thoroughly damaged knight in rusty armor, now?"

"Ouch! Hey, it wasn't my fault getting sidelined by my fuck-twit cousin."

"Yeah, about that. It seems it wasn't as random an act as you might think."

"What do you mean?"

"Well, I don't have any real way to prove it to you, but Beau wanted to see me at lunch. Sort of a 'you can't refuse this' kind of deal. I knew we had plans for lunch, and he said it was already being handled and I should just be at the quad at lunchtime for a little chat with the football gods."

He was silent. Considering my words, maybe there was more than just a hunch on my part. I didn't say anything for a moment.

"Els?"

I sighed. "It's just that when you dropped me off for English Lit and Marco wasn't there to sit beside me, Beau did."

"Well, that can't be good."

"Yeah, it wasn't. Though the really scary part is how calm he was about it all. He'd been scheming this whole thing from the start it seems."

"How do you mean?"

"Well, from day one, he was pretty adamant about Marco choosing to sit next to me instead of with the other jocks at the back of the class. Marco stood up to him; he was truly amazing. I didn't want him to, of course. It was all just too new to me. I thought I was too much trouble."

"Get to the point, Els. That was in the past—let's speed it up to why you think my ankle has to do with any of this."

"But it's all related! Don't you see? Christ, this is what Marco fails to see. Beau hasn't liked me for—well, I dunno, since I was born and he didn't even know I existed but he still found some speculative part of his heart that had blackened itself against me, I guess." He sighed at my waxing poetic on Beau's absolute hatred for all things gay. "I'm getting to it! But you have to see the bigger picture. This isn't random at all, despite what Marco thinks about it. I know. I've seen their glances when we pass, and they think Marco and I aren't looking. It's dark, and evil. I know people bandy that about, but I've no doubt about Beau's intent. Marco's corrupted and I did the corrupting. Well, according to Beau anyway. I guess there's just no way to convince him it was Marco who pursued me. I've tried."

"Okay, you're all over the place with this now. Concentrate. So, why is my ankle in the middle of all of this?"

I sighed audibly from the sheer frustration that there was so much to say and not any real way of conveying what I'd been piecing together in the back of my mind for a while now. "Okay, I'll start with that and you can ask questions, and maybe it will all make sense. So, the bottom line is I think Beau put Stevie up to sidelining you at PE because he knew you and I were going to have lunch together and he needed you out of the way. See?"

"Wait, so you're saying Stephen did this to me 'cause he was put up to it?"

"Now he's catching on... Way to bring up the rear on this whole machismo bullet train."

"Hey, excuse me for missing out on some key meetings."

"Yeah, well, I guess I shouldn't give you too much shit 'cause at least you've got an open mind on the topic. Marco thinks I am whacked out of my head on it. But I know what I've seen. I mean it, every time I spared a second glance or took a little longer than Marco to look away—it was there. The cold hard glares, the smiles completely wiped from their faces. But they put on one helluva show for Marco, I can tell you that."

"Huh." That was all he had for me.

"Huh, what? Was that a 'huh—I think you're totally off your rocker but don't want to piss you off' or a 'huh, now it's all making kinda sense to me'? Whose side are you on?"

"There aren't any sides, Els. God, you're cute as all fuck when you get flustered."

"Aw, shit. Not you too. Look, can you give it a rest for a few? I'm really sort of worried. I mean, think about it. Just for a moment, accept what I am saying is the truth, that Beau has had his guys in play today because they knew Marco was going to be away at Stanford."

"Do you think he told them?"

"I don't think there was any way for the team not to know. I mean, he is taking off for an entire day. I know the championship game isn't until the following Friday, but still, he had to have asked about going because it's still sort of close to the big game. So yeah, I think they all knew. Beau's not one to let an opportunity slip by him. He's far too clever for that."

"You mean opportunistic. That's not necessarily the same thing as being clever."

"No, he's clever. I know. If I had any doubts before lunch, I don't now."

"Why? What'd he say?"

"Oh, just that I was the worst thing to have entered Marco's life. That Cindy's pregnant with his child, how I am stealing all of his—"

"Wait a fucking minute! Child? What the fuck?"

"Oh, yeah. I guess you missed that particular meeting of the fag council, didn't you? You need to stop running off, Gandalf. We elves have complicated lives, it seems."

"But a fucking kid?"

"Yeah, that's how they usually come into this world—unless of course you are some sort of magical fairy or the blessed virgin fagboy. God knows Marco and I have tried to have kids on our own. But, yeah. Cindy and he fucked. It wasn't his doing, and I know that sounds like I am rationalizing a helluva lot, and I guess I am. I've forgiven him. Not that there was a lot of forgiving to do, mind you. He had beaten himself up really hard over it. There was little left for me to even be mad at. But yeah. There's a kid evidently, though Marco still doesn't know. I just sort of figured it out when Beau spoke to him on my phone at our lunch date that we were supposed to have but Beau ordered a football mafia hit against you and, well, it seems your cousin is now some sort of mafioso gangster—he's probably reveling in that. Probably makes his pole-dancing days sink further into the background."

"Not as far back as you'd like to think."

A beat.

"We boffed the day before yesterday. He fucked me twice. He's a decent top and I like getting fucked from time to time, so there ya are."

"And you were going to tell me this, when exactly?"

"Hey, you elves sometimes miss when we wizards post our carnal pleasures on the interweb thing..."

"You didn't!"

"Yeah, figured I better since he was giving you a hard time. He was fairly obvious about it too. You can clearly hear him say that he fights wanting to bone guys, that he still regrets not taking you up on your offer those many years ago. It's all caught on blessed Gandalfian digital bits and bytes. I just have to edit the fucking thing and then send him a little clip and his gangsta days are over. He'll probably quit the team in absolute fear of what they'd do to him. By the way, when did this infamous boink moment between our beloved Marco—he still is our beloved, isn't he? I didn't miss the score on that one, right?"

"Yes, you're still in the wings, sexy, stay focused. Marco is still in the driver's seat here. I don't think that will ever change. Not unless he wants it to, then god help him 'cause Francesca will have his balls on a platter and she'll do the deed herself."

"Yikes, mine just hiked themselves up into my hips just thinking about that. She's hot and all, but I could definitely see her being fucking ruthless as all fuck."

"Yeah, I am so glad she's on my side."

"But we're way off target here... Can you just tell me how pole-hungry Stevie became such a gangsta bitch for Beau Hopkins? I know Stevie—more than you obviously—and I gotta tell you, his whole tough-boy thing is such an act. He is fucking scared beyond anything that Beau and the guys will find out about him. It's sorta sad, but now I'm just pissed because if he gave in to Beau's pressure to take me out, then I am so going to kick his ass when I see him next."

"Yeah, well, Stevie may not be my BFF"—Dan snorted at my little admission, but I continued—"but I do remember some of his faults—fear being one of them."

"Dude, I better be your GBF now. I've seen you fuck. You can't get more bestie than that."

"Yeah. You are. No worries there. Even if you didn't witness Marco and me boning each other. I still can't believe we did that. Well, yeah, it's Marco and he's talked about it for a while, so I knew it was coming one way or another..."

He chuckled. "Coming...funny."

"You're nasty. Anyway, he may not be my best friend anymore, but that doesn't mean you should go too hard on him. It can't be easy being a jock and having those feelings. To be honest, I don't know how Marco managed it all, or how he still does. But he has held it together so far. I guess Stevie just may not be as resourceful or may not have been smart enough to take Marco's lead."

"Maybe. But it still doesn't excuse his being a bitch for possibly ruining my dance career—such as it is. I won't be able to dance for several weeks now. Not that there are any auditions in my future, but it'll take me off my game, that's for sure."

"Is it that bad? I never asked. Sorry."

"Nah, it's cool. I know you care. You do care, don't you?"

"Of course, I care. Probably more than I should say actually."

"Really?"

"Behave. I'm still Marco's, and I will be as long as he'll have me."

"Which is like, forever and always, right?"

"Always."

"Yeah, okay."

"I got some good news though..."

"Well, I'm glad someone did."

"I got into Stanford. You're the first to know."

"Dude, that's awesome. Stanford's a great school."

"Yeah, don't know how my folks will pay for it."

"I'm sure they'll work out something. They've been planning on it, right?"

"Yeah, there's a college fund. Don't know how much is in it or how long it'll last."

"I'm sure Marco might have a thing or two to say about that. He'd do just about anything to keep you close to him. Even if he had to get his parents to pay for it."

"Yeah, about that. Turns out he's loaded."

"Well, we knew the family is rich."

"No. I mean, *he's* loaded. As in solo, beyond his parents. A trust fund came into his control when he turned eighteen. I figured it was a couple thousand or maybe even a couple hundred thousand, ya know?"

"It's bigger?"

"Try one hundred and fifty million. And that's just the liquid assets!"

He whistled. "Fuck me!"

"No, that's my territory—back off." I chuckled though; thankful I was still able to find some humor in it all. That was a plus.

"That's not loaded; that's fucking monumental, that is." My brows furrowed over his confirmation of what I'd been struggling with in the back of my mind.

"I guess. But I couldn't use any of it. That's his money."

"Dude, he would so argue that. To him you mean everything. He'd hand it all over to you, if you asked."

Silence.

I didn't know what to think. It was a lot of money. But I really didn't like to think about it. It was monumental. But not in the whole *I'm a gold digger* kinda boyfriend. It was monumental because it was like Monty, the silent elephant we'd have to haul around. I fucking hate silent pachyderms. They're the worst.

"I would never ask. It's his. Period. And I don't want to talk about it anymore."

"Wow. Okay. But there's a helluva lot hidden in that last sentence you might want to spend some time thinking about."

"I know. Fuck, it's so something I never wanted to know. I would be just peachy if it was something he'd take care of and I'd never have to know about it. Now I do, I want Francesca to take it back. But she said I'd have to tell him I know. Something about a family curse that he'd know I know but just wasn't saying. Or some fucked-up Sforza shit like that."

"Yeah, they are kinda golden, aren't they? I got a fucking hard-on just from watching Francesca float around the room."

"Duuuude, argh, I so didn't need to hear that. She's like my future cousin-in-law or something. Like a sister. That's just so many shades of wrong."

"Yeah, all right, all right. I getcha."

"No, actually you don't. 'Cause she sorta has that effect on me as well."

He laughed so fucking hard at that.

"What's so fucking funny? I could fuck a girl, you know. I do have the equipment."

"Yeah, I don't doubt that. I've seen it in action, remember?"

"Yeah, well, you hurt my feelings when you did that."

He got silent for a second.

"Dude, I'm sorry."

Silence. I picked at a loose thread on my comforter, letting him stew in his guilt juices for a bit.

"Dude? Els?"

"I'm just fucking with you." I chuckled. "I so can't imagine me doing it either. I am such a power bottom. I was born to please cock. It just is."

He laughed again, a big snorty kind of laugh that sounded like there was some snot involved.

"Yeah, I noticed."

"Behave."

"Always."

"So, you think I oughta call Marco and tell him about the letter from Stanford? I was debating that before you called."

"Definitely."

"Even if he's at a meet and greet function now?"

"Well, you could text him; then he can call you when he has a moment."

"Doh!"

"Yeah, Homer."

"Okay, well, I think I am gonna go. I got too much pent-up energy. I think I'll text him and see where he is in his day. At least he'll know we're going to the same school."

"You should go online and do the acceptance thing. Reserve your spot immediately. Your letter is sorta late."

"Yeah, what's up with that? Marco got his like a couple of weeks ago."

"Budgets, I guess. Smaller staff, maybe? Who the fuck knows anymore? Customer service is shit these days."

"Yeah, I guess. Okay, I'll catch up with you later."

"Later, E-man."

"God, you are so straight-sounding sometimes. It sorta scares me."

"Nah, you like us straight-sounding boys."

"Yeah, you *bi*-boys do sorta rock my world."

He chuckled. "Love you, Els."

I quirked my lips. I knew he meant it too. Way more than I was willing to admit. But I guess as long as he kept it in check, we'd be okay.

"Yeah, love you too."

"I know..."

"Really?"

"Just say goodbye."

"Bye."

"Good. You're learning to let people love you. And we do, Elliot. Always." He rang off.

Always.

The word hung in the air. The men in my life seemed to find that one above all others to solidify their feelings for me. I supposed I should do as they say and let it be. Enjoy it. *Lord knows, it won't be like that forever.* I'd fuck it up, somehow. I seemed to have a talent for pushing those I love away. Just had to look at my dad to see that glaring example. Fuck, I did it so well I pushed him to the wilds of Alaska to make things work for him. *Who's to say that it won't happen with Marco or Dan?* I had precious little to call my own as it was. I knew I should be thankful for their devotion to me and try like hell not to shake things up too bad. Setting aside those dark thoughts I huffed and brought my phone up to text Marco about the good news. But how to say it? I should be brief because if he looked when I sent it, I didn't want him reading the *Reader's Digest* condensed version of *War and Peace.*

"Keep it short, Donahey."

I ended up with three words and a dash: *Stanford—I'm in!* Followed by a smiley face.

I pressed send and smiled, then got up off the bed, went to my backpack, and fished out my laptop. I fired up the MacBook and waited for the desktop to pop. I went back to my phone and continued perusing the photos I had of Marco. I realized there was a photo I didn't have but I wanted most of all: one of him sitting on our stump out in the forest behind my house. I wanted one of him to capture what he used to do, hanging out there and waiting for some brief glimpse of me. That was romantic on so many levels. My heart ached for how he wanted everything to work out for us, and just how long he'd been wanting that. It did have history. It did have weight. Like a blanket of love, it was palpable.

I navigated to the Stanford website indicated on my acceptance letter. I logged in using the temporary access they provided to create an account on their system. I had just reached the actual acceptance form page when my phone rang—it was Marco.

"Heya, babe!"

"Whoo-hoo!" he screamed. "I knew you'd get in! We're so totally set! This day just gets better and better!" He was so full of exclamations that my smile grew so wide it began to hurt. Then as suddenly as it arrived, it faded; my Emo-ness began to creep in as a small pang worked its way into my heart. He was having fun, it seemed. Fun without me. I didn't want to feel so damned needy, but with the day I'd been having I sorta wished I was bored tagging along with him today, enjoying his glory, basking in everything that was him. At least I could've spent the day watching him having fun. That would be so much better than what I'd been through.

"Yeah. I guess. So, things are going well?"

"Better than well, actually. They had a quarterback a couple of seasons ago who was openly gay with the team, but they didn't make any big deal of it in the press. Took a DL approach just to minimize the drama and let the sportscasters concentrate on how the team was playing rather than any personal dirt they could dig up. So, there's a total precedent—I'm not the first. I told them about you, and the guys seemed supportive. Angus, the ginger guy, said he was glad there was going to be someone else besides him on the team. So yeah, gaydar was totally working on that score. They all chimed in that now he'd have competition. It was all in good fun. Guess it's why Stanford has such a gay-friendly rep among the schools."

"Yeah, I guess."

"So what're you doing now?"

"Just filling in the acceptance form online."

"Cool. I'm gonna make a couple of stops before I head out. We're sorta wrapping it all up here. Since I'm attached there's no need for the stripper club they planned—not like I'm of age, so I think they were going to do some sort of private party thing. I dunno. I guess they all thought I'd be up for it though 'cause the other guys looked sorta hopeful. I told them to go on without me, I'd be there in spirit or whatever."

"Okay. You gonna stop by here on your way home? Do I get to see you first, I mean?"

"Of course! I think there's a little celebratory lovemaking on our horizon."

"Mmmm, I'm looking forward to it."

"'Kay, well, I better get running so I can take care of things and get back to you."

"Yeah, okay. Be careful driving back, okay? I worry when you're away from me. I don't like it very much."

"I hear you. But this should be a one-time thing. After I get back, I'll never leave your side, babe. Fuck, we may not even wait for us to graduate. I think I may pop the question soon. So, yeah, be prepared."

"You aren't supposed to tell me that!"

"Oh, yeah, like we haven't been discussing marriage at all. So totally Elliot random there. My bad."

I chuckled, finding the urge to stretch. I can't help it. Talking to Marco creates all this pent-up energy that builds until I need to release it somehow. If I don't have my cock out, then it turns into a long cat-like stretch starting from the tips of my fingers and radiating down my body to the curling of my toes. A good healthy stretch.

"I'll take care of all that energy you've got going on. I can hear it. You got an itch and I'll do the scratching. 'Kay, babe?"

"'Kay..." I yawned, though I tried like hell to stifle it.

"Wow, you better not crash on me."

"Well, it'll take you a couple of hours to get back, so maybe just a little nap to keep my reserves up. Something tells me I'm gonna be worn out tonight."

"Uh-huh," he drawled in that sexy husky voice of his. It made my toes curl knowing what was buried in that singular phrase.

"'Kay. Well, I gotta get so I can wrap shit up and head home. See you soon?"

"Yeah, you know where I live."

"Brother, do I ever."

"Love you..."

"Love you too babe."

"Sweetheart?"

"Yeah?"

"Be careful...okay?"

"Always."

He rang off.

I spent the next hour typing up the online stuff to accept my offered placement from Stanford. That set, I thought I should give my mom a call to let her know the good news. I called her while I was prepping a shower for myself.

"Yes..."

"Hey, Mom. Just wanted you to know the good news."

"What's that?"

"I got into Stanford!"

"That's great, sweetheart. I know your dad hoped you'd get into his school, but I know you were sort of set on Stanford, which, from my perspective, is totally fine because it puts you closer to us."

"Yeah." Inwardly I was debating on telling her I had the acceptance letter from Dad's alma mater but had stashed it, hoping against all hope I'd get the letter I got today. I was so glad that it had all panned out. I yawned again. "I just got done completing the acceptance forms online. I got a couple of appointments to set up with guidance counselors and financial aid and stuff, but the ball's definitely rolling now. It's sort of great that I don't have to worry about that."

"What about the boyfriend? Where's he going?"

"Uh, mmm, Stanford?" I said, not bothering to hide the small amount of guilt I had for burying the other option.

A beat. Never good where my mom was concerned.

"How long did you have the letter from Berkeley before you got the one today?"

How the fuck does she always know?

"Uh, maybe only a few days..."

"Elliot, you better be glad you got your Stanford letter because if your father knew you were holding out on his alma mater he'd be a little hurt."

"Yeah, I know. Believe me, it tugged every day I didn't get this letter. But I did, so can't we just be happy for that?"

Another beat.

"I suppose... It can stay between us."

"Thanks, Mom."

"So, you okay for dinner? I didn't remember to make anything."

"Yeah, I think I'm okay." Actually, I remembered I had the deconstructed and possibly wilted BLT in my lunch sack. I pulled it out of my backpack and gingerly examined its state. It was fairly okay. I'd have to replace the tomato and lettuce, but the rest looked okay. Though the mayo in the small container should be thrown out too. All fixable. "Yeah, I'm good."

"Okay, sweetheart. I've got a bit of sorting to do here after we close, so I'll be home around nine forty-five or so, okay?"

"Sure, Mom. See you then."

We said our goodbyes, and a small chill ran over my body from head to toe. Like when someone walks over your grave or something like that. A piss shiver the guys called it. Well, I didn't have to pee and I didn't appear to be chilled. The house was cool but not unseasonably so. I shook it off, literally. With the mention of food from my mother, my stomach growled.

"So now you're hungry?" Another gurgle. "Yeah, okay. Let's eat."

I grabbed the lunch sack and what contents I had to replace and moseyed over to the kitchen. Ten minutes later I was on the couch watching Ina Garten extol the wondrous things that could be done with a chicken breast. I liked her style of cooking, though she tended to favor dill a lot which wasn't my favorite herb. I made a mental note on writing her about what substitutes could be used when you didn't like dill so much. I finished my sandwich along with some baked potato chips Mom bought because I begged her for some sort of junk food in the house and she gave up the ghost but modified it by only buying me baked chips instead of the fried variety. Hey, I was glad I got any chips in the house, so I wasn't about to argue about the particulars.

Sandra Lee was up next, and I debated the pros and cons of watching her. I was conflicted because I saw her as a boozy sort of chef who just couldn't wait to get to the cocktails and tablescapes. I mean seriously, what is up with tablescapes? I think Ina had it right; tablescapes give me a pain—and not a balls-to-the-hip good kind that my boyfriend gave me either. The other side was Sandra was a big-time supporter of the gay cause, so yeah, conflicted. I ended up watching though, even knowing my homework was nudging the back of my mind, prodding me to do the right thing rather than lying on the couch like a big wet noodle.

My phone vibrated on the coffee table. I reached for it from my supine position on the couch, the tips of my fingers just barely grazing the edge of the phone. I was really being lazy. I seemed to need it given the wacky, goofy, fucked-up day I'd had. I was so relieved just knowing my guy was on his way back to me. I brought the phone to my face. A text from Marco.

Wrapping it all up, be there sooner than you think.

I smiled broadly at the words glowing from my phone. I actually flushed from toe to head. I snuggled a bit back into the sofa. My guy was closer even as I lay here. Things were going to be okay. I texted him back that I would be waiting here with open arms or something cheesy like that with a small giggle bubbling along my lips.

I finally worked up the gumption to get off the sofa. I needed to take a bath if I was going to welcome my guy back the way he deserved. He had spent the whole day on our future together. The least he deserved was to be welcomed back into my waiting arms. Well, that's how I was putting it together in my head anyway.

Twenty minutes later I was soaking in the tub with the phone sitting on the small side table. I put things there I needed to have within reach—my nail kit, exfoliating brush, the iPhone stand. Normally I didn't bring the phone anywhere near the tub—I could be quite the klutz—but today I was chancing it because I simply didn't want to miss a moment of his texts. I knew he wouldn't text me as he was driving. We had a strict no-texting rule generally whenever we were on the road. The call this morning was a pseudo-exception that I forgave him as it was the first time we were going to be apart with a great deal of distance between us—it was as stressful for him as it had been for me. It made me realize just how entrenched he had become in my life. I relished how pervasive he was in every corner of who I was. I always thought if I'd ever have someone special in my life it would be compartmentalized. But nothing could be further from the truth than how things were between Marco and me.

The table rumbled with the phone receiving a text. I opened my eyes and cleared away some of the bubbles from my arms and shook out the excess water as much as I could before I rolled onto my side and gingerly picked up my phone and unlocked it.

On the road.

I sent back that he was to be careful and not to speed. I wanted him back safe and whole.

I gotcha on this.

That was my guy. I smiled and gently put the phone back and rolled the table back a bit. I didn't want to press my luck that somehow all of its contents would end up in the tub with me. My mother was right; that ass-over-tea-kettle tumble down the ravine wasn't a complete surprise. I'd been known to do some fairly unusual but truly spectacular dives, spills, and free falls that defied not only gravity but logic. It was best not to take chances with the only link to my baby as he wended his way home.

Satisfied I had put enough distance between me and the side table, I relaxed for a few minutes among the just-beyond-warm waters with enough bubbles to make the crew of that old Lawrence Welk show a bit sentimental. I know, I'm too young to know about those things—yeah, never underestimate the power of a gayboy to absorb what went on before him. Media history was a priority with me—thanks to Mom and her old-time Hollywood days. And I was a sucker for Kristen Wiig's twisted take on it on *Saturday Night Live* too.

Some time passed. How much exactly I cannot say for I dozed off at some point. When at last I roused myself from sleep, the water had cooled considerably and there wasn't a bubble to be found. I drained the tub and began to run a shower to finish bathing when a familiar baritone voice at my door nearly had me jumping out of my skin.

"Mind if I join you, babe?"

Chapter Ten

The Obtenebration of Cassiel Elliot Donahey

Marco!

　But how?

　Fuck it, I didn't care. It must be a helluva lot later than I realized.

　"Baby! But how'd you get here so quickly?"

　"Huh? Oh, I sorta cheated. I *may* have been on the road already when I first called. Why? You disappointed? I could go back..."

　"Like fucking hell, you will!" I started jumping up and down in excitement for him to come to me, jangling my dangly bits which caught his eye, and he came to me in a flash.

　"Sweetheart, you are so beautiful!"

　He scooped me up from the tub. I barely had a chance to shut the water off, and he was carrying me to my bed to have his way with me. I was perfectly okay with that. Outside lightning flashed followed by a shuddering crack of thunder. Thor's hammer bellowing upon the rooftop caught us both by surprise. After a beat where we were just staring at the ceiling, he squeezed me to him, and we chuckled before he walked us back to my room.

　He gently flung me onto the bed. I giggled and so did he as he struggled like a mad man to scramble out of his clothes.

　"I gotta be quick though, sweetheart. At least, at first. Mom made me promise to come straight home when I got back. But you come first."

　I snickered at the door he left open with that last remark. "More like you want to nut first, then see to your mother."

　He gave a mock look of horror that I put ejaculate along with this mother in the same sentence. "I'd never..."

　"Uh—huh. Get over here you big lug and give me what for... I've missed you, dammit!"

He quirked his lips in the way that always got my blood roiling—making my danglies not so dangly. I spread my legs slowly and ran a finger between my legs, gently stroking my hole to entice him. His gaze became inflamed. He shucked his pants, no underwear this time around—that was new—and kicked off his trainers—no socks, either. He hadn't bothered with the T-shirt which was another odd thing. He wanted me, badly. He stood there in all of his half-naked glory, yet somehow something was different, something in the heat of the moment that was off, yet familiar, electric all at the same time.

"Well? I'm waiting." I raised a brow, and he emitted a low growl in his throat. I tossed my head back and laughed deeply. He was on me in a flash, his muscular body taking possession of me with all the ravenous power he could muster. And my mister could muster quite a lot.

I tried to be there every way he wanted me, but lord, did one day make him over-the-top hungry for all things me. His mouth couldn't decide if it wanted to devour my mouth, my chin, my neck, so he took in a bit of each—making the rounds among them all. I ran my hands up into his shirt and tweaked his nipples hard. He arched into it, his eyes flashing the brilliant verdant shade that captured my imagination so.

"Fuck, baby, I ain't going anywhere. Day-um, baby! Okay, yeah. Take what you want. I'm not gonna stop you."

He chuckled darkly as he nudged his cock against my hole.

"C'mere, you. I need to fuck you in the worst way right now."

"Just the worst way? How 'bout you do it in the best way possible? You know, the slow driving, making me ache with each thick inch of you as you screw your hips in the way that makes my eyes want to take up residence in the back of my head and my toes curl from the pleasure and pain of only what your cock does to me? You know, *that* kind of fuck? 'Cause, baby, I can sure use that sort of sex right now. I got an itch deep inside me, baby. I need you to scratch the fuck out of it with that cock of yours."

His eyes lit up as I spoke of how much I wanted him to do me.

"I love it when you tell me what you want," he murmured lustfully. He reached up and pulled me down on top of him and then rolled me over onto my back as we kissed.

"You wanna get the lube?"

I reached up to the cubby just above my head. He batted my hands away, and I chuckled. "Well, I don't know why you just didn't get it yourself seeing how you're so needy this evening."

His smile was so warm and sexy, and I was home; I was where I always wanted to be. I had my guy back in my arms and he was about to fuck the daylights out of me and I wanted to feel every maddening inch of him.

Somewhere outside I heard something move in the backyard. Bloody fucking deer, probably. They were always nosing around back there at odd times. I liked them well enough unless they got into shit. Which was often. I returned my gaze from the direction of my window back to Marco.

"Burn me, baby. I want to feel it."

He nodded as he sat up and brought his thick cock up to my face. I reached up and cupped his ass in my hands and drew him into my mouth, letting him slip to the back of my throat in one long move, swallowing him whole. I brought my hands around to his nips again, and I began to play with them while he fucked my mouth for a bit, letting me get it all wet for a good fucking. He pulled out and slid down the length of my body, hoisting my legs up onto his shoulders—my all-time favorite position. My eyes never leaving his. I knew how much he loved watching me as he breached my body with a slathering of lube on his cock and took possession of me for our mutual pleasure.

I moved my legs to accommodate the breadth of him. His lovemaking was always intense. Whether slow or fast, Marco liked to ravage me thoroughly. It was the one salient part of our lovemaking I'd come to enjoy the most. Tonight, however, he was far more frenzied. Whatever was driving him as he fucked, it had a desperation to it, like I'd fade away or something.

"Baby, I like what you're doing," I hissed loudly, "but I'm not going anywhere. We can go as long as you want—or well, at least until my mom comes home."

He put fingers to my lips. "Shhh, less talking. Let me love you as you should be loved."

I nodded and moved my body so I could meet his thrusts, our bodies cracking as our hips collided. I moaned as he did those things to me that never failed to make my toes curl. His kisses were probing as they were ravenous.

"You're mine, you know that? Mine."

"I know, baby. I know."

We kissed again as he started to fuck me with a ferocity even I didn't know he possessed. It burned, it hurt, but it was all him, just the way I liked him.

He came with little warning, just a rush of him as he poured into me, bucking wildly to where we nearly tumbled off the bed. In the last throes of his passion, he pulled me up to straddle his lap, staying planted within me, with the slow movement of his hips while he kissed me, thanking me over and over for being there for him, for my understanding, for being his.

I didn't understand it. I didn't really attempt to. We'd had a day being separated that had started to right itself. It was all I needed to know. Marco was back. He was mine and I was his. Case closed. With another round of kissing, his semi-flaccid cock became aroused again, so naturally, he picked up where he left off, and we began again. It had gotten to where one time for us was often never enough. I was just glad I had the stamina and desire to have him take me as much as he wanted. It was truly the one thing I would give everything else up in my life for: to be in his arms and feel him move within me. So I clung to him like he wanted me to and met his lust with my desire for him. It made him happy; it made me happy.

After our third round of sex we lay together in a slimy sweat-coated heap. His shirt clung to him in a sweaty mess. I chided him for it. He said he didn't know why he didn't take it off sooner, but he must have figured he could dress faster if we ran overlong. I shook my head and rolled my eyes at his obtuse logic. He kept telling me how much he loved me and how thankful he was that I was in his life. I smiled and told him it wasn't necessary to say those things. I knew he did, and we were good again, better in fact, because we'd survived the whole mess that came before.

He was nuzzling my neck as he spooned me to him, whispering sweet nothings as he slipped back inside me. I smirked and settled in for another good screwing when his teeth grazed the tendon along between my neck and shoulder that he favored. This time his bite was a bit harsher than I'd ever recalled.

"Babe, that's a bit rough."

He gurgled, "Mine..." but continued to bite and suck upon that part of me as his cock began to snap inside me. I moaned, but he didn't relent. This was a whole new thing for him, something he'd never done. I didn't know if he needed this because of how badly the whole separation had been today and I wanted to be there for him, I did, but this was darker. His hands were far more forceful, aggressive to the point where he was manhandling me. All the while he kept up that mantra of "mine" over and over. His biting had moved to other parts of me—even going so far as to bite the back of my neck as he rolled me onto my stomach and plowed me vigorously.

"Love breeding you..."

This was way off base, a place we'd never gone to before. It was dark, dominating, and rough. I didn't mind rough. It's what often drove our passion for each other. But here Marco wasn't taking my pleasure into consideration. He wanted to fuck; he wanted to breed; he wanted to seed. It was all about him and his dominance over me. He'd had a whacked-out day—I guess. So many things that were new to us both. I'm sure on some level it was scary kind of new. I knew that, so I thought why not just let him have what he needed? I could do that for him, and then we'd talk about it later. So I endured his aggressive possession of me. As he drove to another orgasm, he finally had me flipped onto my back, but the look of lust was very dark, almost animalistic. I actually found it hard to look into his eyes.

"Look at me, Elliot! I need to see you."

"I know, but it's hard 'cause you're really hurting me, baby."

"Mine."

"I know. I am."

"No, Elliot, you're *mine*!"

"I..."

Lightning cracked over the house, shaking the walls and rattling the windows. Somewhere outside I heard someone yelp. That was odd. Our next-door neighbor must've been outside when it went off.

"*Non di mio fratello, sei mio!*" He found his release, hard, full long thrusts as his cock pulsed with his spent juices flowing into me again. "*Sei mio!*" Crack! A flash of light cut through the room. "*Sei...*" Slap...his hips colliding with my own. "*Mio...*" He collapsed on top of me panting wildly, his cock still throbbing—pulsing within, leaving his mark. I ran my hands up and down his back as he nuzzled in and dozed. I lay there pondering what had just happened. Mentally, I tried to translate what he spoke in Italian. I wish I'd been paying more attention, but through his orgasm and the noise from the storm, it all was a jumbled moment in my head.

He was out. Completely. And he was extremely heavy. I'd slept underneath him before, and it was always a pleasurable experience, being surrounded by him. The problem I had now was that I needed some perspective of what this whacked-out day had brought. Given the last round of fucking, I didn't think we were out of the woods yet. What had just happened? I thought we were going to have celebratory sex. That certainly seemed to celebrate everything aggressive and possessive in us, but not quite what I had in mind nor what he had alluded to when we last spoke. That was far more playful. This was darker, brooding, inherently hungry.

I suddenly didn't want to look any deeper. Like Scarlett O'Hara, I'd think about it tomorrow. *Yeah, look where that got her... Maybe you'd better rethink that whole idea.*

"Be quiet, bitch," I whispered to myself.

"Who's a bitch?" he mumbled against my neck.

"Nothing, babe. Just me chastising myself."

"Don't. You're perfect." He slowly raised his head as he came out of his little nap. His eyes slowly stoking the fire back in them, radiant, like Greek fire.

"I'm sorry, sweetheart, about earlier. I just needed to possess you so much." He shrugged. "I won't let it happen again."

I nodded and we kissed. Familiar and yet, not quite—as if he were holding out on me about something. Cindy's little baby-bomb, perhaps? Maybe he figured it out and was worried about talking it over with me? I'd better let him bring it up then.

I heard a phone buzz. Had to be Marco's as I didn't have mine on vibrate only—and mine was still in the bathroom; this was closer. He leaned over the side of the bed and tugged at his pants' pocket, fishing out the phone. He glanced at it. His brow quirked a bit, and he bit his lip for a second before punching something in with great speed, far faster than I'd ever seen him text before. I just shrugged it off that I'd never really paid it much attention before now. He set the phone back into his pocket and started to get up.

"I gotta get to my parents' house. Mom is looking for me. Is it all right if I come back later? You know, after I check in with them and do the dinner thing?"

"Sure, but we have school tomorrow, so do you just want to catch up tomorrow instead? I know you must be tired from all that driving."

He yawned, his eyes widening as soon as his mouth closed. Evidently, that yawn had caught him by surprise as well. He smiled lazily.

"Yeah, I guess so. Didn't realize I was so tired."

"Well, we did go a few rounds in a row. So maybe I tuckered you out?" I wiggled my eyebrows, and he growled and nuzzled into my neck, making us both giggle as his hands moved about me. They were incredibly soft. Not what I was used to.

"Wow, that's, uh, different."

"What?"

"You using a new hand cream, babe? Your hands are usually a lot rougher. Not that I'm complaining. It's just a marked difference, that's all. Was wondering what you were using." A beat passed between us before he answered.

"There's that new working hands cream they've been advertising on the TV lately—well, I got me some of that. Do you think it's working?"

"Fuck, yeah. Though I gotta say, I had nothing against your rougher hands before. I kinda liked the sensation of them against my fair skin."

"You like it when I do rough, don'tcha?"

"Fuck, yeah. What? You don't?"

"No, I didn't say that. Listen, I know that last time I sorta got…"

I smirked, thankful that here was the more heartfelt emotion behind his apology. "I know, sweetheart. Don't worry. I can take it when you need that much from me. Just give a guy some warning, will ya? I'll never deny you. You have every inch of me, down to my soul, if we've even got one of those."

"Oh, we do." He looked at me pointedly, almost menacing for a fraction of a second that I ever doubted the divine in us; then his gaze softened, and he continued, "And yours warms mine."

I smiled, though I couldn't help the feeling that Marco did perhaps have a religious streak in him we hadn't fully discussed yet. We're both Catholic, so maybe it meant more to him than I thought. I made a mental note to bring it up later. I scrambled slowly out of bed, walked him to the bathroom, and started the shower. I lathered him up from head to toe, spending a great deal more time than was necessary around his privates as he kissed me deeply. A sudden shiver passed over me, and I brought our kiss to an abrupt halt, startling Marco.

"What's the matter?" he murmured as he kissed me lightly along my cheek. My brow furrowed as I strained to listen to whatever had caught my attention from beyond the open bathroom door. I knew it was too early for Mom to come home, so I didn't know what else it could be.

"Nothing, I guess. Just thought I heard something, that's all."

I pressed him under the showerhead to rinse while I took care of my body with far less care than I'd shown him.

"Hey, that's supposed to be my duty." He smirked as the water ran down his face, making his eyes sparkle with far more allure than I'd ever seen in them. God, he was still hungry for me.

"Babe, your mother is waiting. I don't fancy her finding out what was keeping you. We can meet up again tonight if you really want to."

He quirked that infamous Marco brow of his, stirring my cock and making my ass twitch just from the thought boiling over in those eyes.

He spun me into the water stream while he knelt and helped me rinse off my crotch before he began to suck me a little. He hadn't done this for a while, so it took me by surprise and I yelped from the unexpected sensation. He giggled softly but continued to work me toward an orgasm. A minute or so later and I was about ready to shoot. I kept nudging him that I was going to, thinking he might want to pull off. He didn't. He hungrily lapped up every drop as I convulsed above him. I got a deep guttural growl for my efforts. He hummed softly as he nursed what he could from me. I began to convulse far more than usual because suddenly it had all become far too ticklish. He finally released me, stood, and took me into his arms. He kissed me—delighting me with what he'd collected from me to share between us before sucking it down his throat. We kissed for a while longer. He held me close, making my head swim with the largeness of him as he enveloped me. This was indeed the man I knew I would marry. The man who I would follow to the ends of the earth, if he required it of me. He was the dawn promising a new day and the gloaming light of dusk. My man, my Marco.

"I better get going."

I nodded, turning off the shower. He climbed out and held out a hand for me to step out as well. He started to move to the bedroom when I tugged upon his arm, stalling him.

"You should brush your teeth, sweetheart. I don't fancy my future mother-in-law smelling my cum on your breath." I indicated the sink behind me with a jerk of my head.

"Good idea. Guess that's why I'm marrying you, huh? You know just how to take care of me."

"Always will."

"Always?"

"Uh-huh. You've got me for good, sweetheart."

He kissed me on the end of my nose, bringing a smile to my lips.

"Toothbrush, please?"

"It's in the same drawer it always is, in exactly the same case."

"I know, but I'm tired—long drive and all. Can you get it for me?"

My brow furrowed a bit, but then he did the pouty face that would melt all my defenses and I caved, like I always do.

"Oh, you poor baby," I said as I reached behind me without bothering to take so much as a peek.

I could do it in the dark if I needed to. So could he. I didn't quite get the whole "I'm tired" thing, but if he wanted me to pamper him, it's the least I could do. I produced the toothbrush case and began to hand it to him, only to yank it back as he reached for it. A look of surprise lit across his face.

"You sure you don't want me to brush them for you too?"

"Oh, hardy-har-har. No, I got this."

"Are you sure? 'Cause I would hate for fatigue to set in halfway through and I'd have to come back in here and perform CPR or something—I don't fancy a toothpaste-flavored rescue operation. Okay?"

"Got it. None of the fainting will ensue whilst I am tending to the cleansing of my mouth," he said in a fake British accent that wasn't too unlike Benedict Cumberbatch. Who knew he could do impressions?

"Oooh, that's very good. I didn't know you could do that."

He shrugged. "I may have a surprise or two left up my sleeve."

"Wow, uh, any chance of a preview of coming attractions?"

He nuzzled in, pulling me into his warm, wet body. I was in hog heaven.

"I'll give you coming attractions, you sexy piece of man."

I batted my eyelashes at him, saying in my best Southern belle voice, "You just know all the right things to say to a girl, don'tcha, Mister Sforza?"

"Girl? I don't see any girl here. I've got me a bona fide stud in my arms."

I chuckled. "Yeah, well, this stud is going to get you into trouble if you don't get a move on. Your mother can be ruthless."

He shrugged. "Yeah, that's true."

I slowly extracted myself from his embrace. I reached for a towel and began to dry myself off as he went about brushing his teeth. A couple of minutes later I chucked my towel to him, and he dried himself off quickly before putting the toothbrush back into its case and returning it to the drawer.

"Babe?"

"Ummm?"

"What's this?"

There were only two things in that drawer. One of them he had in his hand and was returning. The other was a hand soap dispenser that at one time had Dial hand soap but now had been filled with an entirely different liquid.

"What do you think it is?" I asked with an impish grin on my face.

"It looks like...cum." He turned to me, quirking his brow, letting me know that my next answer would either satisfy his curiosity or he would be boning me again on the bed.

"It's lube, sweetheart."

"Lube that looks like cum?"

"Uh-huh. I found it online from a company catering to gay men. Pretty fucking wild, huh?"

"But why's it in this old soap dispenser?"

"Because the bottle was too damned suggestive. I didn't want my mother finding it with that label. It's called Cum Lube, which doesn't leave much to the imagination. This way I can hide it in plain sight. I just have to pray she doesn't run out of soap and come in here to see if I've got a spare. That would be rather awkward."

He snorted and shook his head.

"Why didn't we use it today?"

"Oh, I just got it a couple of days ago and transferred it last night. I'll have to show you the website. I think you'll have tons of ideas of what we can play around with from there."

He wiggled his eyebrows. "I can't wait."

"Yeah, yeah. Now get dressed so you can get back home. I don't want to get you into trouble with your parents."

He put the bottle back in the drawer and placed the toothbrush case back as well before closing it. His face flushed with all the dirty thoughts I knew he had roiling around up there. My guy was extremely inventive when it came to our lovemaking. He knew if I was suggesting a website, it was going to become a new favorite of his. My desires never went unheeded by him.

"I feel an overused bookmark coming on."

"Oh yeah, when I found the site, I spent hours late one night just imagining all the fun stuff we could get into. They even have porn clips showing you how to use the toys and gear and stuff. That site fucking rocks."

He came over to me. "It's a done deal then. I'll do whatever I have to keep you sexually satisfied."

"You already do, lover."

"You know I'm gonna ask you soon, right?"

I blushed but couldn't find words to say that I thought were satisfactory. Plus, I really didn't trust my voice at the moment, so I sort of shrugged instead.

He put a finger under my chin and brought my eyes to meet with his. "I know we've talked about it, but I guarantee you, just knowing I will propose and how it actually happens are two very different things. When I do, it will be spectacular and as awe-inspiring as the love I feel for you. You'll see, babe. I'm so going to blow your socks off."

I looked up at him from under my brow, using my eyelashes to their greatest effect. "I don't have any socks on now, big boy." I batted them at him, and he laughed a deep belly laugh, pulling me tightly to him. We kissed—though it was chaste because I hadn't brushed yet either.

My next words were so soft I wasn't sure I was even saying them aloud. But I seemed to have his undivided attention, so I think he heard them just the same. "You know, as wonderful as it all sounds, you don't need to do anything spectacular to wow me. You do every time you say you love me. Nothing ever will equate to that. You could move mountains, bring me the stars from the sky, even shower me with all the things I desire. Nothing will equate to those simple words and the look in your face when you say them to me. They are the greatest gift you give me. They are everything to me. So, while I appreciate the thought, the planning, and the drive you have to blow my socks off, just know that you do every time we're alone together and you look at me the way you do."

He blushed. I could see that what I'd said really got to him.

"I'm the luckiest guy on the earth. You know that?"

I pushed out my lower lip and looked up into those fiery green eyes—so much love there. "I'd argue that with you. I'm the lucky one. I never thought I'd ever have a chance with someone as hot and special as you. Never thought I was special enough to gain anyone's attention."

"Now what would possibly make you think... Wait, this isn't some *oh, poor me* thing, is it?"

I shrugged. It sorta was. I was just me. I could draw and sing a little, but beyond that there wasn't anything spectacular about me.

"We've talked about this, I'm sure of it."

I nodded, feeling like a complete fool for taking us down Pathetic Road, though it was a path I'd often traveled by my lonesome. That was pathetic in and of itself; why'd I have to drag Marco along for the ride?

"Baby, you are the most important thing in my life. I cherish you above anything else." He took my face in his hands. Smooth hands—a completely strange feeling. That was some miraculous hand cream. I might have to buy some and see if it worked on heels too, as mine tended to be a bit calloused. "You are the love of my life, and the life of my love. Nothing will ever change that."

I nodded slowly, my eyes tearing up from the incredible amount of love he had for me. Me. Who woulda thought?

He kissed me softly, pulling me even tighter to him. In a very real way he was nearly crushing me to him, but I didn't care. I'd endure anything from him. I melted into him, relaxing into his tight embrace. He slowly broke the kiss.

"See, your body knows. It knows it belongs with me. I am yours and you are mine. Always."

I nodded again, letting my eyes slowly gaze up the length of him to meet his.

"Always," I murmured.

"C'mon. Let's get me dressed so I can do the parent thing."

He tugged us out of the bathroom, and he scooped up his clothing from the various points he'd tossed them to the floor. I got a brilliantly sexy view of his ass as he bent over to put on his pants. I leaned over and kissed one cheek gently as he shucked himself into them. He glanced over this shoulder, a big shit-eating grin across his face. He wiggled his ass just a bit and got a small nip from me for his efforts. He yelped before putting on his pants. Fun time was over—at least for a while.

He took me back into his arms. I snuggled into his chest, shivering a bit in the coolness of the room against my naked body.

"You need to get a robe on or something. I don't want you catching cold."

"I'm not cold if you're holding me."

"But that's the point, sweetheart. I have to go, so you need to put something on, silly boy."

I smirked and looked up into his face. There was something different about him. Perhaps because he had glimpsed our future and it had matured him? Maybe he was already becoming the man he was going to be—regardless of Beau's thoughts on the subject. He was still my Marco, but like a new sweater or hoodie, he had a fresh layer of confidence—as if that were even possible. But somehow it was. There was an intrinsic change in him. Something that wasn't there before. The words were the same, but the inflections were altered—as if from a man who'd been in the world and saw beyond the insular environment of high school. It wasn't beyond the realm of possibilities. This was Marco, after all. Marco was a prime example of someone in a constant state of transcendence. Marco rose above the melee of life. I wished it weren't true sometimes, because he seemed so unattainable, so über-natural, as it were. Then he would look at me, ablaze like brilliant Greek fire—golden and verdant all at the same time—and I knew he saw me. All of me. Pushing past any and all defenses I'd mastered as if they were smoke and air. And he would see the me I hoarded, the me I protected against everything I perceived as a threat to my welfare. And he would consume me—in everything that was glorious and rapturous about him. Folding me into his arms, claiming me above all others. It was spectacular. It was thrilling and awe-inspiring, and it scared me half to death. Every breath when I was near him bespoke of the sweetness in life, those things you experience and are indelibly carved into the fiber of your being. My mind, body, and spirit were riddled with where Marco had left his imprint. There was so much of him that was me. This is why I could never deny him. This is why I'd never leave him. I was his, in every way a human can be to another. I was his. Absolute.

"Always," I whispered softly to him. It was disjointed. He hadn't asked me anything at all. But he knew what I was speaking of, nonetheless.

He chuckled. "Yeah, I'll always love you too. Now get into a robe or some sweats or something. Much as I like you naked, I don't want you getting sick on me—especially with the holidays right around the corner."

"Okay..." I moved off to collect my bathrobe from the back of the bathroom door. I slipped into it as he went to put on his shirt. I snagged it from him and handed him a shirt he kept here for just such an occasion.

"You can't put that smelly thing back on after a shower. I'll wash it for you and put it back in the drawer for next time, okay?"

He slipped on the Mercy High shirt, and I took the sweaty one in exchange and held it up to my nose, inhaling him—allowing his scent to flood my senses. He chuckled warmly as he came up to me and tied the robe off at the waist for me before walking me over to the bed. He sat down on it and brought me to him, hugging me so his head was against my chest.

"Hmmm, my favorite sound." I knew he was listening to my heart. I understood that. Because I had the same sentiment over his. I squatted down and helped him into his shoes. He beamed as I did so. I think he kinda saw how we would be with one another as we began our lives together. I am sure the honeymoon phase would end at some point, and dressing ourselves would return to the banality of life that it was for most people. But a secret part of me wanted to hold on to the absolute joy it brought me to do simple things like this for him. After lacing up his trainers and tying them off for him, I reached for his jacket from my writing desk and handed it to him.

Fully dressed, he kissed me again. A snap of a twig from outside my window caught our attention.

"Fucking deer," I said to him, rolling my eyes as I helped him put on his jacket.

"I'll scare 'em away when I get out to the car, I'm sure."

I shrugged. "Yeah, but if it's a buck, then watch yourself. They can be a bit skittish and might even charge you. They're pretty gutsy at times."

"With this rain? Listen to it."

It was rather a deluge outside.

"Are you sure you're going to be okay getting home?"

"Is that an offer to stay?"

"Would that you could, lover man."

He kissed me again. He was in a very, very kissy mood at the moment. He grunted/groaned that he knew our time together was up.

"Yeah. Guess I better git then, huh?"

"Yeah. I guess."

I walked him to the back door of the house because he usually parked toward that end whenever he was bold enough. We kissed again at the door. It turned into a fit of giggles for us both before he pulled back slowly, small chuckles still bubbling along my lips.

"Gosh, you sure are beautiful, Els."

"Right back atcha, babe." I winked at him. He looked down at me in my sea-foam-green robe trimmed in white eyelet type lace piping—a quirk curled the one side of his mouth.

"I really need to buy you a new robe, one that's a little less prissy."

"What? You don't think the colors bring out my eyes?"

"No, sweetheart—they actually clash."

I pouted. "Well, it is my mom's. She didn't much like it, and I needed one. Way I figured it, no one was gonna see me in it. Or so I thought." I looked up at him from under my brow, making sure to put out the sexiest look I could muster. I hoped I mastered it by now, but it was my body. It had a habit of betraying me at the most inopportune times.

"Stop... I'll get into so much trouble if you do that. I won't leave."

"Good! It worked. Whew! I was thinking I'd come off looking like I was sick or something. You never know with me. It's always a fucking coin toss when I try a look on you. I wish I was better at it."

"You do just fine. As long as you save those icy-blue eyes for me, that's all I care about."

"They're just for you."

"Always?"

"Always." He kissed me again. "You want an umbrella or something?"

"Honey, I'm a rough and tough son of a bitchin' football player, remember?"

"Yeah, yeah, you don't need no stinkin' umbrella... Okay, tough guy. Get a move on or I'll kidnap you for the night. Mom be damned."

He popped open the door, and we were hit with a torrent of water. He had to holler to be heard over the storm. Lightning flashed, and I thought I saw something move in the distance. Probably the deer being startled by Marco like he thought. By the time the second flash hit, the backyard was clear. It had evidently run off into the forest.

"Get back inside. I'll be fine. I'll call you when I get home. Okay?"

I nodded and kissed him again quickly before I let him hike his letterman's jacket over his head and make the dash to the Impala. In a way I was very thankful for the black steely beast of a car. It was like he'd be more protected as he cruised the rain-drenched roads back to his house. That car was like a mobile fortress—not like those tissue-paper cars we have built today.

I closed the door but looked out of the back window, still shivering from the cold water that had covered me within seconds of the door opening. I wanted to wait to make sure he got started up and out of the yard okay. I heard the old girl rumble up... She glided back, not even a slip of her tires in the muck and mud of that side of the house. She was a very capable car, and in that easy glide across the side of my house I gained a newfound respect for her.

"Take care of him, old gal. He's all I got."

As if she heard my plea, I heard him gun her a bit, knowing he was slowly bringing her about on the side of the house to head back home. I walked from the back door to the front of the house to see the car pull to the road. A brilliant flash of lightning—the car for one bright, shining moment illuminated in silvery-blue highlights. A beast of a car. Powerful, protective—everything Marco was to me. My heart swelled that I was his, and he was mine.

"Always."

And then he was gone, the rumble fading into the ruckus that was the storm around us. I started to make my way back to the bedroom. I glanced at the phone—odd. He hadn't called or texted. It was a given. He always did that. I began to look for his phone in case he'd forgotten it. If he did, I wanted to have it handy for him so he wouldn't spend too much time out in the rain.

I didn't see it anywhere. The thunder was cacophonous, shaking the house to the foundation. It was a bad storm, and we hadn't seen the worst of it yet from the sound of it.

"I hope he makes it there okay."

I fought the impulse to call him, primarily because I didn't want to distract him from his driving in this weather. I scratched my head, thinking what I should do next. Homework? I really wasn't into it. I'd catch hell for having to make it up over the weekend, but maybe I could study with Marco. That'd be an excuse to have him to the shop. Not like we needed one, but hey, every little excuse I could come up with made me warm and fuzzy inside that I had a boyfriend I could make up excuses for—how twisted was that?

A hard pounding knock rattled the back door. Even with the disturbing rumble of the storm, the banging was loud enough to startle me. Had Marco come back? Did he lose his phone in here? Best not to keep him out in the rain any longer than I had to. I dashed down the hall and around the wall that led to the kitchen. A flash of lightning briefly illuminated the letterman's jacket in a silvery silhouette. I reached for the doorknob and began to open it.

"Babe, did you forget your phone?"

Those were the only words I got out of my mouth when two sets of hands gripped me by the collar of the robe and I was flung headlong into the air to come crashing down on the rain-drenched mud in a clatter of gnashed teeth, a bumped chin that somehow managed to find hard soil under the waterlogged earth. The cold of the air swirled around me—biting into my flesh nearly as bad as the crash I'd made as I collided with the ground. I was winded. I couldn't get any air into my lungs, try as I might to suck with all my strength to do so. A flash of brilliant light accompanied a sharp pain to my rib cage.

"Fucking faggot!" I heard a man's voice, loud—thundering against the wind and rain to be heard.

"We told you not to go near him again!" Another kick, this time to my cheek. A cry of pain somehow found its way out of me. The pain was excruciating. Searing flashes of blue-white light exploded in my head with each successive pummeling of my body. I tried like hell to curl up as I struggled for air. Beau, it had to be. No other explanation for it.

Like Satan himself climbing out of the murky hellish depths, Beau's face was silhouetted against the dark gray clouds above. I could barely make him out as he gripped the collar of my robe and pulled me up so my face was even with his.

"You couldn't do what I asked. I guess you're not as smart as you said you were. *Pity*."

He hauled me to my feet. Somewhere in the outer reaches of my tattered nerves, I felt a layer of mud and muck sliding down my leg. Then a fist cut across my mouth. I staggered to the side, finally collapsing onto my knees.

Another flash of lightning. My hands, what I could see out of my eyes, for one was quickly swelling shut, were covered in blood. My blood.

"Hold him."

Four hands lifted me up onto my feet. Another flash of lightning—followed quickly by a rolling clap of thunder that I could feel into the ground beneath my cold bare feet. I knew this was the end. I was going to die out here. Beau would see to it. I knew the kind of darkness that was in him. There was no way I could come out of this alive. My breathing was ragged. I hurt everywhere.

Be happy, Marco. Find love. Find peace. Find family. I love you, baby. With every piece of my heart.

Two quick jabs to my stomach and chest caused me to collapse forward. Just when I thought the pain couldn't get any worse, a fourth boy moved into focus, just beyond Beau. If I had to guess, the other two were Mack and Will. The backfield was complete. I knew they saw I was the threat; I was the one who was damaging them, causing them to descend into chaos and madness. That's how it was for straight boys who got too close to my kind.

Another clip to my jaw and I felt something painful crack. I couldn't move my mouth. I found I just wanted it to end. I wanted it to all be over. It had happened so fast you'd think I couldn't feel so much in such a short span of time. You'd be wrong. Those few seconds stretched into infinity. I was being punished for loving a god. I was being punished for tempting them, all of them, in one way or another.

A loud swat against my shin and searing pain raced up my leg. I shuddered and panted. I knew it was broken. In the intermittent light, I could see Stephen holding the two-by-four in his hands. The pain was almost too much. I began to lose any ability to feel anything. It was all simply too much. I started to sag between Will and Mack.

"I said hold him!"

"You fucking broke his leg, you asshole. This is fucked!" Willem bellowed back at Beau.

"You said we'd rough him up... This is fucking going too far!" Mack echoed Will's thoughts.

"Listen, you pussies, fucking get a grip or you'll be next! And you know I can do it. We're almost done here."

It was here that I checked out—one of those out-of-body experiences. I don't know if it's because chemicals are released in the brain and you ethereally feel like you're having an out-of-body moment, but that was what it felt like, despite my knowing there was nothing supernatural to the whole set of events. Just my brain finding a way to unplug from the onslaught of Beau's attack. Beau leaned in and gripped the hair on my head to push my face back. One eye was now truly closed from when I'd been kicked in the face.

"I should fucking rape your faggoty ass. But I know you'd enjoy it too much. Too bad really, 'cause I bet I woulda made you forget all about your lover boy. Don't worry though; I'll make sure he lives up to his responsibilities. He may not marry Cindy, but he'll sure as hell support them. Don't you worry about him. The guys will rally around him and keep him close. He'll become the man he was supposed to be before you came and poisoned it all." Then to the other guys, "Hold him steady. Time to send this little faggoty demon back to hell!"

I saw his fist coming at me, the rain droplets glancing off of it as it sailed so slowly through the air. Lightning cut across the darkness, illuminating it in sharp relief of silvery lights and harrowing shadows. Thunder rattled, as if this was a decision of the gods, Thor's hammer signaling the death knell of a little fairy boy. The ground shook beneath my battered body. This was my doom; this was what would end it. Beau didn't just mean to knock me out; he meant to take me out of the game for good. Like a true gladiator, you didn't just injure your opponent; you made sure they never got back up again, or you just hadn't done your job. If anything, I knew Beau was a closer. He took very few chances in life. While this was a huge risk on his part, on balance I realized how much they seemed to care for Marco. In their own way, they thought they were doing right by him: a brother looking out for a brother. I was the disease that needed to be rooted out and destroyed. Then everything would go back to being all right in their narrowly defined world. But I knew Marco. He'd never buy any of it. I hoped he'd survive it. He said he couldn't bear a world that didn't have me in it. He'd follow me anywhere. Just as Beau's fist collided with my face, my words came back to haunt me—*oh, shit—now Marco's gonna suicide on everyone and it's all my fault.*

I don't know if my face had been damaged beyond all feeling, but I never really felt the impact of his fist. There was just a searing unimaginable white light—filled with so much pain it was like my head had exploded on impact. Somewhere lightning struck. My body was wracked as if jolted by a million electrified needles—searing me from within.

"Fuck!" someone yelled.

Then...

Musings and Notes

Have faith…all is not lost with my boys of Mercy, California. They all have a great deal left to tell. Elliot may be down for the moment, but he is certainly *not* out. He will rise, in ways greater and more monumental than even Marco realizes when he picks up the story in his first book—which is the next in the series.

While I have liberally used the incredible work of Jay Brannan throughout the series, I would be remiss to not explain why his work has influenced my own. Though at the half-century mark myself, I craved men's voices like Brannan's in my life. His passion for the work he does would've given me strength where I never thought I had any. As a teen, like Elliot in my world, Brannan would have easily been my celebrity crush. I would've fanboy-ed all over him. Who would need wallpaper if I could cover the walls with him?

Angels came to me while I was listening to Jay's *Rob Me Blind* (the reason it is crucial to the series). It was this collection of thoughts and emotions Jay poured into his work that I wanted to play with, to find and create two boys who would be deeply rooted in those emotive moments of hope and fear, of love and the potential for abandonment in asking for that love in return.

My boys all have angelic names. Elliot's first name is *Cassiel*—the angel of tears and regrets. Marco's middle name is *Raphael* (the archangel—it is really his story to tell—everything hinges on him and his actions), and there is another whose name is *Azreal* (the avenging angel—the angel who sits in judgment).

This is not happenstance.

Each boy embodies these thematic elements, and I use those angelic positions to create the world they occupy. This is not a Christian work. It is not meant to be. My Angels are metaphorical. I am a humanist by nature. I am also a gay man living in a world where we are constantly reminded that we are not like everyone else. As queer people, the media hounds us each day that our love is still the unspoken one. Commercials, print media, the internet, you name it—it is dominated by the heterosexual normative berating us every day that *we*, despite our strive for equality, are not like *them*.

Angels of Mercy is a character study. It was far more important to me as its author that the reader come away with the whys of Elliot's choices in how he navigates his often-tumultuous world. The same can be said of Marco who will pick up the tale with *The Sins of the Solstice*. I've read much queer literature, and what I find rather interesting is that for the majority of it, very little is written about the character's headspace. When you live in a world where you constantly have to be vigilant as you navigate through, it can make for some very powerful storytelling. That is my goal in writing these boys' lives. I want the reader who may not be queer themselves to come away with what it might be like to be in a gay boy's shoes—constantly polling and pulse-checking your world because your very survival depends upon it. All of that while you hope, you secretly pray you'll find someone who will see you too and find they can't live without you in their world. A small slice of happiness to call your own. And though you do everything to keep to yourself, you may still run into those who find your very existence threatens who they are and how they think the world should run.

But love is love, as they say.

What I do know is that when it is present, it is all-consuming and all-encompassing. It tears down walls, it shatters lives, and it rules the head and heart as no other can. I know that because I am happy to live it with my own husband of twenty years (as of the writing of this book).

Brannan's *Rob Me Blind* is where my boys spring from. It is their emotive core; it is the root of everything they are. You want to hear what they're about? I highly recommend that you listen to the album. They're there. I listened to it constantly while writing the series (well, that, and anything by another amazing gay composer—you might've heard of him too, Pyotr Ilyich Tchaikovsky. It is no coincidence that I am pairing these two gay men's work with my own). Men's voices, gay men's voices are important to me. When rooted in our collective consciousness of who and what we are and how we fight to eke out any happiness in this world, it can be a powerful place from which to create. Marco, Elliot, and one other boy who I've yet to reveal, voices are all trying to evoke the very hopes, fears, and struggles that we, as gay men, face in an increasingly alternating world of acceptance and intolerance.

As an artist, I am deeply respectful of Brannan's work. I am grateful that he has the courage and the drive to do what he does. What's more, I am inspired by it. He is, in many respects, my muse for the work. He didn't ask for it; he never knew it was. But his voice gave me my own for my boys of Mercy, California, and the dark, powerful, and turbulent story these boys have to tell.

Angels is not an easy series to write. These men face some very difficult and emotive times ahead. Men struggle with the expression of emotions. Even gay men struggle with how to express ourselves and gain acceptance and recognition of our voice being out there in the mainstream at all. It takes a certain courage to do that.

But Jay has been my light in that. His courage to constantly get out there and keep doing it, for putting a powerful and emotive voice into a very turbulent world, I can't help but be inspired. For that, I am deeply grateful and very respectful of how I use his work to influence my own. I asked him for permission to do so. It was important—one artist to another—that I gave him a moment to comment, to allow or deny what I wanted to say when quoting his work in my own. I could've easily created a character based on Brannan and his work. I could've spun a different set of songs that carried the same emotive weight.

I felt I couldn't do that.

I thought it would not give Brannan his proper due.

His work, though unrelated directly to mine, is my light for these boys as the find their "Ever After Happily"—it won't come easy, it won't be without a price. But life is like that. Life can be dark, it can be cruel—but it doesn't mean the spark of hope you will endure, the love you have for another will fail you. It is this singular point that presses me to write *Angels*. That pinprick of light, the emotive shard of hope that is constantly threaded in Brannan's work is my muse—it is what will give my boys what they desire.

I hope you stay with me for the journey.

And I hope you seek out Brannan's work. You'll no doubt find it will pay you in emotive dividends as it does me.

Words, however powerfully composed, simply fail me to express the depth of gratitude I have for Brannan's *Rob Me Blind* and the world it brought to me. It is a debt that will go unpaid until I breathe my last.

Thank you, Mr. Brannan, in ways I can never truly express. My boys exist because you do. Were Marco, Elliot, and an unnamed boy (to be revealed shortly) alive, I know they would thank you too.

Acknowledgements

To my cocreators of WROTE podcast, Jayne Lockwood and Vance Bastian. Your dedication to what we've created, your generosity and support—both in spirit and in heart—are my constant guiding light as I move through this crazy thing we call life. You both mean so much to me—you've become family.

To Wendy Stone and Michael Rumsey, and Paul Berry, you hold my boys of Mercy High in as much regard, warmth, and love as I do. The evolution of this project would be nothing without you. I am truly blessed.

Lastly, but no less important, to our "*Studio 9* Crew": Lawana Bailey, Jeffrey Merrell Davis, Don Garcia, Lorna Laughlin, Cheryl Petersen, Israel Platero, Frank Remiatte, Yvonne Stanley, Pam Stompoly, Robert Villa, and Teresa Wiley, you were my cast of characters (as much as family) around the same age as Elliot is in this book. One day, I'll write our story, as wild and fun as it was. But until then, know you were major influencers of my life and I am deeply humbled and honored to know you.

About the Author

SA "Baz" Collins hails from the San Francisco Bay Area where he lives with his husband, and a Somali cat named Zorro. A classically trained singer/actor (under a different name), Baz knows a good yarn when he sees it.

Based on years of his work as an actor, Baz specializes in character study pieces. It is more important for him that the reader comes away with a greater understanding of the characters and the reasons they make the decisions they do, rather than the situations they are in. It is this deep dive into their manners, their experiences, and how they process the world around them that make up the body of Mr. Collins' work.

You can find his works at sacollins.com and as a cohost/producer of the wrotepodcast.com series.

Email (public address): sacollins@sacollins.com

Facebook: www.facebook.com/sacollinsauthor

Twitter: @sacollinsauthor

Website: www.sacollins.com

Other books by this author

Beware Mohawks Bearing Gifts

Angels of Mercy Series
My Summer of Love

Also Available from NineStar Press

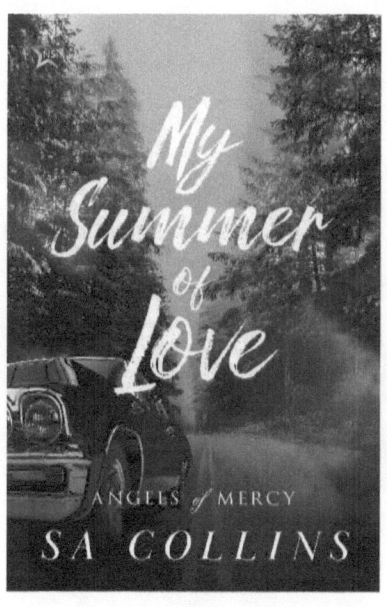 

Connect with NineStar Press

Website: NineStarPress.com

Facebook: NineStarPress

Facebook Reader Group: NineStarNiche

Twitter: @ninestarpress

Tumblr: NineStarPress

www.ingramcontent.com/pod-product-compliance
Lightning Source LLC
Chambersburg PA
CBHW030051100526
44591CB00008B/101